Greenhill
Books

The Art of Renaissance Warfare

Other Greenhill books include:

THE TEUTONIC KNIGHTS
A Military History
William Urban
ISBN 1-85367-667-5

THE BARBARY CORSAIRS
Warfare in the Mediterranean, 1480–1580
Jacques Heers
ISBN 1-85367-552-0

THE SCHOOL OF FENCING
With a General Explanation of the Principal Attitudes
and Positions Peculiar to the Art
Domenico Angelo
Edited and Presented by Jared Kirby
ISBN 1-85367-626-8

ITALIAN RAPIER COMBAT
Ridolfo Capo Ferro
Edited and Presented by Jared Kirby
ISBN 1-85367-580-6

THE RENAISSANCE DRILL BOOK
Jacob de Gheyn
Edited by David J. Blackmore
ISBN 1-85367-561-X

Greenhill offer a 10 per cent discount on any books ordered directly from us.
Please call 0208 458 6314 or email sales@greenhillbooks.com.

For more information on our other books and to enter our 2006 draw to win
military books worth £1,000, please visit www.greenhillbooks.com. You can also
write to us at Park House, 1 Russell Gardens, London NW11 9NN.

The Art of Renaissance Warfare

From the Fall of Constantinople
to the Thirty Years War

Stephen Turnbull

Greenhill Books, London
MBI Publishing, St Paul

Greenhill
Books

The Art of Renaissance Warfare
From the Fall of Constantinople to the Thirty Years War

First published in 2006 by Greenhill Books/Lionel Leventhal Ltd,
Park House, 1 Russell Gardens, London NW11 9NN
and
MBI Publishing Co., Galtier Plaza, Suite 200, 380 Jackson Street,
St Paul, MN 55101-3885, USA

British Library Cataloguing-in Publication Data

Turnbull, Stephen R.
The art of Renaissance warfare: from the fall of Constantinople to the Thirty Years War
1. Military art and science – Europe – History – 16th century
2. Military art and science – Europe – History – Medieval, 500–1500
3. Europe – History, Military
4. Europe – History – 1492–1648
5. Europe – History – 476–1492
I. Title
355'.02'09031

ISBN-13: 978-1-85367-676-5
ISBN-10: 1-85367-676-4

Library of Congress Cataloging-in Publication Data available

For more information on our books, please visit www.greenhillbooks.com,
email sales@greenhillbooks.com, or telephone us within the UK on 020 8458 6314.
You can also write to us at the above London address.

Edited and typeset by Wordsense Ltd, Edinburgh
Maps drawn by Derek Stone
Printed and bound in Great Britain by Creative Print & Design (Wales), Ebbw Vale

Contents

List of Illustrations

Line Art

Maps

Maps

EUROPE ~ 1453~1618

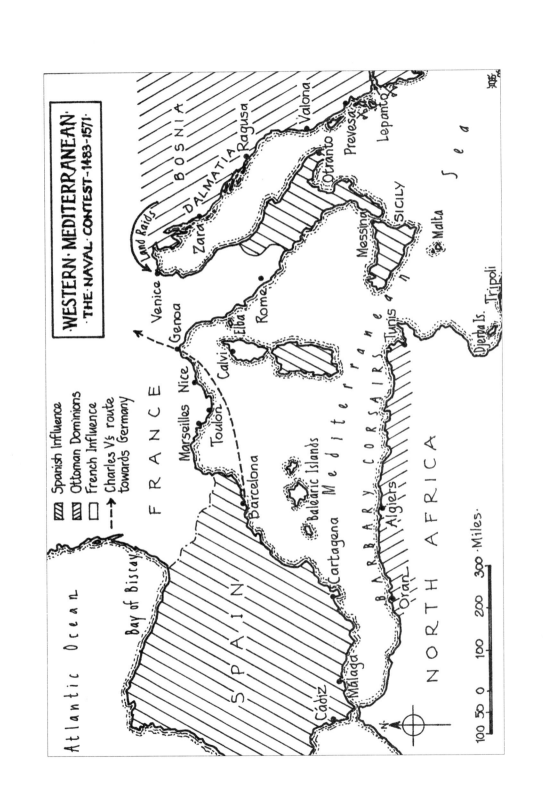

·WESTERN·MEDITERRANEAN·
·THE·NAVAL·CONTEST·1483-1571·

Spanish Influence
Ottoman Dominions
French Influence
Charles V's route towards Germany

Atlantic Ocean

Bay of Biscay

S P A I N

F R A N C E

Cádiz
Málaga
Cartagena
Oran
Barcelona
Toulon
Nice
Marseilles
Genoa
Venice

Balearic Islands

Algiers
Tunis
B A R B A R Y   C O R S A I R S
N O R T H   A F R I C A

Calvi
Elba
Rome
M e d i t e r r a n e a n

Djerba Is.
Tripoli

Malta

Messina
SICILY
Otranto
Prevesa
Lepanto
Valona
Ragusa
DALMATIA
Zara
Land Raids
B O S N I A

S e a

100 50 0   100   200   300 ·Miles·

N

THE·DUTCH·REVOLT·
·1566~1600·

0 ____ 50 km
0 ____ 50 miles

·N·

North Sea

Jemmigen
21 July 1568 ✕
GRONINGEN ●

FRIESLAND

Heiligerlee
23 May 1568 ✕

DRENTHE

Alkmaar ●
1573

Zuider
Zee

OVERIJSSEL

Haarlem ●
1573

Amsterdam ●

IJssel

Zutphen ●
1583

Leiden ●

Utrecht ●

GELDERLAND

HOLY

Delft ●

Brielle ●

Rotterdam ●

UTRECHT

Mookerheyde
✕ 14 April 1574

ZEELAND

Middelburg ●

Breda ●
1580

Maas

Lippe

Vlissingen ●

LANDS OF THE GENERALITY

UPPER
GELDERS

Goes
1572

BRABANT

Ruhr

Gravelines
1578

Bruges ●
1584

Antwerp ●
1585

R O M A N

Ghent ●
1584

Calais ●

F L A N D E R S

Ypres ●

Brussels ●
1585

LIÉGE

Maastricht ●
1579

Cologne ●

LIMBOURG

Aachen ●

Tournai ●
1581

Gembloux
31 January 1578 ✕

Liège ●

Rhine

Mons ●

A R T O I S

Arras ●

Sambre

Namur ●

NAMUR

✕

E M P I R E

Cambrai ●

HAINAUT

BISHOPRIC

LUXEMBOURG

106
·05·

Introduction

Renaissance and Revolution?

In 1438 a traveller from Spain called Pero (Pedro) Tafur visited the great city of Constantinople, where he shared with its citizens a rather exciting moment when the Ottoman sultan passed close to the walls:[1]

> During my stay in the city the Turk marched forth to a place on the Black Sea, and his road took him close to Constantinople. The Despot and those of Pera, thinking that the Turks were going to occupy the country, prepared and armed themselves. The Turk passed close by the wall, and there was some skirmishing that day close to the wall, and he passed with a great company of people. I had the good fortune to see him in the field, and I observed the manner in which he went to war.[2]

Tafur's good fortune had in fact provided him with what proved to be the last sighting of an Ottoman army near Constantinople prior to the great siege of 1453. In that fateful year a much larger army returned and surrounded the city, and as a result more than a thousand years of the Byzantine Empire came dramatically to an end in what has long been regarded as one of the pivotal events in world history. A new chapter had been opened, and in the most dramatic hyperbole of all it was reckoned that the knightly and chivalric world of the Middle Ages had finally ended. The period of creativity in both art and warfare that we know as the Renaissance was about to begin.[3]

The modern world tends to take a rather different view of the significance of the fall of Constantinople. Instead of standing on the walls with Pero Tafur, and seeing something approaching that appears to be alien, threatening and mysterious, the modern scholar looks down on a map and discovers that even fifty years before the siege the Ottoman Empire already stretched from central Anatolia to the borders of Hungary, taking in Bulgaria and much of northern Greece. If distinctive colours are used on the map to show who controls which bit of territory, then the relative insignificance of Constantinople becomes even more apparent.

The Ottoman Empire is now one wide splash of uniform colour, broken only by small contrasting patches that represent trading colonies such as Genoese Pera, but of Constantinople and its great Byzantine Empire there is little sign other than a black dot representing one city.

This book is concerned with the changes in warfare that occurred between the fall of Constantinople and the outbreak of the Thirty Years War. As change in warfare is almost always ongoing, any choice of dates must be somewhat arbitrary and in need of justification. I have chosen to cover almost exactly the same period of a century and a half that was used by J. R. Hale in his classic study *War and Society in Renaissance Europe 1450–1620*.[4] Having dealt with the Hundred Years War in my earlier book *The Knight Triumphant*, my choice of a point of departure on Europe's eastern frontier is the same as Hale's.[5] So is my point of closure where, to use Hale's own words, there were 'international relations so taut with mutual suspicion, from Spain to Poland and from Sweden to Italy, that in 1618 a riot in Bohemia could release tensions that delivered the centre of Europe over to the unprecedented horrors of the Thirty Years War'.[6] The present work, therefore, describes warfare as it was fought during the period that lay between the end of Europe's longest conflict and the beginning of Europe's worst.

The years between 1453 and 1618 were a time of transition and innovation: a time, perhaps, when both military technology and military thinking were moving forward in accomplishment and backwards in morality. It was also a period that has provided fertile ground for the identification of a 'military revolution', a phrase that is now very familiar – but one that was itself revolutionary in 1955 when it was used to sum up the military methods and innovations of Gustavus Adolphus in the seventeenth century.[7] Subsequent studies have challenged this view, and have tended either to identify the occurrence of such a 'military revolution' during the sixteenth rather than the seventeenth century or to extend the time period during which the revolution is supposed to have taken place to a span of almost three centuries.[8] The danger in any such quest is that in an obsessive search almost for the actual moment of occurrence of the military revolution it fails to notice the great sea of change that is happening all the time.

My approach will be to examine the evidence for military development within the context of an overlapping narrative history, identifying in particular any periods of accelerated change during what is undoubtedly a long-term revolution in military affairs that had begun before 1453 and was to continue long after 1618. Armoured knights provide the most colourful example of the changes that were taking place. Fully armed, they would fight battles for many years to come as they made their transition towards becoming cavalry troopers. Other aspects of warfare and technology, all of which were to be heralded as evidence of a military revolution, were equally dynamic, some being firmly in place by 1453 or at various stages of development. Yet all the evidence that one can glean has to be examined with great caution before any conclusions can be drawn. For example, an increase in army size is often taken as proof that a military revolution was taking place, but do army sizes on paper translate realistically into army sizes on the battlefield? Similarly, drill manuals of the early seventeenth century indicate a new precision in infantry behaviour, but are their systematic schemes still as precise when the drill yard is abandoned for the chaos of actual conflict? There is also the awkward presence on many battlefields of successful anachronisms, whether they are Polish cavalrymen carrying out successful charges against 'modern' infantry, or supposedly clumsy and unwieldy Spanish *tercios* defying linear formations of musketeers.

The century and a half under question also saw huge developments in gunpowder artillery – a factor that had the potential to be truly revolutionary. Its successes, however, dated from early in the fifteenth century, when the dukes of Burgundy were genuine innovators and Ottoman skills with cannon were demonstrated at Salonica in 1430 and the Isthmus of Corinth in 1446.[9] The fall of Constantinople to Ottoman bombards was gunpowder's greatest contemporary success, but how effective overall was siege artillery? Its use certainly led to developments in fortifications such as the angle bastion, a form of design that provided better protection but also allowed guns to be used as effectively in defence as they had been in attack. The guaranteed wall-breaker had, temporarily at least, met its match. Subsequent sieges may therefore have taken longer, even if they yielded the same results, so once again a military innovation may have had less effect on the outcome of an operation than upon its conduct. In most cases besieged places either surrendered or were relieved, but there are always exceptions to challenge any rule. The case of the Siege of Pskov in 1581, when a comparatively old-fashioned fortress withstood a long siege conducted by a commander who used his mounted troops almost as mobile siege works, stands the notion of a military revolution on its head. The military revolution is nevertheless a useful concept, provided that it is not embraced too slavishly. It is one that will run like a thread through the chapters that follow, as we study a century and a half that lay between two great wars, but encompassed more than enough wars of its own.

Chronology

1509 Spanish capture Bougie and Tripoli
Siege of Padua
1510 Battle of Djerba
Siege of Ferrara
1512 Siege of Brescia
Battle of Ravenna
1513 Battle of Novara
Battle of Guinegatte (the 'Battle of the Spurs')
1514 Peasants' Revolt in Hungary
1515 Battle of Marignano
1516 Siege of Algiers
1520 Accession of Suleiman the Magnificent
The 'Field of the Cloth of Gold'
1521 Ottomans capture Belgrade
1522 Battle of Bicocca
Second Siege of Rhodes
1524 Death of Bayard at La Sesia
1525 Battle of Pavia
1526 Battle of Mohacs
1528 Blaise de Monluc is wounded at Forcha di Penne
1529 Khereddin Barbarossa captures Algiers
Siege of Vienna
1532 Siege of Güns
1535 Spanish capture Tunis
1537 Ottoman raid on Italy
1538 Battle of Prevesa
1543 Siege of Szekesfehevar
1544 Battle of Ceresole
Siege of Boulogne
1547 Battle of Mühlberg
1552 Siege of Erlau
1554 Siege of Siena
1557 Battle of St Quentin
1558 Siege of Thionville
Ivan the Terrible invades Livonia

1559   Treaty of Cateau–Cambresis
1560   Battles of Ermes
1562   Battle of Dreux
1565   Siege of Malta
1566   Siege of Szigeth
       Death of Suleiman the Magnificent
1567   Battle of St Denis
1568   Battle of Heiligerlee
1569   Battle of Montcontour
1570   Siege of Nicosia
       De Monluc is wounded at Rabastens
1571   Siege of Famagusta
       Battle of Lepanto
1572   William of Orange lands at Brielle
       Relief of Goes
       Siege of Zutphen
       Siege of Naarden
1573   Siege of La Rochelle
       Siege of Alkmaar
       Siege of Haarlem
1574   Battle of Mookerheyde
       Siege of Leiden
1576   The 'Spanish Fury' at Antwerp
       Stefan Bathory becomes King of Poland
1578   Battle of Gembloux
1580   Imprisonment of François de la Noue
1581   Siege of Pskov
1584   Assassination of William of Orange
       Siege of Antwerp begins
1585   Fall of Antwerp
1587   Battle of Coutras
1590   Battle of Ivry
1591   Death of François de la Noue
1593   Death of Duke of Parma
       Battle of Sissek

In memory of Jo Turnbull, 1950–2002,
who shared so much in this book

Chapter 1
A Tale of Two Cities

Even though the fall of Constantinople is no longer seen as a strict dividing line between the Middle Ages and the Renaissance, the events of 1453 are of fundamental importance if the process of transition is to be properly understood. Central to that understanding is a need to place its military significance into its proper context. It is not enough simply to demonstrate that Ottoman artillery shattered the medieval walls of Constantinople, because if this success was indeed the herald of a military revolution then an explanation also has to be offered for the failure of the same army under the same commander with same weapons at a similar city three years later. The experience of the Siege of Belgrade in 1456 therefore makes any discussion of Constantinople into a tale of two cities, not just the one.

Sailing to Byzantium

In spite of the significance loaded on to the loss of Constantinople, it has first to be recognised that by 1453 the 'New Rome' of Constantine the Great was no longer the power it had once been. Its influence, and indeed its territory, had shrunk to almost nothing beyond the land that was enclosed within the city's still-mighty walls, from which communication had to be made almost entirely by sea. Everything immediately across the Bosphorus was already in Ottoman hands, and their capital of Edirne (formerly Adrianople), captured in 1361, actually lay to the west of Constantinople, in Thrace. In terms of surface area there was not much left either to capture or to care about, an attitude that was reflected in the paltry concern that was voiced about the city's fate prior to its taking. Because Constantinople had once been sacked by the armies of fellow Christians during the Fourth Crusade of 1204, the tendency in western Europe was to look upon the Byzantine Empire as an embarrassing elderly relative who was taking a long time to die.

The fall of Constantinople in 1453 was therefore no sudden event but an act long foreseen and lamented most widely in those lands where the least effort was made to avert it. Contemporary observers of a cynical yet religious mind may well have speculated that, so far, God had spared the city more for the holy relics it contained than for anything else. In reality the attitude towards Constantinople's fate was expressed most acutely in the reluctance of anyone to come to the city's assistance, relics or not. To those of an optimistic and romantic inclination Constantinople was still a symbol of eternal Rome. It had withstood numerous sieges in the past and surely would continue to do so. As recently as 1422 an Ottoman force employing artillery had been beaten off by a citizens' army inspired by a vision of the Virgin Mary on Constantinople's walls.[1]

Linked to this touching belief in the capacity of the city's mighty fortifications to withstand changing military technology was a contempt for, and an underestimation of, the fighting power of the Ottomans – a delusion that was to last for centuries after the fall of Constantinople.[2] At a conference held in Florence in 1439 Byzantine officials of the Emperor John VIII estimated that it would take only one month for a crusading army to conquer Turkish-held territory in Europe, and one further month to take the Holy Land![3] In an oration delivered in Rome in 1452, Aeneas Sylvius, who afterwards became Pope Pius II, appealed to his audience to recognise that 'the Turks were unwarlike, weak, effeminate, neither martial in spirit nor in counsel; what they have taken may be recovered without difficulty'.[4]

Yet somehow these optimistic attitudes towards going on crusade to assist Constantinople and throw back the 'weak and effeminate' Ottomans were never actually translated into action. The experience of Nicopolis in 1396, a Christian disaster brought about by the self-same 'unwarlike' Ottomans, had been a very painful one. From that time onwards, whenever crusades to save Constantinople were discussed, one common feature that always prevented them from happening was a serious overestimation of the numbers of Christian princes who would be willing to participate. Philip the Good, Duke of Burgundy from 1419 to 1467, was one of the few European rulers who even contemplated sending a force to confront the Turks, but he was after all the perfect crusader. Philip had been born in 1396, the year of the Nicopolis crusade that had been organised by his grandfather Philip the Bold and led by his father John the Fearless, and he maintained throughout his life a keen interest in this manifestation of knightly virtue.[5]

Also, unlike many other potential crusaders, Philip the Good's knowledge of the lands of the infidel was based on sound intelligence. In 1421 he sent a certain Guillebert de Lannoy on a grand tour which included Constantinople, Russia, Rhodes, Jerusalem and Crete. Much of the information Guillebert brought back was in the form of military observations of the balance of power on the Muslim frontier and details of the fortresses that guarded it.[6] Intelligence notwithstanding, a crusading expedition remained an exercise on paper until 1441, when a Burgundian fleet set sail for the Mediterranean under the command of Geoffroy de Thoisy. The ships were not primarily intended to assist Constantinople but were instead a response to an appeal for help from the Knights of the Order of Hospitallers of St John of Jerusalem on the island of Rhodes, who were under threat from the Mamluks of Egypt. De Thoisy's fleet was already cruising the Mediterranean when a request for assistance from the Byzantine emperor was received in Burgundy. In response, further ships were hired in Venice and in 1444 these followed the existing fleet to support an advance against the Ottomans by a largely Hungarian army. The Burgundian fleet was given the small but important role of preventing the Ottomans from crossing the Bosphorus at its northern, Black Sea, end. A combination of bad weather and Ottoman artillery fire neutralised their presence and allowed the Ottomans to engage the Christian army at Varna, where the crusaders were annihilated in the biggest disaster since Nicopolis.

The result was that when Emperor John VIII passed away in October 1448 it looked very much that his successor would be isolated when he faced the greatest challenge in the Byzantine Empire's long history. There were some minor stirrings to the contrary. In early May 1451 the news of Mehmet II's plans for taking Constantinople reached Mons, where Philip the Bold's Knights of the Golden Fleece were gathering for their annual celebration. It was the perfect setting for chivalric plans to be laid so, full of enthusiasm, Philip despatched ambassadors to France, Austria, England and Hungary proposing a grand crusade to save Constantinople. There was a modest reaction, but by March 1453 Philip's own commitment was weakening because rebels in his own territories demanded attention. So in May 1453, when Mehmet II was setting up his siege lines around Constantinople, Philip the Good was to be found at Ghent, performing a similar operation against enemies of his own.

The Fall of Constantinople

The city that had been founded in AD 324 by Emperor Constantine to be his new capital lay on the shore of the Sea of Marmara where it was entered by the Bosphorus, the strait that leads up to the Black Sea. Now known as Istanbul, it was built on a formidable triangular promontory and was defended to the north by the natural harbour known as the Golden Horn. The weakest point of its natural defences was the landward side, so this area was defended by some of the finest fortifications that the medieval world could provide. The largest section, known as the Walls of Theodosius, dated from the fifth century AD and had withstood sieges for almost one thousand years (see plate 1). It stretched roughly from north to south with a total length of about four miles and consisted of an outer and inner wall. These strong, if old-fashioned walls were joined to the sea walls that encircled the city to make a complete defensive system. Although repairs were made to the walls following the siege of 1422, nothing had been done to convert them to withstand the new challenges that mid-fifteenth-century siege cannon could now provide. The economic plight of isolated Constantinople probably rendered the expense unthinkable.[7]

The great Siege of Constantinople was conducted personally by the Ottoman Sultan Mehmet II, known to posterity as Mehmet the Conqueror, a military genius who was to be revered as one of the greatest sultans of his line and whose devotion to the military calling was noted by his contemporaries.[8] A meticulous planner, he took interest in the minutest details of operations and is described as sketching plans of the city and the location of his cannon and siege engines. Every aspect of the siege operation was known to him, and influenced by him, for months before he came within sight of Constantinople's walls. His existing strategy of isolating the city from all sides was transferred to the micro level with the taking of all the remaining Byzantine possessions on the Black Sea coast, and most important of all he was determined to have full command of the sea. During previous sieges Constantinople had been able to continue receiving supplies by ship, and as recently as the Varna campaign the Turkish army had depended upon Genoese help to cross the Bosphorus. Steps were now taken to make both these factors irrelevant in the campaign that lay ahead.

On the Asiatic shore of the Bosphorus lay an Ottoman fortress called Anadolu Hisar. In 1452 Mehmet II built a castle opposite it on the European side of the straits. Named first 'the cutter of the straits' or 'the cutter of the throat', and later simply as Rumeli Hisar 'the European castle', the new fortress allowed the Ottoman artillery to control all shipping in and out of the Black Sea in a way that was never before possible. In November 1452 a Venetian galley was sunk by a cannonball fired from Rumeli Hisar. The days of relief armies arriving by sea were over.

In March 1453 an Ottoman fleet assembled off Gallipoli and sailed proudly into the Sea of Marmara while an army assembled in Thrace. This time there were no Burgundian vessels to hinder the ships' progress, and the sight from Constantinople of the Ottoman navy passing its sea walls while the army approached its land walls was one that struck terror into the inhabitants. To add to the lesson already delivered from Rumeli Hisar concerning the potential of the Ottoman artillery, there soon lumbered into view a tremendous addition to their fire power.

In almost every account one reads of the fall of Constantinople a great emphasis is placed on the part played by artillery.[9] Early in his reign Mehmet II had ordered his foundries to experiment in producing large cannon. Although he was not the great innovator in artillery that earlier admirers claimed for him, Mehmet II was an enthusiast for the subject, and appreciated quite early on that siege cannon would be a very important resource in his future plans. He had long immersed himself in illustrated western works on fortifications and siege engines, and was well served by European advisers, whose presence was to lead to accusations that the sultan managed to capture Constantinople because of Christian treachery. A well-known story (recounted originally by the chronicler Dukas) tells how a Hungarian artillery expert named Urban approached the Byzantine emperor with an offer to cast guns for the defence of the city.[10] Because the price he demanded was too high, and a supply of raw materials could not in any case be guaranteed, he was sent away disappointed. Urban therefore deserted the Byzantine cause and immediately turned to the sultan, who cross-questioned him, asking if Urban could cast a cannon capable of breaching the walls of Constantinople. When Urban replied that he could cast a cannon capable of destroying the walls of Babylon, Mehmet II hired him for four times the fee he had originally asked at Constantinople.

Within three months Urban had produced the large-calibre weapon that was mounted on Rumeli Hisar and carried out the sinking noted above. This demonstration was so impressive that Mehmet II ordered Urban to build a gun twice the size of the first that could breach the land walls. The resulting monster needed fifty yoke of oxen to move it, and required a total 'gun team' of 700 men. It was cast at Edirne and was test fired where:

> . . . public announcements were made . . . to advise everyone of the loud and thunderous noise which it would make so that no one would be struck dumb by hearing the noise unexpectedly or any pregnant women miscarry.[11]

The noise was heard for miles around. The cannonball travelled for a mile and sank almost six feet into the earth when it landed. Urban's big gun and other smaller pieces were then laboriously dragged to Constantinople by seventy oxen and ten thousand men.

Following the advice of his artillerymen, the sultan positioned his siege guns against the weakest and most vulnerable parts of the wall. The targets included the imperial palace of Blachernae at the north-western corner of the city and the Romanus Gate (now the Topkapi Gate) in the middle wall. The bombardment, which was to last fifty-five days, soon began to cause massive destruction, and the chronicler Kritovoulos has left a fascinating description of what happened when one of the enormous stone balls hit its target:

And the stone, borne with enormous force and velocity, hit the wall, which it immediately shook and knocked down, and was itself broken into many fragments and scattered, hurling the pieces everywhere and killing those who happened to be nearby.[12]

From the Byzantine side the defenders hit back with their own artillery weapons, but they faced several problems, one of the most serious being that the flat roofs of the towers in the medieval walls were not sufficiently strong to act as gun emplacements. As Leonard of Chios noted, the largest cannon had to remain silent for fear of damage to their own walls by vibration, and Chalkondylas even wrote that the act of firing cannon did more harm to the towers than did the Ottoman bombardment.[13] As a consequence they were unable to use their cannon effectively. The sultan, by contrast, had the leisure to mount his bombards in the places where they would do the maximum destruction, and thereby achieved results that under any other circumstances would have been regarded as most unlikely. It was therefore the careful use of artillery, not merely its possession, which was to be such a crucial factor at Constantinople.

On 20 April there occurred one of the few pieces of good fortune which the defenders experienced during the entire siege, when three supply ships braved the Ottoman blockade and entered the Golden Horn. This natural harbour, across which a stout chain had been slung, was the only sea area that the Byzantines still controlled. But two days later the defenders' elation turned to despair when Mehmet II put into motion an extraordinary feat of military engineering. A wooden roadway was constructed from the Bosphorus to a stream called the Springs, which fed the Golden Horn, and with much muscular effort some eighty Ottoman ships were dragged overland and relaunched far beyond the boom.

Seaborne attacks could now be mounted from much closer quarters, but there were rumours concerning the approach of a relieving army from Hungary. This prompted Mehmet II to launch a simultaneous assault against the land and sea walls in the early hours of the morning of Tuesday 29 May.[14] The Byzantine emperor had concentrated his troops between the inner and middle walls, and when they were in position the gates of the inner wall were closed. There was to be no retreat. The Ottoman irregulars went in first but were driven back, as were the Anatolian infantry who followed them.

A final attack by the janissaries took the middle wall, and when a wounded senior commander of Constantinople was seen being evacuated through the inner wall into the city the impression was given that he was retreating. Resistance began to fade, and when the emperor was killed in a brave counterattack Constantinople fell. Ottoman military skill had finally extinguished the small dot on the map that had challenged and embarrassed them for so long.

A New Crusade

When Constantinople was finally captured, the previous European attitude of dismissal rapidly changed to one of horror and regret. Among the varied emotions that were expressed, some observers entertained pious hopes that the possession of Constantinople might satisfy the young sultan's ambitions. This soon proved to be an illusion. Having captured the greatest city in the world anything now seemed possible to Mehmet the Conqueror, as he soon became known.

Some of the reaction from western Europe came in the form of calls for a crusade for the recapture of Constantinople, and no one expressed the new feeling better than Philip the Good, Duke of Burgundy. In February 1454 Philip presided over a magnificent gathering of the Knights of the Golden Fleece at a banquet where the centrepiece was a live pheasant decked in precious jewels. At this 'Feast of the Pheasant', as it became known, Philip announced that he was ready to depart on a crusade to recapture Constantinople. The Knights of the Golden Fleece followed the example set by their leader. One vowed not to sleep on Saturday nights until he had fought a single combat with a 'Saracen'. Another swore, somewhat unhelpfully, that he would not wear armour on his right hand until he had entered battle against the Turks. But the enthusiasm waned as soon as the effects of the wine wore off, until by February 1455, by which time the departure was no more imminent than it had been a year previously, a certain knight of Hainault felt it necessary to write to Philip excusing himself because of his bad leg.[15]

There is every reason to suppose that Philip the Good was perfectly serious about his intentions. In 1454 his son, the future Charles the Bold, wrote to the authorities in each of his father's territories to announce a crusade with the overt intention of recapturing Constantinople and of relieving the other countries, particularly Hungary, which were threatened by the Ottomans. By 1456, a detailed plan of campaign had been drawn up. In the sections dealing with the composition of the army artillery is particularly mentioned, with it being noted that 'five or six hundred gunners, carpenters, masons, smiths, pioneers, miners and workmen will be needed with their tools, armed and equipped with pikes, ready to fight if necessary'. Later in the document we read of 'three hundred lances at four horses per lance, each comprising a man-at-arms, his page, a valet armed and equipped as above mentioned, and a crossbowman'.[16]

Yet Philip the Good never went on crusade to Constantinople or anywhere else, every attempt at setting out being either postponed, cancelled or cut short.

In 1464 the personal commitment to the cause of Pope Pius II underwrote a token expedition of three thousand men under Philip's bastard son Anthony. They set out from Sluys, but when they called in at Marseilles for extra galleys the news reached them of the death of the enthusiastic pope, so the expedition was promptly cancelled. The following year the intentions of Philip's heir Charles against France led to the former zeal for crusading being channelled into a completely different direction, and by the time of Philip the Good's death in 1467 the notion of a Burgundian-led crusade to recapture Constantinople had disappeared for ever.

The Siege of Belgrade

While western Europe talked, eastern Europe acted. In 1454 John Hunyadi, the Regent of Hungary, led an army across the Danube and defeated the advancing Ottomans at the Battle of Krusevac in Serbia. Hunyadi had led campaigns against the Ottoman threat for many decades, and had fought at the Battle of Varna in 1444.

He pursued the Ottomans as far as Bulgaria, but the experience proved to be only a minor setback for Mehmet the Conqueror, who returned to Serbia in 1455, where he captured the castle of Novo Brdo in Kosovo along with its precious gold and silver mines. The next stage was to continue his advance northwards and strike at the gateway to Hungary that was represented by Belgrade, the key fortress on the Danube.[17]

The city of Belgrade was Constantinople in miniature. There was a similarly shaped promontory, where the rivers Danube and Sava played the role that the sea and the Golden Horn provided at Constantinople. Their confluence formed a headland two-and-a-half miles long and three-quarters of a mile wide that rose about 130 feet above the rivers to provide a natural defence on three sides. Belgrade also had land walls, but none of these has survived to allow a comparison to be made with Constantinople, although some sections of the medieval walls round the inner citadel are extant and indicate a fine contemporary defensive system (see plate 2). These walls defended the town that in 1456 lay below the main citadel on the Danube and Sava sides and was connected to it by a wooden bridge.

Among the written accounts of the siege one stands out because of its discussion on why the siege failed. This is the document known as the *Memoirs of a Janissary* by Konstantin Mihailovic, a Serb who fought for the Ottomans and survived to write his memoirs.[18] He was probably not an actual janissary but served instead in a supporting role. Mihailovic first provides his own views on one important decision at the start of the campaign. On arriving outside the city the sultan held a council of war as to the best way of capturing it, and considerable disagreements arose. Karaja Pasha, one of his finest captains, strongly urged against any assault on Belgrade at all. He reminded the young sultan how his father had besieged Belgrade in vain for six months in 1440. To prevent the repetition of such a blunder he advised his master merely to surround the place with a small force that would act largely in an observing capacity. Meanwhile the Ottoman host should engage itself in devastating the region between the Danube and the Sava and Drava rivers so that the city became as isolated from immediate support as Constantinople had been.[19] But the sultan would not listen to counsels of delay, although, according to Mihailovic, he was cautious enough to want to cross the Danube and take up a position with cannon to frustrate any possible relieving army. This was not, however, carried out, because other captains persuaded him that it was not necessary.[20] The siege therefore went ahead, and Karaja Pasha, who had urged so strongly against it, became one of its first victims when a stone torn from the wall by a cannonball struck him in the head and killed him instantly.[21]

Just as at Constantinople, Mehmet the Conqueror placed great faith in his artillery, and there was no shortage of pieces. Estimates vary of the number of guns he had, but he appears to have put about three hundred cannon into action, of which about twenty-two were large-calibre siege guns, reported by an eyewitness to be twenty-seven feet long.[22] Many were cast in foundries that the Ottomans established in Serbia, where large numbers of cannon founders came from Europe to work. Once again, Mehmet II showed his skill in the effective use of his cannon, not merely of their possession, and concentrated the bombardment at Belgrade on the land walls, where the guns could get close enough to bring about real damage.

It is clear from the accounts of the siege that the destruction wrought by the guns at Belgrade proved to be even greater than the comparable situation at Constantinople. A twelve-day bombardment was carried out, and the sound of the firing was said to have been carried by the south wind as far as Szeged, a distance of nearly one hundred miles. Yawning breaches were made in the land walls. There was however very little loss of life from the bombardment alone, because watchers were posted on the walls who signalled with bells when a ball was spotted on its way. The citizens could then clear the area of the expected target. The continued bombardment nevertheless made it impossible for the defenders to repair the breaches adequately, because their laboriously applied materials were soon scattered again. In his report on the siege John Hunyadi recorded that only a few tottering towers were left when the final attack began, while the larger part of the ramparts was level with the ground, so that Belgrade 'non est castrum sed campus' (is not a castle but a field).[23]

It was at that point that the situation changed radically from the similar position at Constantinople. That city had been isolated and almost abandoned by its allies, but, when the walls of Belgrade were beginning to look like a stone yard and the garrison had only forty-eight hours of food and supplies left, a relieving army arrived. The army was led by John Hunyadi, who had seen his first task as being to break the naval blockade that Mehmet II had so sensibly placed across the Danube. The Christian fleet sailed down the river and after five hours of bitter fighting succeeded in breaking the iron chain that joined the sultan's ships together. The Hungarian crusaders entered the city, bringing supplies and inspiration. Mihailovic claims that the sultan wanted to continue the bombardment for another two weeks, but again his generals persuaded him against a course of action, and advised him to trust in the janissaries to take the city by assault. The garrison took the enormous gamble of allowing the Ottomans to enter the lower town unmolested through the crumbling walls. Thinking that the place had been abandoned, the troops began looting and were then subjected to a fierce counterattack. A battle began around the flattened walls, and the Ottomans were eventually driven back from the assault positions they occupied in the ditches by the expedient of throwing vast quantities of burning materials down upon them.

The following day saw the decisive moment of the Siege of Belgrade, because accompanying John Hunyadi's conventional crusading army was a mass of peasants, clerics, labourers and vagrants who had been attracted to the defence of the city by the tub-thumping preaching of an elderly friar called John Capistrano. During a lull in the fighting, a handful of these rustic crusaders abandoned their posts in total defiance of Hunyadi's orders and went in search of Ottoman victims. The trickle out of the walls began a stream and then a flood, until even John Capistrano, the leader whom they revered as a living saint, was unable to control them. Throwing all caution to the winds Capistrano raised his crucifix standard on high, and with the friar at their head the crusading rabble advanced against the Turkish siege lines. Alarmed by their approach the Ottomans retreated until Mehmet II himself was forced to rally them. At this John Hunyadi realised that he had to order a general advance, so the entire Christian host fell upon their enemies. Mehmet the Conqueror fought in the hand-to-hand combat until, wounded in the thigh, he was dragged away by his bodyguard to join reluctantly in an unseemly rout.

The unexpected end to the Siege of Belgrade was hailed throughout Europe as a miracle, but the reality of the situation was complex. Thirsting for revenge for Krusevac, and newly confident again after Novo Brdo, the sultan struck against Belgrade too soon instead of isolating it from any support. Being either unwilling or ill-advised to weaken his besieging army by diverting troops across the Danube, he laid himself open to Hunyadi's brave relief. To both sides it was seen as the will of God. 'But the greatest sorrow of all,' writes Mihailovic, 'was that the Lord God did not grant that Belgrade be captured by the Turks.'[24] Although superior both in manpower and artillery, the final result was that the weaker city had resisted while the stronger one had fallen. Siege cannon were not quite the revolutionary guarantors of success that they had appeared to be.

Chapter 2

Of Powder and Pikes

In Edinburgh Castle sits one of the world's best examples of a white elephant. It is a giant bombard known affectionately as Mons Meg, and was given to King James II of Scotland by Philip the Good, Duke of Burgundy, in 1457.[1] The expression 'white elephant' is apt, because it derives from the presentation of these rare and valuable creatures by kings of Siam to visiting dignitaries. As well as being uncommon and precious, the beasts were also exceedingly expensive to keep, and were therefore not entirely welcome as diplomatic gifts. Mons Meg was not only elephantine in size but it was also difficult to transport and slow to fire, and almost obsolete by the time Philip the Good gave it away.

In its way, Mons Meg makes a strange comment on the notion of a military revolution. Damage to walls during the recent sieges of Constantinople and Belgrade had demonstrated the power of huge bombards. Yet Philip the Good was so aware of their shortcomings compared to lighter bronze guns that he could afford to give away what appeared to be the most formidable artillery piece in his collection. But Mons Meg is no less telling as a symbol of the sad fate of the dukes of Burgundy, because artillery was not the only field in which the Burgundian rulers showed unusual foresight. We can also discern in the armies of Philip the Good and his successor Charles the Bold the first stirrings of a military revolution in the form of infantry organisation, uniforms and the combination of troops. One might therefore have expected that such developments would have brought about the Burgundian domination of Europe. Yet this did not happen, and the supposedly modern Burgundian army was to find itself being defeated time and again by a mode of warfare that looked comparatively primitive, until Burgundian power disappeared for ever in 1477 at the hands of what appeared to be squads of simple infantrymen.

The Guns of Burgundy

The Burgundian dukes had always been at the forefront of developments in gunpowder weapons. Froissart credits Philip the Bold, who reigned from 1363 to 1404, with the first successful siege using cannon, at Odruik in 1377,[2] and his descendants were to follow eagerly in his footsteps – an achievement that was partly explained by their continued enmity against the kings of France. By 1453 the royal artillery train, associated in particular with the Bureau brothers, had been instrumental in the expulsion of English armies from France at the end of the Hundred Years War, and developments in technology were carefully noted and jealously guarded. The Burgundians also had the advantage of controlling some well-established centres of metal-working such as Liège. John the Fearless, who reigned from 1404 to 1419, may have had as many as four thousand hand guns in his arsenal. As for larger weapons, when Charles the Bold laid siege to Dinant in 1466 the town capitulated after only a week's bombardment, in spite of having resisted seventeen previous siege attempts mounted without the aid of artillery. But even this was no easy victory, because as many as 502 large and 1,200 small cannonballs were fired during this short space of time, and Charles's frustration was taken out on the citizens whom he tied together in pairs and threw into the river. Artillery warfare required both patience and enormous financial resources.

The Burgundian adoption and appreciation of artillery technology was in marked contrast to the attitude of many of their contemporaries. A certain 'Lord of Cordes', besieging Beauvais in 1472, had only two cannons, which were fired twice during the entire operation, and in 1453 the entire army of Ghent had fled when one of their artillerymen accidentally let a spark fall into an open sack of gunpowder.[3] Accidents apart, such battlefield use of artillery was by no means as efficient or impressive as the firing of cannon against a castle wall. At Montlhéry, for example, the Burgundian cannon were well represented, but only managed to fire ten salvoes at the French during the battle, and at Brusthem trees and hedges impeded their lines of fire.[4]

By the last quarter of the fifteenth century the Burgundians had realised that a number of smaller bronze guns could be more effective in a siege than one or two huge bombards. One vital consideration was transport. The early bombards were arduously loaded on to wagons and then equally as laboriously taken off and prepared for firing – the Ottoman monsters at Constantinople being a good example. Lighter guns could also be designed to sit on permanent carriages, and the model designed in Burgundy was to become the prototype for all later European gun carriages. But even this innovation does not imply any great speeding up of the artillery process on the battlefield. At the Siege of Neuss in 1475 the Burgundians were able to ford the Rhine with their heavy guns while under full view of the enemy, because the emperor's guns were facing away from the river and it would have taken too long to turn them round.[5]

As for Mons Meg, the famous gun was completed in 1449 and at birth weighed in at 15,366 pounds, with a length of fifteen feet and a calibre of eighteen inches.[6] She arrived in Scotland in 1457 and may have been present at the fateful Siege of Roxburgh in 1460, when a gun exploded while being fired and killed King James II. Her awkwardness notwithstanding, the Scots continued to use Mons Meg for many years to come, and the gaping hole in one wall of Norham Castle on the River Tweed bears testimony to how effective she was in 1497. But when the Scots invaded England for the disastrous Flodden campaign in 1513, Mons Meg was not taken along. She ended her active days firing royal salutes, the last of which, in 1680, blew a hole in her barrel. Meanwhile, the Burgundians had not only moved on in terms of artillery development but, against all expectations, had managed to move off the political stage completely. Long before the apparently obsolete Mons Meg had left active service in Scotland, the supposedly modern dukes of Burgundy had disappeared into history, having met with a catastrophe in 1476 against an army that artillery technology had been so far unable to challenge on equal terms.

The Rise of the Swiss
The memories of 1476 and the dramatic military events that surrounded that year are still cherished in Switzerland, whose soldiers brought about the unexpected Burgundian humiliation. A short poem, once taught to every Swiss schoolchild, sums up neatly the events that culminated during the first few days of 1477:

> *Karl der Kühne verlor*
> *bei Grandson das Gut,*
> *bei Mürten den Mut,*
> *bei Nancy das Blut.*

> Charles the Bold lost
> at Grandson his treasure,
> at Mürten his courage,
> at Nancy his life.

Charles the Bold was the fourth, and last, Duke of Burgundy.[7] He was born in 1433 in Dijon, the capital of the original duchy, which by Charles's accession in 1467 had spread northwards in an irregular patchwork to encompass the Low Countries, Brabant and Flanders. Charles had been the loyal supporter of his father during the discussions and plans on first saving Constantinople and then recapturing it. He was also fully in tune with the Burgundian enthusiasm for artillery, and knew how to use his weapons to good effect. During the Siege of Neuss in 1475 a chronicler noted how 'it was pitiful how culverins were fired at (the people) thicker than rain'.[8] Success attended his efforts, and Charles captured Luxembourg and Lorraine during the first few years of his reign.

But from 1469 onwards Burgundian power had also become a threat to the Swiss. These were the days when the word 'Swiss' was just coming into use to describe the loose confederation that dated from the end of the thirteenth century, when the three original canton members of Uri, Schwyz and Unterwalden had created a nucleus. Of the three, the Schwyz attained a particular reputation, so their name was adopted by the whole confederation after their humble spearmen had defeated an army of mounted knights at Morgarten in 1315. By 1469 the Swiss confederacy was becoming aggressive and dynamic. It desired complete independence from the Holy Roman Empire, and was much given to raiding. The canton of Bern now led the Swiss federation, which had its eye on expansion into the Burgundian territories towards the north and the west.

A square of Swiss pikemen, showing the halberdiers enclosed within

The principal weapon used by the Swiss in the early days was the halberd – a heavy, pointed axe mounted on a long shaft that combined the functions of battle axe, cutting weapon and hook. It was deadly when it met its target but was slow and ponderous to deliver, so when the predominantly infantry-based army of the Swiss confederacy began to expand out of its own valleys into areas where cavalry could operate a change in weaponry was required. As a result, one particular weapon came into its own: the pike. This weapon was probably first introduced from Italy, but by the time of an expedition from Lucerne in 1425 it was recorded that 40 per cent of the army of the Swiss confederacy were armed with pikes.

The Swiss pike was wielded by the most experienced troops in the army: men who could be trusted to co-operate with each other and who would hold firm when mounted knights approached. These men sheltered other troops, such as crossbowmen, within the giant hedgehog that they created. The most heavily armoured pikemen formed the front line, the butts of their weapons were grounded to take the shock of a charge, and their usual targets were the knights' horses.

By using pikes in this way the Swiss soon achieved a formidable reputation for breaking cavalry and humiliating the élite mounted knights. The Swiss secret was unity and discipline. A single pikeman, who wore little armour and carried a clumsy weapon, was almost defenceless, so the Swiss never fought as individuals but instead as an organised and self-supporting body of men who made up a unit that acquired a life of its own. Contemporaries referred to the silent and eerie way by which a Swiss pike square seemed to ooze across a battlefield. Deep inside the square were other men armed with the old-fashioned halberds. They caused most of the wounds when riders were unseated or the square entered into a situation of mêlée. At the right moment the pikemen's ranks would open, letting the halberdiers through as a second wave – and none of them took prisoners.

In April 1474 Alsace revolted against Burgundian domination and its inhabitants executed their hated overlord Pierre Hagenbach. The Swiss were heavily involved in this development, so a military confrontation between them and Charles the Bold could not be long in coming. When, in the following year, Charles was heavily occupied in several areas of his territory simultaneously the Swiss initiated the long-expected military collision, but it was not until the Swiss reached Estavayer on Lake Neuchâtel that there was any serious resistance.[9] Fortunately, for the besiegers, many of Estavayer's citizens had decided to flee by climbing down ropes that they had hung from the town walls, and had very obligingly left these escape ropes in place. With their help the Swiss entered the town and a massacre ensued – the first of many such episodes in the Swiss–Burgundian conflict. Estavayer was also looted systematically, including every piece of equipment used in its cloth-making industry. Such behaviour was by no means uncommon in fifteenth-century warfare, but the 'rape' of Estavayer was so extreme that it even provoked a reprimand from the authorities at Bern, who criticised their own army for carrying out atrocities that 'might move God and the saints against us in vengeance'. It was a strangely prophetic remark, save that the role of the Almighty was to be taken by the very earthly Duke of Burgundy.

The Treasures of Grandson

The Swiss advance took them as far as Morges on Lake Geneva, and the fear of sack and pillage resulted in them being paid a ransom from the cities of Lausanne and Geneva. Other Swiss operations effectively cut the Duke of Burgundy's supply lines across the Alps, the route that was used by the Italian mercenaries whom he employed. All was not gloom, however, for Charles the Bold, because in November 1475 he captured Nancy, the capital of the duchy of Lorraine. This was an important gain for Burgundy, and encouraged Charles to make an attempt to recapture the strategic castle of Grandson, which lay near the southern tip of Lake Neuchâtel and was one of the Swiss confederacy's most important gains. Its construction dated from 1279, and the building was to be associated with various Lords of Grandson for many years. One female member of the family even made her mark on English history. This was Catherine, Countess of Salisbury, who became the mistress of Edward III after the death of her husband. It was Catherine's garter that slipped from her leg during the famous ball, leading to the immortal comment from the king and the founding of the Order of the Garter.

Charles the Bold launched his attack on Grandson with twenty thousand men on 18 February 1476. So tight was the Burgundian control of the approaches by lake as well as by land that when a number of boats containing reinforcements made their way across Lake Neuchâtel by night they could not even get close enough to Grandson to inform the garrison of their presence, in spite of desperate shouting and the vigorous waving of spears. The castle held out for ten days, but surrendered to Burgundian terms on 28 February. By this date the battlements had been blasted off by the Burgundian artillery and the garrison's meagre rations of corn had finally run out. According to Swiss sources, false information was given to the garrison that other nearby castles had already fallen, with much slaughter, but that their own lives would be spared if they capitulated. The garrison had little choice but to comply. Because they were facing starvation and had had much of their powder supply destroyed by fire, the defenders gave in to Charles's army. The majority of the several hundred survivors of the siege were either drowned in the lake or hanged from the walnut trees on its shore.

A Swiss relief army for Grandson had assembled at Neuchâtel on 28 February, only to learn two days later that they were too late to save the castle. The force numbered about eighteen thousand men, of which the Bern contingent of seven thousand was the largest. Hearing that the Swiss were concentrated on the northern side of Lake Neuchâtel, Charles the Bold led his army in that direction rather than continuing round its southern tip. A few miles along the shore from Grandson lay a small but strategic castle called Vaumarcus, which dominated the narrowest stretch of road between the lake and Mont Aubert. The Burgundian army quickly seized and garrisoned Vaumarcus, giving itself a further point of defence against any Swiss incursion. The rival armies were now only twelve miles apart.[10]

Perhaps hoping that an attack on Vaumarchus would entice Charles to come out and meet them in battle, the Swiss army assaulted it on the night of 1 March. Whether it was intended or not, the result was a Burgundian advance. Charles the Bold established a new camp two miles from Vaumarchus at Concise, the village that was to lend its fields, if not its name, to the forthcoming Battle of Grandson. With Vaumarchus safely masked, the vanguard of the Swiss army advanced on Concise by two routes: the high road through the woods on the slopes of Mont Aubert, and the road along the side of the lake.[11]

Historians still dispute whether this initial advance was a tactical move or just the wayward forward progress of certain army units. Whatever the intention, there was a brief clash with Burgundian scouts, and late in the morning the Swiss vanguard emerged from the forest to see the entire Burgundian army advancing on the slopes and plain below. Keeping to the high ground, the Swiss sent urgent messages to the rear, and waited for the arrival of the main body.

Meanwhile the Burgundians, who were as yet oblivious of the nearness of the Swiss, were also on the move, in their case by three columns – one along the shore, another across the plain and a third through the edge of the woods – when the Swiss vanguard suddenly came into view. Charles ordered a limited tactical withdrawal, in the hope of replying with an encircling movement, and then launched a series of unsuccessful attacks, including at least one cavalry charge that was repelled by the phalanx of pikemen.

How was Charles to break the formation and the resolve of the formidable hedgehog of pikes with its core of halberdiers? One answer that lay in his hands was the powerful Burgundian artillery arm. With long bronze barrels that offered a considerable accuracy of fire, and mounted on carriages with a sophisticated mechanism for changing the gun's elevation, these cannon were capable of a range of eight hundred yards. There were, however, problems about bringing them into action at Grandson: the Swiss were still on the slopes above the Burgundians, which made elevation a problem, and Charles's own army was constantly engaging the enemy, thus denying the Burgundian gunners a clear field of fire. Charles needed to pull back part of his army again. Unfortunately for him, the retiring of his front-rank troops was perceived by the rest of his army not as a further tactical withdrawal but as a retreat. Panic soon spread and the erroneous perception of a rout became a grim reality. To add to the confusion, the main body of Swiss troops had now arrived to join their comrades and announced their presence by the blowing of alpenhorns and the uttering of blood-curdling yells.

As fears grew the Burgundian army took to its heels and fled before the expected pursuit, but no pursuit occurred. Having inflicted only a few hundred casualties on Charles's army the Swiss simply let them go – a strange decision that is totally explained by what the Swiss found in the Burgundian camp. The ostentatious Charles the Bold had been planning to set up a new fortified position, and in addition to his abandoned weapons, artillery, flags and tents the Swiss found innumerable chests packed with treasure ready for the move. No contemporary army could possibly pass it by, and the Swiss began to enjoy a frenzy of plunder among what was to prove to be one of the richest hauls of booty ever taken in battle up to that time. Tapestries, books, reliquaries, plate, jewels, diamonds, gold, not to mention Charles the Bold's throne and his pearl-encrusted hat, were among the items grabbed, broken up, hidden inside jackets or loaded on to carts. The Swiss rule that all booty should be taken in common and then divided up was gleefully ignored in the massive act of appropriation. For the next quarter of a century this immense booty was to provide many a legal wrangle for the confederacy's leaders, whilst continuing to provide them with a healthy bank balance.[12]

Somehow enough members of the Swiss army managed to tear themselves away from their newly acquired wealth to cut down the bodies of their comrades that were still hanging from the walnut trees outside Grandson. Only thirty Burgundian troops still remained in the castle, and after battering the door down the Swiss calmly threw each of them to his death from the battlements. Only one aristocrat, who pleaded that he was worth ransoming, was spared from the general slaughter. The Burgundian garrison at Vaumarchus quickly learned of the disaster down the road at Concise, and managed to slip away at dead of night through the siege lines of the Swiss, whose energies were probably occupied in prising rubies out of reliquaries with their daggers.

Massacre at Mürten

The abundance of loot prevented any immediate follow-up to the victory of Grandson, and it was the loose organisation of the Swiss Confederacy that ruled out any further strategic move to take advantage of their enviable situation. Their policy of disbanding and returning home after a victory left the initiative with the Burgundian court, where Charles the Bold displayed a remarkable capacity for recovery. On 9 May he was to be found reviewing his troops in preparation for a new campaign, although this was against the wishes of several of his counsellors. All was not well within his army either, because its heterogeneous contingents of mercenaries often quarrelled with each other. In March there had been open conflict between the English and Italian units that had resulted in many casualties on both sides. 'The English are proud people without any respect,' commented a perceptive chronicler, 'and claim superiority over every nation.' A week after Charles's review of his troops these same English archers mutinied and surrounded his headquarters, brandishing their longbows and demanding to be paid. The duke, who spoke excellent English, persuaded them to calm down and even succeeded in getting them to kneel and ask his pardon.

The new Burgundian army that Charles assembled consisted of about twenty-two thousand men, including 2,100 heavy cavalry and 5,700 archers. He could choose two possible routes for an attack upon Bern from the direction of Lausanne. Each had in its path a fortified place; one was Fribourg and the other was Mürten (Morat). Charles chose the latter route, which would involve a siege against this little fortified town whose walls touched the shore of Lake Mürten. In spite of having lost nearly all his artillery, Charles was supremely confident. After all, the Siege of Grandson had been a resounding success – it was only the battle that he had lost.

Duke Charles arrived at his objective on 11 June and surrounded Mürten with impressive siege lines. Trenches were dug by night because of the artillery fire from within the town, and on 17 June the Burgundians commenced a bombardment from the nearby hills. From his excellent vantage point at the top of the hill called the Bois Dominigue, Charles watched with glee as huge holes began to appear in the town's walls, but on 18 June a fierce Burgundian assault was repulsed after bloody fighting. Unlike Grandson, the town had been well prepared for a siege, both physically and psychologically. The fate of the massacred defenders of Grandson was reason enough to continue resistance, a matter of which the Burgundian besiegers reminded them in letters fired into the town attached to crossbow bolts.[13]

It was at this point that Charles the Bold made an extraordinary strategic blunder. Instead of concentrating all his forces on taking Mürten, Charles divided his army, keeping part of it to continue the siege and sending the rest on towards Bern. Three attacks on the approaches and river crossings before Bern were repulsed, and, worse still, encouraged the mobilisation of the other Swiss cantons, whose men were soon on their way towards Mürten.[14]

Charles the Bold's response was to draw up lines of battle outside Mürten on 21 June in anticipation of a Swiss attack. He chose a potentially strong position behind a green hedge, with mounted knights on his right flank, and the remaining Burgundian field artillery covering the left, where there was a gap of one hundred yards between the end of the hedge and a deep depression. When no attack came, Charles concluded that the Swiss had decided on a purely defensive operation, and relaxed his guard. Heavy rain that night and on into the next served only to convince him that he was right, but in fact the delay was simply due to the fact that the Swiss were still assembling their army. The Zürich contingent had marched ninety miles in three days, leaving their stragglers by the roadside, and arrived in Bern on the afternoon of Friday 21 June. After a few hours' rest they continued their march overnight to go into battle on the Saturday morning, but the weather and their lack of both sleep and breakfast had left the Swiss troops tired and uncomfortable. A mounted reconnaissance force was sent on ahead to scout the Burgundian positions, while the wet and bedraggled army proceeded to move through the dense woodland, pausing only for the traditional ceremony of knighting some of the more prominent young noblemen (see plate 3).

In spite of reports by his own scouts, Charles the Bold still remained convinced that no attack was forthcoming. Nearly all the troops who had been lined up in battle order the day before had now been stood down. According to a reliable report from the duke's war treasurer, at 10 a.m. on that fateful Saturday Charles became engaged in the vital task of paying his men's wages (see plate 4). The picture this conjures up – of hundreds of Italian and English mercenaries jostling each other in an untidy scramble to get their hands on their pay before any Swiss attack materialised – may not be very far from the truth. In fact, the war treasurer recorded that one particular wages clerk was given a considerable sum of money just one hour before the battle began. He had loaded the cash on to his horse, which 'left hastily with the others, and there has been no news of it since'.

As pay day began, the Swiss army emerged from the woods half a mile away from the Burgundian front line, which now consisted of only a handful of troops behind the long green hedge, and within twenty minutes the entire Swiss army was revealed. The attack was halted temporarily at the hedge by English archers who were supported by artillery fire from the flank. But soon this line was broken and piecemeal actions by isolated mounted units were brushed off by the Swiss pikes.

Charles, observed by an eyewitness to be 'paralysed', had only just succeeded in putting his armour on. Some of his army were even less well prepared and were slaughtered in their tents. As at Grandson, there was a panic and a rout, but un-like Grandson looting was replaced by a bloody pursuit. When Mürten opened its gates the Burgundian soldiers were hunted down like rats. Hundreds of them were driven into the lake, where they were either cut to pieces or drowned under the weight of their armour. Some hid in trees or managed to swim to freedom, a distance of two miles, but others were shot with arrows or handgun bullets as they swam across the lake. Still more were rounded up and had their throats cut as if on an slaughterhouse line. Female camp followers alone were spared, being compelled by the victors to confirm their gender by exposing their breasts or genitals to the leering soldiery.

At the Battle of Mürten the Swiss army lost only four hundred men, mostly during the initial action at the hedge. The Burgundian casualties may well have been as high as twelve thousand, many of whom were massacred in cold blood. What plunder had been to Grandson, so slaughter was to Mürten, in one of the most sanguinary battles of the fifteenth century.

Nemesis at Nancy

In spite of the huge loss to his army, Charles the Bold had again survived and was destined to suffer a third and final defeat against this same enemy. It happened at Nancy, the capital of the duchy of Lorraine, which had become a Burgundian possession in 1475. But the examples set by the duke's defeats at Grandson and Mürten had encouraged a revolt, so that, by August 1476, Nancy was the only part of Lorraine still in Burgundian hands. During that month, Nancy was subjected to something of a half-hearted siege by Duke René of Lorraine. The first round went to the Burgundian garrison, who arranged for a messenger to be captured with letters on his person containing the false information that Charles the Bold was coming to Nancy's relief. The besiegers were completely fooled and fled, leaving six carts of good Alsace wine behind them. It was a minor compensation for the booty of Grandson, but it proved to be only a temporary respite when the Duke of Lorraine rallied his men and restarted the siege.

On 25 September Charles the Bold set out with a relieving army, but by now he was too late to save them. The garrison of Nancy had capitulated, propelled towards that end by a mutiny among the English archers. All of Lorraine was now lost, so Charles's advisers urged him very strongly to leave matters as they were and retire to winter quarters in Luxembourg. The bold duke ignored them, and laid siege to Nancy in October. It was a calculated risk, because the Duke of Lorraine was still without sufficient allies to challenge him, but Charles's behaviour at the Siege of Grandson made the Nancy garrison that much more determined to resist.

If, as they reckoned, they were all going to be hanged anyway, so much the better reason for trying to hold out to the last drop of blood.

Charles the Bold was certainly right about the lack of enthusiasm among his enemies to fight Burgundy, but an army of six thousand Swiss volunteers was collected at Basel on 15 December. Meanwhile the weather grew colder, and the Siege of Nancy became more and more unpleasant for both sides. The defenders were reduced to eating dogs, cats, rats and mice. On Christmas Eve four hundred Burgundian soldiers froze to death in the lines, and a certain Burgundian knight who suggested that Charles the Bold should be placed in a bombard and fired into Nancy was hanged for his impudence.

In a sad repetition of Mürten, Charles the Bold refused to accept that an enemy army was marching towards him, but advancing they were – albeit slowly due to the wintry weather. The Swiss contingent had left Basel on 19 December, but had suffered casualties on the Rhine when a drunken soldier fell overboard and the rush of his comrades to the side made the boat capsize. The main body of Swiss set out on 26 December and advanced through Alsace, making a point of attacking Jews on the way and looting their property. It was not long before they had joined the other allies of the Duke of Lorraine, beside whom flew the banners of Duke Sigismund of Austria and the bishops of Basel and Strasbourg.

It was 5 January 1477 when Charles finally became convinced that a relief army was marching towards his siege lines. He evacuated the bulk of his army from the siege trenches around Nancy, and drew them up in a defensive position across the approach road. From this location Charles the Bold commanded his army of five thousand frozen, exhausted, demoralised and unpaid men, and prepared to receive an attack from an enemy four times the size, in which were many veterans of Grandson and Mürten.

It was snowing heavily when the battle began. Visibility was very poor, and the first sign of Burgundian life that the allied army came across was a scout who was in a church tower acting as a lookout. He was thrown to his death. The allies responded to the menace from Charles the Bold's artillery by a wide flanking move to their left, which involved an awkward march over broken ground and across frozen streams. The whole manoeuvre was carried out in secrecy, partly because of the weather and partly because Charles had not sought to patrol or reconnoitre a long ridge which concealed their movements. Soon after midday the alpenhorns sounded, just as they had at Grandson. The knights on Charles's right flank began to give way, and once again the artillery were powerless to support them. A frontal assault followed, and for the third time a Burgundian army was in full retreat. This time, however, there was a difference – Duke Charles himself was in the thick of the rout and every man in the allied armies was after him. A chronicler described the scene, which had many echoes of Mürten:

> On the next day and for three days afterwards the peasants were still killing the fugitives along the roads as far as Metz so that, for five or six leagues on the way towards Metz, one found nothing but people killed and stripped by the roads. At that time it was freezing and it was more horribly cold than ever, so that many of those who hid died of hunger, of cold and of discomfort.[15]

The snow-filled moat around Metz soon became filled with a frozen multitude begging to be allowed in. When the gates were opened a panic ensued as they crawled and crushed their way to safety. Back at Nancy, the victors found the mangled body of Charles the Bold, Duke of Burgundy, after two days of carefully searching the battlefield. A blow to the head had killed him after he had been dismounted in the flight. His corpse had been stripped of its jewels and his face was half eaten away by wolves, but knowledge of the location of his past battle scars provided a positive identification.

Thus did the fourth and last Duke of Burgundy lose his life's blood at Nancy, along with his courage and the treasure that had already disappeared on the fields of Grandson and Mürten in that fateful and memorable year of 1476. His enthusiasm for military innovation had been unable to save him from three defeats and an early death at the hands of an apparently primitive army. There can be few other examples in history of such a David-and-Goliath struggle, where a comparatively small organisation like the Swiss confederacy overthrows a larger one so completely that it disappears for ever. The heir of innovation had betrayed his forebears by his own incompetence, but had thrust into the limelight a very different set of innovators, whose clumsy weapons promised a very different sort of military revolution.

Chapter 3
The Guns of Granada

The Granada War of 1481–92 marks the beginning of a process by which medieval Spain transformed itself from being an unimportant feudal backwater of Europe to a nation that controlled a world empire. The achievement was both political and military, and it began with this vital ten-year-long campaign of reconquest whereby the old Moorish kingdom of Granada, Spain's last outpost of Islamic rule, was overcome using tactics and technology that were to pave the way for Spain's future greatness.[1]

The military significance of the Granada War is considerable. The mountainous terrain through which it was conducted meant that the campaign tended to become one of sieges rather than knightly cavalry battles, with an overall strategy of trying to break down and occupy Muslim territory piece by piece. The infantry who played such a vital role in this then went on to become the core of the Spanish army that was to fight in Italy and the New World, trained and experienced in ways of warfare that required them to withstand extremes of heat and cold and considerable discomfort. The commanders who were to lead these men, such as Gonzalo Fernández de Córdoba – 'El Gran Capitán', also learned much of their trade in the Granada campaign.[2] Finally, the latter part of the campaign was very much an artillery war. Cannon began to play a major part in sieges, so that the Granada War marks the transition from trebuchet to gun, with the development of the latter on a massive scale.[3]

The Long *Reconquista*

The Moors had ruled their territories in Spain for seven centuries, and had been challenged for these possessions for almost as long. The thirteenth century had seen several important centres regained by the Christians. Córdoba had fallen in 1236, and Seville in 1248, but every Muslim loss seemed to make further Christian attempts at reconquest more difficult to achieve because the border was driven further south and became more tightly defined. Following the capture of Seville, a new demarcation line between Christian and Muslim territory surrounded the kingdom of Granada. It was ruled by the Nasrid dynasty, which enjoyed excellent relations with the North African Islamic world across the Strait of Gibraltar and was an enthusiastic supporters of the Ottomans.

In spite of the religious and ideological differences between the Christians and Muslims of southern Spain, the communities enjoyed a co-existence which, if not actually peaceful, fell far short of the terrors that would later overcome them both. There were still frequent hostilities in spite of a formal proclamation of truce in 1478, but these consisted largely of border raids conducted on a private basis, and the only recent example of a serious drive against the Muslim hegemony was the Christian capture of Gibraltar in 1464. Apart from this, any impassioned exhortations to crusades against the infidel merely resulted in a local baron raiding his neighbour for reasons that were anything but religious. His rewards consisted simply of loot with the occasional chance of knightly immortality in the pages of a future romantic chronicle, works of literature that somehow always managed to transform the most demeaning operations into gallant and chivalric pursuits.

A major change in attitude came with the union of the crowns of Aragon and Castile through the marriage of King Ferdinand and Queen Isabella in 1469. Christian Spain was now a united force, but because of civil war and a Portuguese invasion it was not until 1482 that Muslim Spain was to feel the brunt of this powerful union. In fact, it was the Moors who struck the first blow. In late 1481, seeking revenge for the Christian raids he had suffered, the amir (ruler) of Granada, Abû'l-Hassan 'Ali (reigned 1464–85), carried out an attack on the fortress of Zahara, the defence of which, he had been informed, was much neglected. Zahara was built on the tip of a rocky hill, one edge of its tiny keep being flush with the sheer side of the western face, and it commanded the plains for miles around. Its position had led to it being regarded as perfectly defended, but Abû'l-Hassan 'Ali attacked using the threefold coincidence of Christian complacency, a fierce stormy night and the fact that it was 26 December. The weather covered both the Muslim approach and the raising of scaling ladders against Zahara's walls, behind which the entire garrison appeared to be sleeping off the effects of the Christmas festivities. The surprise was total, and its capture so easy that daybreak found the entire population of the town freezing in the public square while they waited to be marched off to Granada as captives.[4]

The Challenge Is Accepted

The sack of Zahara provided the justification that Ferdinand and Isabella needed to launch a further phase of the centuries-long *Reconquista*. Their general Don

Rodrigo Ponce de León, Marquis of Cádiz, was first into the fray. In an operation very similar to that against Zahara, the marquis was informed that the Nasrid fortress of Alhama was only lightly garrisoned and thus open to the possibility of a surprise attack. However, unlike isolated Zahara, Alhama lay in the heart of Moorish Spain, thus necessitating a hazardous approach deep into enemy territory. The marquis therefore set off with three thousand *jinetes* (light cavalrymen) and four thousand infantry on a circuitous approach that avoided the populated valleys and stuck to the rugged defiles of the largely uninhabited mountains. They marched by night and rested during the day, and after three days of undetected advance came within sight of Alhama on 28 February 1482. Once again the forces of nature favoured a commander's boldness, and heavy rain reduced the garrison's vigilance as the vanguard under Juan de Ortega placed scaling ladders against the citadel. After a fierce assault the walls were secured and the gates opened for the Marquis of Cádiz's main body.[5]

The loss of Alhama was a tremendous shock to Abû'l-Hassan 'Ali, who tried twice to retake it during the following months. Neither attempt was successful, in spite of fierce assaults that were met by equally determined resistance. Alhama was a Christian prize well within the Muslim lands – isolated but powerful, threatening but also challenging. The days of restrained border raids had now passed. Moorish Spain was fighting for its very existence. To lose would mean religious, cultural and personal extinction.

The immediate result of the loss of Alhama was the creation of a serious division within the Nasrid house itself. Blaming Amir Abû'l-Hassan 'Ali for the fall of Alhama, his rivals marched on Granada with the amir's son Abû 'Abd 'Allah, whose name was to be corrupted in Spanish chronicles into the form by which he is usually known: Boabdil. Muslim Spain now had two rival amirs: Boabdil in Granada, and the old Amir Abû'l-Hassan 'Ali who set up his headquarters in Málaga. It was a situation which Ferdinand and Isabella were keen to exploit.

The main strategic problem now facing the Christian monarchs was Alhama's isolation, so a major campaign was planned to take the fortress of Loja, from which it would be possible to open up communications with Alhama. The attack was led by King Ferdinand himself and proved to be a disaster. The first fight was for some high ground overlooking Loja that could be used as an artillery position. Many of the Christians ascended the hill, only to discover a number of Muslim cavalrymen approaching from another direction. The Christians fled back down, only to be trapped by hundreds more of the enemy who had been waiting for them. By the time they were relieved and the Muslims had withdrawn into Loja many lay dead, including the master of the knightly Order of Calatrava, who had been killed by crossbow fire. The Christians still holding the hill were ordered to withdraw, whereupon Muslims rushed to take their place, but the sight of Muslim banners on the hill convinced the main body of Ferdinand's army (who had not been told about the planned withdrawal) that their comrades had been defeated. Panic set in, and the commander of Loja, 'Ali al-Attâr, sallied out to add to the Christian misery during Ferdinand's retreat.[6]

Not long afterwards, certain of Ferdinand's commanders launched their own campaign against the western half of the divided Nasrid kingdom by marching on Málaga. This action proved to be every bit as disastrous as the eastern operation. The Christian knights advanced as far as the walls of Málaga itself, where Amir Abû'l-Hassan 'Ali was waiting for them along with his brother Muhammad, who was later to be known by the sobriquet al-Zagal 'the Valiant'. Restraining his men from attacking rashly, the brave brother took out a small force of cavalry to engage the enemy while the old amir encircled the unsuspecting Spaniards with his main body of troops. When the surprise attack came the Christian army began the difficult process of finding its route back in the dark. The Muslims lit fires to guide their own men and to highlight their increasingly confused enemies, and it was not long before the Christians realised that they were trapped in a valley. All discipline and organisation collapsed as the Spanish tried to make their own way out, and hundreds were captured.

Back in Granada, Boabdil saw his estranged father's victory as a challenge to his own prestige, and resolved to achieve his own share of glory by capturing the fortress of Lucena. In April 1483 he laid siege to this castle, but when a relieving force was spotted Boabdil overestimated its strength and pulled back. A Christian army then pursued him towards a swollen river where fighting began. During the battle, Boabdil's loyal general 'Ali al-Attâr was killed, but worse was to come when a group of Spanish foot-soldiers came across a wounded man hiding in reeds who turned out to be Boabdil himself. He refused to surrender to anyone but a knight, but one was easily found to take back to Ferdinand and Isabella the great prize of the leader of their enemies.

The ruler of one-half of the divided Moorish kingdom was now a captive. In spite of earlier reverses the final conquest of Moorish Spain now appeared to be a distinct possibility. The royal prisoner Boabdil was treated with great courtesy, but the Spanish monarchs soon realised that more trouble could be caused to the Muslims by releasing Boabdil than would be served by keeping him. He was therefore granted his freedom after a secret understanding was made that he would become a vassal of Christian Spain if the king and queen helped him regain his kingdom from his father.

The Artillery War

During the next few years there were only raids and small-scale actions between the rival armies. Early in 1485 the old amir Abû'l-Hassan 'Ali suffered a stroke and was replaced by Muhammad the Valiant, but there was to be no decisive shift in the military balance of power between Christian and Muslim until Ferdinand laid siege to the crucial Nasrid town of Ronda. Dramatically situated, Ronda lies on a rocky escarpment that is split half-way along its length by a dramatic, deep yet very narrow gorge. The high-level bridge that now spans this gorge did not exist in 1485, so the amazing natural feature of these sheer cliffs was able to play a full part in the defence of the town. The part of Ronda now known as the old city was surrounded by strong walls that reached to the very edge of the drop. Its water supply was assured by access to the river provided by hundreds of stone steps cut within the cliff itself by Christian slaves, a pathway that was heavily defended against any enemy troops who might occupy the opposite cliff top such a short distance away. It is not surprising, therefore, that Ronda was considered impregnable.

To capture Ronda, Ferdinand and Isabella made telling use of their superiority in artillery, which they had been slowly acquiring since the campaign began.[7] Guns had been used sporadically since 1482, but they had been in short supply. In 1484 King Ferdinand established royal arsenals in Seville and Córdoba, where a steady stream of foreign gunnery experts plied their trade on his behalf. One statistic will suffice to illustrate how far this technological advance progressed in a short space of time: in 1479 only four master gunners were in the service of the Spanish monarch; but by 1485 there were ninety-one of them. Between 8 and 22 May the artillery of King Ferdinand blasted Ronda from every direction. It is also at Ronda that we read for almost the first time in European warfare of deliberations concerning the siting of guns, their ranges and estimates of the number of shots needed to create a breach.

As the Siege of Constantinople had shown, for a fifteenth-century bombardment to have anything like a chance of success close gun emplacements were a necessary risk. Close-range artillery fire therefore became a characteristic of the Siege of Ronda, but more conventional and old-fashioned siege engines also played their part. Thousands of men waited with scaling ladders, because, even if artillery created breaches more efficiently than ever before, a city still had to be captured over its rubble and physically occupied. Guns were just the start, and a chronicler described the bombardment of Ronda as follows:

The bombardment was so heavy and continuous that the Moors on sentry duty could hear one another only with difficulty. They did not have the

opportunity to sleep, nor did they know which sector needed support, for
in one case the cannon knocked down the wall, in another the siege engines
and *curtows* destroyed the houses, and if they tried to repair the damage
wrought by the cannon they could not, for the continuous hail of fire from
the smaller weapons prevented the repairs and killed anyone on the wall.[8]

The term *curtow* (*quartao* in Spanish) refers to a large-calibre, short-barrelled gun.
The above passage also neatly reflects the two prongs of an artillery siege that
were to become the norm throughout Europe over the next century. The first was
the use of cannon to blast holes in the fortifications. The other was the use of arquebuses to harass any of the defenders who tried to make repairs.

The decisive blow to Ronda, however, came probably from a trebuchet, which
threw a massive incendiary bomb into the centre of the town and caused a major
fire. At the same time, a detachment of Spanish troops, using good, old-fashioned,
hand-to-hand fighting, made their way into the gorge far below the walls and captured the steps that gave access to the river and the water supply. Not long after
this Ronda surrendered, having illustrated what could be achieved using artillery
in conjunction with solid and determined infantry work. It was a lesson for the
rest of the campaign. Accordingly, in May 1486 King Ferdinand returned to Loja,
where he had once been so humiliated. The combination of guns and gallantry reduced Loja within a week, and the army then advanced upon Ilora, where his men
scaled the broken ramparts, brought down by the guns.

The Siege of Málaga

The most dramatic use of artillery in the whole Granada War occurred in 1487 at
the Siege of Málaga, the kingdom's main port.[9] Málaga was defended by a most
impressive castle complex overlooking the harbour, much of which survives to
this day. At the foot of the hill lay the Alcazaba, which was formidable enough as a
fortress, but this area was connected by a long double wall running up the spine of
the hill to an even more solid structure known as Gibralfaro castle.

The first action against Málaga was close-combat work designed to secure
positions in which the Christian siege guns could be located. The site of the castle
required that the guns be fired at a high elevation, which tested fifteenth-century
cannon to their limits. It is not therefore surprising to hear that most of the summer of 1487 was taken up with fierce fights to secure siege positions for the Christian artillery. It would appear that the Christian besiegers were surprised when
the Muslim defenders also used cannon against them, resulting in a long artillery
duel for the control of Gibralfaro. The Muslims' ranging was good too, and on one

occasion they succeeded in placing a shot into Ferdinand's rather conspicuous tent. It also looked as though the Christians would soon run out of ammunition, so requests for supplies were sent as far afield as Sicily and Flanders. Iron cannon-balls do not appear to have been used during the Granada War, both sides relying solely on shaped stone. Old stone balls were collected for recycling from where they were still lying on the ground at the site of Algeciras, having been collected for trebuchet use a century and a half earlier![10]

With both sides growing increasingly desperate, the Muslims despatched a suicide assassin into the Christian lines. Claiming that he had information for the king's ear alone, the man, who was not even searched for concealed weapons, was escorted into the royal quarters. On seeing a finely dressed nobleman, the assassin assumed he was King Ferdinand and stabbed his victim using a dagger. He was immediately apprehended and killed on the spot. As a grim warning to the garrison, the assassin's body was cut into pieces and thrown into the castle from a trebuchet. The defenders recognised his body and stitched it together with silken thread, fit for a hero's funeral. Then, in retaliation, they killed a high-ranking Christian prisoner, tied his body to a donkey, and sent it off towards the Spanish lines. It is interesting to note that this gruesome use of a trebuchet is probably the last written reference to the employment of these weapons in western Europe.

Meanwhile, the siege continued with the artillery bombardment complementing the more traditional techniques of mining and assault parties. Starvation, nearly always a companion in a long siege, also began to take its toll, with the people of Málaga being reduced to eating donkeys, dogs and leaves. In the end it was gunpowder that decided the issue, not cannon: a mine was buried beneath a vital tower and its bridge. When the mine exploded the tower collapsed. Its loss convinced the citizens of Málaga, if not at first the garrison, that a negotiated surrender had to be arranged, and Málaga capitulated. Many may then have wished that they had fought to the death when almost the entire population was sold off into slavery.

The Fall of Granada

The loss of Málaga severely threatened the ultimate survival of the Nasrid kingdom. Boabdil again indicated his willingness to surrender it to the Christian monarchs in return for his investiture as a Castilian noblemen and jurisdiction over certain towns held by his uncle. As a consequence the Spanish campaign from 1488 onwards was largely directed towards acquiring these towns. In 1489 Baza fell, and the Amir Muhammad the Valiant surrendered to the Catholic monarchs rather than submit to his hated nephew. The war should now have been over, but at that point Boabdil repudiated his former vows and prepared to defend the city of Granada, which was now all that was left of his former kingdom.[11] In spring 1490 the Christian army began their arrangements for a long siege by building a new city, named Santa Fe, to serve as their headquarters. It was designed on a grid pattern, and its formidable appearance alone was to provide a striking challenge to Granada.

There was much fighting around the walls of the beautiful Alhambra palace, which was Boabdil's last refuge. Once more the Christians' guns opened up on a defended place, but Boabdil did not have the stomach for a long siege. By the end of November 1491 terms were agreed, and he surrendered Granada to Ferdinand and Isabella on 2 January 1492. Their banner and a Christian cross were raised from the Alhambra's highest tower (*see* plates 5 and 6).

As Boabdil rode away he turned and wept when he reached the point that gave him his last view of the Alhambra. According to legend, his mother reproached him, saying, 'You may well weep like a woman for what you could not defend as a man,' but with that 'last sigh of the Moor' the long history of the *Reconquista* came to its end.

The sadness felt within Islam found its counterpart in the joy within Christendom.[12] The fall of Constantinople was felt to have been avenged, and in a strange way a new era really was beginning. Four months later, in that same siege camp of Santa Fe, the final agreement was given for Christopher Columbus to set out on his epic voyage that was ultimately to lead to new wars of conquest in a world as yet undiscovered – wars that would be fought by the same soldiers who had learned their trade in the savage schoolroom of the ten-year fight for Granada.

Chapter 4

Breaking the Square

The destruction of Charles the Bold, Duke of Burgundy, at the hands of Swiss pikemen in 1477 gave the Swiss a reputation for invincibility that soon threatened to transcend reality. But, as the myth grew, the Swiss capitalised upon it, both to create fear among their enemies and as a way of making their services look more desirable to the European monarchs who increasingly employed them in a mercenary capacity.

The picture the Swiss liked to present of themselves was of a furious and unstoppable, yet controlled, mass of men that crushed all opposition beneath a steady and inexorable advance. Unfortunately for the Swiss, those who employed them as mercenaries were not totally taken in by the myth and watched constantly to work out ways of defeating them, just in case the Swiss became their enemies one day. It was a battle of wills as much as muscle, a conflict between maintaining a myth of invincibility and a determination by other armies to discover the secret of how to overcome a formidable but stereotyped tactic, and finally 'break the square'.

Pike versus Pike

Any careful observer of the Burgundian Wars would have concluded that meticulous manoeuvring was not the most important element in the success of the Swiss. This was demonstrated again during the Swabian War, which took the form of a series of battles fought along the Swiss confederacy's northern and eastern borders in 1499. The immediate cause of the conflict was Swiss opposition to an imperial tax imposed in 1495, and the ultimate result was the final assertion of Swiss independence from the Holy Roman Empire. During this war the Swiss were forced to fight against a mirror-image of themselves, because the Holy Roman Emperor Maximilian had introduced his own corps of pikemen into the imperial army. These were the famous *landsknechts*, heavy pike-wielding infantry whose name was to become well known on battlefields in the sixteenth century.[1] The Swiss responded by reorganising their pike square formations so that the proportion of soldiers using pikes increased to two-thirds, leaving a smaller number of halberdiers inside. At the Battle of Frastanz the Swiss showed their superiority over the newcomers in a fight where they claimed to have suffered eleven casualties against their opponents' three thousand!

The result of bringing two pike armies together was the first manifestation of what was to become known as the 'push of pike'. The opposing forces seemed to lose all individuality as they literally pushed against each other, the only sign of life being at the interface where the front lines met and tight, bloody and fatal hand-to-hand combat took place. Whichever side won, the push tended to decide the battle, because the losers of it now had their backs to the victors. In the absence of 'push of pike' a pike square could actually charge, and, given the right conditions, it could move surprisingly quickly over unbroken ground. At Dornach the Swiss pikemen moved so rapidly against the unsuspecting enemy camp that they managed to put the imperial artillery out of action without even one shot being fired.

The Treaty of Basel, by which the Swabian War ended, severed all links between the confederacy and the Holy Roman Empire, but once independence had been achieved the united but heterogeneous cantons appeared to lack a common

The moment of interaction between two pike units, leading to the 'push of pike'

objective. Far from being an emerging great power, the Swiss were to enter the sixteenth century as the most sought-after mercenaries in Europe, a process through which the myth of Swiss invincibility was mercilessly propagated.

The Swiss in French Service

An early employer of Swiss mercenaries was King Charles VIII of France, who hired them when he marched into Italy in 1494. His campaign to regain Naples (an old Angevin possession to which Charles believed he was entitled) marked the beginning of more than half a century of warfare that would involve French, Spanish, Swiss, Italian and German armies. The operations are known as the Italian Wars, because it was chiefly on that peninsula that the fighting was conducted. Later, when the fighting had spread, it is by the names of the two rival houses of Habsburg and Valois that the conflict is known. In military terms, Charles VIII's advance also ushered in an important period of development, because Italy became what The Netherlands was to be almost a century later – Europe's laboratory of warfare, where new ideas concerning infantry, artillery and fortifications were tested and tried.[2]

Charles VIII marched into Italy with a head full of romantic ideas about chivalry and unromantic, but no less unrealistic, legal precedents concerning the family trees of Angevin kings and Byzantine emperors. His army was just as impressive as his mental state. Charles had with him squadrons of knights in glittering armour, phalanxes of Swiss pikemen, and, just to show that he was as modern as the next monarch where it mattered, an artillery train that was unmatched in Europe.[3] It was the largest army assembled for a century, and it is interesting to note that the ten thousand Swiss troops in his ranks were there in open defiance of a ban placed by the Swiss authorities on unregulated mercenary enlistment. In future, Swiss mercenaries would be supplied to France by contract, but in 1494 they went of their own accord, and the large size of the host reveals how popular such adventures could be.

With such men behind him Charles expected little opposition. In addition the French were currently on very friendly terms with the royal houses of both Savoy and Milan. He had also wisely secured his rear by a treaty with the Spanish monarchs Ferdinand and Isabella. The wisdom in so doing, however, was somewhat offset by the means thereof, because it had involved ceding virtually all French control over the Pyrenees, but Charles obviously thought he had struck a bargain. As for the petty Italian states and the papacy, Charles treated them with undisguised contempt, and his rapid arrival in Naples seemed to justify both his plans and his optimism.

The French passage through the peninsula was eased by fear, which had been generated when the news spread southwards of a massacre, involving the Swiss, at Mordano, one of the few fortresses to have resisted them. As the French army approached his capital Ferdinand, King of Aragon and of Naples, fled to Sicily. This left Charles in undisputed possession of the whole kingdom, except for a few minor outposts. Ferdinand's dynasty had never been entirely popular, but any initial welcome Charles received soon changed to opposition when he made grants of land to his followers and allowed his mercenaries to run rampage.

The Battle of Fornovo

But a storm was brewing in the north. Ferdinand of Aragon joined forces with Venice, Milan and Pope Alexander VI in an alliance called the League of St Mark. The treaty of alliance was signed only a month after Charles's triumphant entry into Naples, and because a considerable naval force was also involved the result was that the French king was in full possession of his objective but had no way of getting home either by land or sea. Charles's only hope was to force his way through. So, leaving part of his army in Naples, he began a fighting retreat through what was now hostile territory. The members of the League at first thought to intercept him at Rome, but at the request of the pope they decided instead to trap him and fight a decisive battle in the Apennine mountains. The Marquis of Mantua, commander of the host, did not want merely to stop the French – he wanted to annihilate them. He planned to allow the French to pass over the Apennines and into Lombardy down the Taro Valley, where it was hoped that the League's abilities in mounted warfare could be displayed to best advantage. The other factor involved in forcing the French to use a high mountain pass was the hope that this would cause them to abandon their artillery train, but on their way north the Swiss contingent in the French army had sacked a certain town in defiance of orders. As punishment Charles required them to drag his cannons up paths that were impassible to draught animals.

The Marquis of Mantua laid a trap two miles north of a village called Fornovo. He knew that the French would have to march in a long column along the road that headed north on the west bank, and there, where the river bed was shallow and the banks were firm and stony, he would ford the river and take them in the flank. The French would first be bombarded by cannon fire, and then various units of horsemen would cross the river to engage them. The Italian army was divided almost equally between fully armoured knights and lighter-mounted troops such as mounted crossbowmen and six hundred *stradiots*. They were the much-feared light cavalry, chiefly composed of Albanians, whom the Venetians had raised in the

Balkans. As an unusual incentive the *stradiots* were promised one ducat for every French head they brought back, a scheme that was abused by at least one *stradiot* who cut the head off a local priest and presented it for his reward.

The one element in the allied plans that did not proceed as favourably as anticipated was the crossing of the River Taro, because when the French first came into contact with their reception committee some very bad weather during the night made the water level rise considerably and stirred up the formerly firm surface of the river bed. Vigilant scouting ensured that the presence of the allied army came as no surprise to King Charles VIII, so he deployed his army to make it easier for their positions on the march to be readily converted to a line of battle by a simple 'right face'. As the core of his army were the Swiss pikemen, such a simple manoeuvre was unlikely to cause many problems. So it proved, because the Marquis of Mantua opened up with his guns, which did little damage, and crossed the swollen river, which provoked little alarm in their enemies. He then engaged with the French, which proved to be a disaster. The League's army was defeated in less than a quarter of an hour. There was some minor compensation when the *stradiots* hit the king's baggage train, but when the Milanese knights came upon their French counterparts their courage failed them and they fell into disorder. Meanwhile, the porcupine that was the Swiss pikemen repelled every other mounted attack and crushed the Milanese infantry in classic manner. The numbers of Milanese dead figured highly in the final total of seventeen allies killed to every one Frenchman. It was a fine victory both for traditional heavy knights and for the solid mass of Swiss pikemen, with the overall lesson being that both these arms had to be used in combination with each other.[4] The latter force did particularly well out of the success, because when King Charles VIII finally regained the safety of Piedmont in July he found that his uncle had been besieged in Novara. Charles's retreating army could not help in its current state of depletion, so he sent one of his generals to hire five thousand more Swiss for the French army. The result was a recruiting sergeant's dream of heaven. Not five thousand but twenty thousand men descended from the cantons in response – one-fifth of the confederacy's entire male population!

No Money – No Swiss!

The escape of King Charles VIII from Italy was a shock every bit as great as his unopposed entry into it had been, and recriminations soon began.[5] In Machiavelli's view, the double disgrace was due to the Italian states having relied for too long on the *condottieri* system of mercenaries. This statement, of course, ignored the fact that at the heart of the conquering French army lay the best-known mercenaries

in Europe – the Swiss and their pikes, an arrangement that King Charles VIII for-
malised a year before his death by forming the first permanent company of Swiss
in French service as his personal bodyguard. The unit eventually became known as
the Compagnie des Cent Suisses, and would serve successive French monarchs in
this capacity until 1791.

Fornovo may have been a remarkable victory, but it was a battle won in the
course of a fighting retreat, and Charles had little to show as a result of the precipi-
tate campaign that had brought it about. It was therefore not long before another
French army was seen in Italy, because when Charles died in 1498 his successor
King Louis XII reawakened both the French claim to Naples and to the duchy of
Milan. The French army of invasion included twelve thousand Swiss mercenaries.
They easily captured Milan from Ludovico Sforza, but Louis subsequently failed
to pay them, so six thousand men from the Swiss troops crossed to Sforza's side at
nearby Novara and vowed to recapture Milan for him.

The pro-Sforza Swiss were then besieged in Novara by a French army containing the rest of the Swiss troops, a potentially nightmarish situation of Swiss
killing Swiss which the confederacy's regulatory laws had been designed to avoid.
An armed confrontation was happily avoided by negotiation, although a plot to
smuggle Sforza out of the city was betrayed to the French by a Swiss officer in return for a bribe. All in all, it was a most unsavoury operation, and did nothing for
the reputation of the Swiss other than the creation of a saying that was often to
be used to blacken them in the future – 'No money, no Swiss'. This was somewhat
unfair, because very frequently it was the hirer who failed to keep his side of the
bargain. In 1507, for example, the Swiss formally withdrew all troops from French
service because they were not being paid.

Following Louis's capture of Milan, it was diplomacy, not war, that went some
way to securing his other objective, thanks to the Spanish monarch betraying his
cousin in Naples. So Ferdinand of Aragon ended his days in comfortable exile in
France, and the French and Spanish divided up his territory between them. Yet
this amicable division did not last for long, and the resulting split was finally to
place two veteran armies at each other's throats: the Spanish who had learned their
trade in Granada, and the Swiss who had learned it almost everywhere else.

El Gran Capitán

Spain's war against the French and their Swiss mercenaries in southern Italy was
conducted by a remarkable leader called Gonzalo Fernández de Córdoba, known
to all as 'El Gran Capitán' (the great captain) (see plate 7). Like so many of his
men, he had learnt his trade during the Granada War, where he had distinguished

himself at the head of attacking forces. During one skirmish de Córdoba had his horse shot from underneath him. At the Siege of Montefrio he had strapped an infantryman's shield on to his back, placed a large helmet on his head and led the way up the scaling ladders. At Tajara he constructed a makeshift *testudo* for his assault party out of house doors covered in cork. Such successes had led to him being relied on to take charge of every attack, and his reputation had grown rapidly.[6]

His first encounter during the Italian campaign was the Battle of Seminara in 1495, a battle that El Gran Capitán would probably have preferred to forget. He had sailed from Spain to Calabria with an army of six hundred horse and fifteen hundred foot. Of the mounted troops, on which the Spanish preferred to rely, one hundred were heavily armoured knights, while the rest were lightly army *jinetes*, an arm peculiar to Spain whose main weapon was not a spear or lance but a javelin, which they threw at the enemy. They also carried swords and heart-shaped shields for close combat. His infantry were a mixed bunch of sword-and-buckler men, crossbowmen and a few arquebusiers. When the Battle of Seminara was joined, the French knights swept the *jinetes* from the field while the Swiss pike phalanx crushed the foot-soldiers. Stunned by the defeat, Gonzalo de Córdoba took to guerrilla fighting for a while, but then concentrated on building up a reformed Spanish army, and it was a very different force that returned to Italy to take on Louis XII. The first results of de Córdoba's considerations were demonstrated at the Battle of Barletta in 1502. He now had pikemen of his own, but he still had his sword-and-buckler men, and used them in a way that capitalised upon the rigidity of the Swiss pike square. They were kept to the rear of the Spanish pikes, and when the front rows were locked together they were sent in to slip between the shafts and cause damage.[7]

One way of breaking the square had therefore been demonstrated, and the following year de Córdoba was to show one more in a battle that destroyed the mounted knights as much as it did the pikemen. At the Battle of Cerignola in 1503 de Córdoba was faced with heavily armoured French knights who were used to breaking an enemy position by a fierce frontal charge. De Córdoba had the privilege of selecting his own position, so he chose to act defensively by digging a ditch, reinforcing it with stakes and creating a front line in which as many as two thousand arquebusiers may have been deployed in four ranks. The comparatively few Spanish knights waited at the rear, while the *jinetes* harassed the French to encourage them to deliver the frontal attack for which de Córdoba had prepared so well. The *jinetes* performed their role so efficiently that the French had no opportunity to reconnoitre the battlefield and discover the trench. Their fresh knights led the charge, but came to a halt in front of the Spanish position, where arquebus fire put them into disorder and their commander, the Duc de Nemours, was shot dead. In spite of the disorganised knights a French infantry assault followed, led by the Swiss pikemen, but again the ditch came into its own and broke the supposedly unstoppable Swiss advance. It also allowed the arquebusiers to cut significant holes in their front ranks.[8]

When he sensed that his enemy was reeling, El Gran Capitán ordered into action two flank attacks from Spanish knights, and when the French began their retreat the *jinetes* pursued them. The Italian *condottiere* Fabrizio Colonna, who fought for de Córdoba that day, made the somewhat sneering remark that it was neither the Spaniard's tactical genius nor the deployment of modern weapons that had won Cerignola for him, but a 'little ditch and an earth parapet', a remark that was as perceptive as it was unkind, but Colonna was a knight through and through.[9]

In fact the trench and stakes of Cerignola were not conceptually very different from the stake line at Agincourt. De Córdoba's tactics would also probably have worked just as well if he had used archers instead of arquebusiers, although the noise and smoke of guns added a further dimension to the surprise of a controlled volley in the way that skilled generals were to exploit for many years to come.[10] De Córdoba possessed heavier guns than arquebuses, but a fire in the powder store just before battle was joined placed them out of action so it was the arquebusiers who became the heroes of the hour. Cerignola is usually regarded as being the battle where a new way was discovered of defeating mounted knights, but the repulse of the Swiss pikemen by requiring them to advance over trenches and broken ground was every bit as significant. Yet for these sorts of tactics to succeed there has to be an attacking general who is either inexperienced or stupid enough to let it happen, and any analysis of developments in military history has to allow for the fact that such generals are never in short supply.

The Battle of the Garigliano

El Gran Capitán's next victory over the French was conducted under very different circumstances. Having been defeated at Cerignola, the French army was once more in retreat, so Louis XII hurried to obtain reinforcements, but by the time they arrived on the scene the survivors of Cerignola had barricaded themselves inside the castle of Gaeta. De Córdoba moved against the French relief army, and the two armies soon found themselves facing each other across the swollen River Garigliano, whose wintry spate had turned the surrounding marshlands into a more formidable bog than was usual. The French attempted to cross using a pontoon bridge. De Córdoba waited until the bridge was full of men and then launched a counterattack. The French commander, the Marquis of Mantua, who had fought at Fornovo, tried again later using larger boats shipped up from the harbour at Gaeta. This time he succeeded in forcing a crossing, but although the Spanish fell back he was unable to capitalise on his triumph because of the rapidly deteriorating weather. Instead, he erected his own version of field fortifications so that the area of the Garigliano began to resemble a trench system of the First World War, with the mud to match.

For six weeks both sides endured a cold, wet and unpleasant stalemate, and after a Christmas truce de Córdoba moved into action once again. On 27 December, he erected his own prefabricated pontoon bridge several miles upstream from the French positions. The *jinetes* led the way in a surprise crossing, and the Spanish advance downstream was so rapid that the French infantry, which included the Swiss, had no time to take up a position and started to fall back towards Gaeta. With admirable discipline, they rallied and made a stand at Molo de Gaeta, where a bridge formed an ideal obstacle. Eventually the Spanish forced their way through by sheer weight of numbers, and their horsemen once more started to inflict death and destruction. The French offered to surrender Gaeta in return for a safe conduct, and de Córdoba agreed willingly. He had probably guessed that a promise not to harass the French on their homeward journey by land or sea would not be copied by any inhabitants of the towns they had pillaged on their way down. So it proved, and it was a ragged and demoralised French army that reached the Alps.

The Garigliano was Gonzalo de Córdoba's last campaign. He became Viceroy of Naples, a post which he held for four years before returning to Spain as a hero. He died in 1515, by which time there had been further developments in the military field that capitalised on his own innovations. Other Spanish commanders were now helping to lay down the foundations of a legend of Spanish excellence and invincibility that would eventually equal the myth of the Swiss.

The Battle of Ravenna

The battles of Cerignola and Garigliano effectively ended French ambitions with regard to Naples. For the rest of the sixteenth century, successive French monarchs had to be content with fighting for control of the duchy of Milan, although several attempts to extend France's Italian borders in other directions were to provoke memorable conflicts following the collapse of the League of Cambrai in 1508, an alliance (aimed at Venice) that the French had dominated and from which they stood to gain most. In its place Louis XII was to find his former allies combined with Venice against him in the so-called Holy League.

There was another major change within the French army, because the Swiss had temporarily become Louis's enemies after he had failed to pay them in 1507.

Louis therefore turned to *landsknechts* to provide his pikemen in the coming war. The Swiss joined the Holy League, and, apart from a force of six thousand Swiss pikemen hired by the papacy, fought for the next five years not as mercenaries but as the army of the Swiss confederacy. It was to be a fateful time for them, but the next opportunity to break a pike square was carried out not against the Swiss but against *landsknechts*.

In 1512, instead of drawing in his troops to defend against a possible move by the Holy League towards Milan, Louis XII went on to the offensive. The French commander in Italy was the young Gaston de Foix (*see* plate 8), who captured Brescia and then turned against Ravenna, the most important city still left in enemy hands. With the help of the Duke of Ferrara's artillery, breaches were made in the city's walls. But, before the place could be stormed, de Foix had to deal with a Spanish army sent to relieve the situation. The Spanish dug a defensive trench and awaited the French attack. Theirs was a naturally strong position because it had a river on one flank and marshy ground on the other, but de Foix was determined to take it by frontal assault.[11]

This was not, as one might think, the act of a madman, because de Foix intended to apply the lesson of Cerignola in reverse. By means of his artillery, of which he had an abundance, he would destroy the Spaniards' field positions to leave barren ground across which to advance. The French artillery moved out of the siege lines across a pontoon bridge while the bulk of the French army forded the river and took up their positions. The planned bombardment then began, but it was by no means as one-sided as de Foix had intended, because the Spanish had field pieces too. The French guns targeted the mounted Spanish knights while the Spanish cannon created havoc among the French infantry. One advantage that the French possessed was a greater freedom of ground in which to operate, so two guns were sent back across the bridge and down the opposite bank to fire on the Spanish from a different angle. Fabrizio Colonna, who was taken prisoner during the battle, said afterwards that this short-range fire into densely packed ranks of knights was a turning-point in the battle. One single cannonball apparently killed thirty-three knights, and such slaughter convinced him that they must advance at all costs to find men to fight against, rather than anonymous iron balls.[12] Having concluded such a modern phase of the conflict, the Battle of Ravenna now took a decidedly old-fashioned turn as knight charged against knight, breaking lances when they met.

While this was going on the *landsknechts* in the French army advanced, but here the trench came into its own by slowing their advance and allowing the Spanish sword-and-buckler men to slip under the points of the pikes and get in among them. In spite of emerging victorious the French army suffered huge losses, including its commander de Foix, while the losing Spanish army was almost annihilated. Ravenna was one of the bloodiest battles of the sixteenth century and demonstrated the importance of firepower when it was combined with a flexible use of the mounted arm.[13]

The Battle of Novara

It was to be the Battle of Novara in 1513 before the men from the Swiss cantons were seen in action again. There they fought for the first time against a French army. Louis XII returned to Italy in June of that year, intent on recovering Milan. It was an unwise move, because King Henry VIII of England and the Holy Roman Emperor Maximilian were making the threatening noises that would eventually lead to an invasion of France, but a treaty with Venice encouraged Louis in his gamble. The Swiss troops in imperial service who had been left behind in Italy retreated to Novara, so the French moved in rapidly to capture the town before more Swiss arrived to relieve it. When the Swiss did appear they managed to out-guess the French, who had been expecting them to rest their troops before attacking. But the Swiss had learned a valuable lesson from Cerignola's trench: they realised that they must use the element of surprise to attack the French in their camp before there was time for trenches to be dug. So in charged the pikemen in classic Swiss style, and even their old enemies the *landsknechts* were swept aside as the bristling porcupines defied artillery and arquebus fire to squash everything in their path. It was a glorious victory, helped by the French commander at Novara behaving like his predecessor at Cerignola in reverse – one had charged a fortified position, the other had neglected to provide one.

There was to be a further crop of French disasters in 1513. These will be described in a later chapter, but for now it will suffice to note that after Novara Louis XII formally surrendered all his claims to Milan and Naples. It should have meant peace in Europe, and for one whole year it did – until Louis died and his successor King Francis I proved to be even more ambitious than either of the two previous monarchs who had coveted a place in the sun.

Reversal at Marignano

Novara turned out to be the last great victory that the Swiss pikemen achieved by using their traditional tactics, because when another French king felt the impact of Swiss pikes two years later the results were very different. Francis I had been born in 1494, that glorious year when Charles VIII had invaded Italy and swept all before him. When the young Francis ascended the throne in 1515, he swore to

King Francis I of France, victor of the Battle of Marignano in 1515. The king was taken prisoner during the Battle of Pavia in 1525

regain the territory his predecessors had both won and lost, and he would begin with the richest prize in northern Italy – the duchy of Milan. For the fourth time in twenty years, therefore, the French invaded Italy.

Francis I's crossing of the Alps impressed all his contemporaries, particularly because, for once, there were actually troops there to oppose him. These were the now-hostile Swiss, but Francis cleverly avoided them by crossing over the little-used Colle Madalena. This strategy completely astounded Prospero Colonna, the commander-in-chief who was supposed to have stopped the French from invading. 'Have they wings, then?' he asked when news was brought to him of the crossing of the mountains. Just then a flying column of French, under the great *chevalier* Bayard, burst in on him at dinner.

The invaders faced the first serious resistance to their advance at the little village of Marignano on the outskirts of Milan (*see* plate 9). Blocking their way were Swiss pikemen who had formerly fought for France. The French had once again hired German *landsknechts*, so when the armies clashed there developed one of the most dramatic examples ever of 'push of pike'. In spite of arquebus fire tearing into their ranks, the Swiss maintained the upper hand and continued to push the French back as the day wore on. Only midnight brought a respite from the carnage, because the exhausted soldiers on both sides simply collapsed and slept where they fell, and even the king of France was forced to drink water from a ditch filled with bodies.

But Francis possessed some impressive field artillery, and the combination of cannon plus pikes eventually triumphed over pikes alone. The system that Francis employed was to deliver charge after charge by his mounted knights, while the artillery fired on them during the intervals between charges. The chivalric assaults achieved little by themselves, but the artillery could do its work because the charges forced the Swiss pikemen to form defensive hedgehogs rather than advance.[14] It was the same combination of arms that had worked at Ravenna, although it was used in a different way, and once Francis's Venetian allies had arrived the day was his. The Swiss retreated very honourably, but after this fight that was 'not between men but between ferocious giants', according to a veteran soldier who took part in the battle, twelve thousand men from the cantons lay dead on the battlefield. The power, if not quite the spell, of the Swiss had been broken.

The victory at Marignano made Francis I a hero, and almost everything that a king of France could possibly desire now lay at his feet – almost everything because within months of the battle the throne of the Holy Roman Empire became vacant upon the death of Maximilian. In accordance with an ancient tradition, any successor to the imperial throne was not just appointed but elected, and, in compliance with another old tradition, the 'electoral college', which had all the votes, was highly susceptible to bribery. There were initially three candidates. One of them, King Henry VIII of England, dropped out when he realised what enormous sums were involved. By contrast, Francis I, Europe's new hero, bribed willingly and liberally, but the other candidate bribed better, and Francis never forgave him for it.

This open-handed fellow was Charles of Habsburg (see plate 10), a man who was Burgundian by birth, Spanish by inheritance and German by descent. He was to claim that he spoke German to his horse, French to his ministers and Spanish to his God. He had inherited the territories lost by Charles the Bold, and in 1516, on the death of his grandfather King Ferdinand of Spain, this sixteen-year-old youth ruled an empire of which the Roman Caesars would have been proud. It included lands in Spain, Italy, France, Germany, Austria and The Netherlands, not to mention the mysterious territory of the New World. Unfortunately for Charles, however, much of this impressive patchwork was prevented from being a continuous territory by the presence at its geographical heart of the extensive and politically unfriendly kingdom of France. Not even becoming Emperor Charles V could compensate for that unpleasant fact.

Humiliation at Bicocca

From the time of Charles V's accession, the Italian Wars became the dynastic Habsburg–Valois Wars, and it was not long before Europe was to experience once again the 'push of pike'. Marignano had been an honourable defeat for the Swiss pikemen, but it was not a disaster. That tragedy had to wait until the Battle of Bicocca in 1522, where the Swiss were back fighting for the French. Francis I negotiated a new treaty with the confederacy whereby it agreed once again to supply mercenaries in French service. They had also promised not to declare war on the Emperor – a difficult combination, when the French advance against Charles V meant that they were doing precisely that.

The Battle of Bicocca came about as a result of another engagement near Milan. The imperial commander, Prospero Colonna, had spent the winter of 1521/22 avoiding giving battle to the French. By April 1522 his cat-and-mouse game was beginning to pay off, albeit in an unexpected way, because the twenty thousand Swiss troops now in French service were growing mutinous as a result of not being paid. When the opportunity arose to fight Colonna, who had fortified himself in the grounds of a country house called Bicocca, the Swiss presented the French general Lautrec with an ultimatum: either he fought a battle the next day and gave them a chance to pillage for their arrears of pay, or they would go home.

Colonna had set up a fine defensive position in the way that was now becoming commonplace: the house was defended by a long rampart behind a sunken road lined with arquebusiers. Lautrec was aware of the situation, and as the imperial army contained many *landsknechts* he planned a careful assault preceded by French artillery fire to break the enemy defences. But their Swiss mercenaries were impatient for action. At dawn on 27 April they formed up in two squares each about four thousand men strong and rushed headlong against the enemy in a frontal assault, despite the attempts by Lautrec to hold them back until the artillery had done its murderous work. The squares were in open and undisguised rivalry to be the first to close with the *landsknechts*, and took one thousand casualties before coming to a halt at the sunken road. Here the Swiss were safe from the artillery fire because the guns could not be sufficiently depressed, but there were still those arquebusiers. Those Swiss in the front ranks, the 'double pay' men whom a commander promised to pay twice (and always did, but only to the survivors!) fought as fiercely as ever, but were shot down as they attempted to leave the sunken road. To do this they had to scale the rampart, which was of a height greater than the length of a Swiss pike, and by the time the Swiss gave up the effort three thousand of them lay dead below the rampart.[15]

The Swiss had fought the Battle of Bicocca in a manner that contradicted everything they were supposed to have learned over the past quarter of a century, and it ended the myth of Swiss invincibility on a note of humiliation. For years to come, their contribution to a battlefield would be comparatively muted, and this was to be illustrated by their participation in one of the most significant battles of the sixteenth century – Pavia (*see* plate 11). At Pavia in 1525 the French army, under the personal command of Francis I, was besieging an imperial army until a relief army came along and besieged them in turn. A Spanish unit broke through the French lines one foggy morning. This provoked a French counterattack, and there ensued a very confusing battle that was fought under conditions of low visibility. Neither side was able to make use of prepared field positions. Instead, the soldiers took whatever cover they could, from walls or copses that loomed out of the fog, or simply stood their ground with no cover at all. The Spanish arquebusiers, acting predominately in small units, managed to take a heavy toll both of the French knights and the Swiss pikemen. The Swiss were strangely reluctant to attack – perhaps the memory of Bicocca was too vivid – but the Cent Suisses of the French royal guard fought to the last man during the battle's most important incident: an unsuccessful attempt to save Francis I from being captured. But of the former style of the 'all-crushing porcupine' of the pike squares there were only defeat and withdrawal. Bicocca's status as the end of an era was dismally confirmed.

On being freed Francis I turned his thoughts towards a reform of the French army, which he reorganised in 'legions', a term borrowed from antiquity and thus typical of the Renaissance. The legions combined pikemen and arquebusiers in a pattern similar to the better-known *tercios* of Spain, which are first mentioned by that name in 1534. The *tercio* (Spanish 'third') was the tactical formation that took its title from the medieval practice of dividing an army into three parts – the van, main battle and the rear. On paper a *tercio*'s strength was about three thousand men and consisted only of pikemen and arquebusiers, with no sword-and-buckler men. Pikemen were in a considerable majority. The distinguished French commander and man of letters, François de la Noue, admired such a combination, and quoted with enthusiasm the way four thousand men under Charles V had beaten off almost twenty thousand Moorish horse with minimal losses.[16] The *tercio*, with its four rectangular 'sleeves' of shot at each corner, was nonetheless a clumsy and wasteful way of combining the two arms. The inner files of a *tercio* contributed little to the eventual outcome of the fight, and firepower was greatly restricted.[17]

The Swiss Revival

It took twenty years for the Swiss to recover their *élan* at the Battle of Ceresole in 1544, and it was achieved only after considerable heart-searching and a reorganisation of tactics. The most important development was to intermingle arquebuses with pikemen in a modified version of the pike square. This was no easy task, and when battle was about to be joined it fell to an officer known as the sergeant-major to make the necessary arrangements using a process that required a knowledge of mathematics as well as tactics. In time, such a system – legion or *tercio* – was to become almost universal, but when employed at Ceresole it was clearly still in an experimental phase.

Blaise de Monluc, who survived the battle to write his memoirs, described how he placed a line of arquebusiers between the first and second rows of pikes. They held their fire until the front rank were engaged, and then opened up with very bloody results. However, as de Monluc ruefully noted, the enemy had done the same thing, so it is not surprising that de Monluc recorded 'a great slaughter' at Ceresole: first from the exchange of fire between the arquebusiers, and then from the resulting 'push of pike' between the Swiss and the *landsknechts*. The battle ended when heavily armoured French knights charged the enemy flanks, but at Ceresole the Swiss achieved their rehabilitation. The French army included two groups of Swiss: an inexperienced unit on the left wing and veterans on the right. The topography of Ceresole was such that one flank could not see the other, so when the inexperienced square gave way it did not demoralise those on the right wing, who won a classic pike battle against the *landsknechts*. The *landsknechts* had obligingly marched up a hill against the Swiss, thereby losing their formation in the marshy ground of the valley bottom and blocking their own lines of fire. For once the Swiss acted cautiously instead of rushing into the attack. They also took the unusual step of lying down so that the imperial army's arquebus and cannon fire passed over their heads, and it was only when the *landsknechts* were thirty paces away that they charged into the enemy with great success. They then re-formed and went to the assistance of their disordered comrades on the left flank.[18]

The former image of a Swiss pike square as an all-conquering steamroller, advancing steadily forward and simply crushing everything in its path, had ended at Bicocca. Ceresole was a battle won by being patient and disciplined, and it showed the princes of Europe the new potential of the Swiss pike square as a defensive formation – both for its own sake and as a hedge to protect the arquebusiers who now formed their core in place of the halberdiers. For the rest of the sixteenth century Swiss would be hired to fulfil this role. The myth of Swiss invincibility had died at Bicocca, and it is to their credit that they were able to learn from their defeats and show the world that they were now a modern army.

Chapter 5
The Laboratory of Siege Warfare

In pre-gunpowder days the worst a castle wall could expect was a well-aimed high trajectory stone ball flung from a trebuchet. Projectiles like these could be devastating enough, as sieges such as Acre in 1291 had proved, but cannon could fire balls on a lower trajectory to hit a medieval wall at right angles. Despite this, early fifteenth-century bombards could operate only on a powder-to-projectile weight ratio of 1:13 lest the cannon burst, and King Henry V's Siege of Harfleur ended after three months with the garrison being starved into submission, rather than having its defences battered to the ground. It was only later in the century that the ratio could be increased to 1:2, which greatly enhanced the bombard's hitting power. When the French retook Harfleur in 1449 their artillery-based siege took only sixteen days compared to Henry V's three months. The trebuchet, which had often matched the stone-firing bombard in its destructive capacity, was finally obsolete as a wall breaker.[1]

The other main method of capturing a medieval castle involved assault by siege towers and scaling ladders, against which certain simple countermeasures were very effective. A high defensive curtain wall flanked by even higher corner towers required scaling ladders to be impossibly long. Scarping, the projection of the bases of towers at an angle, had a similar effect by requiring too great an angle for the ladders. Height also gave the defenders some protection against fire arrows, which were aimed to destroy the wooden fighting platforms erected round the tops of towers and along walls. The inclusion of machicolations (stone-dropping holes inside a projecting terrace) allowed a simple method of vertical defence, and if scarping was present the projectiles would bounce off horizontally and fatally from a tower's base. All in all, tall, scarped curtain walls and towers, such as may be seen surrounding the town of Montagnana in Italy, Gibralfaro castle in Málaga or even mighty Constantinople, were a medieval lord's finest insurance policy until gunpowder came along.[2]

At the same time, of course, guns were being developed to make bombardments more efficient and more effective. To some extent this battle of wills has never ceased and is now waged with 'smart' weapons and concrete bunkers, but it is to the Renaissance that we must look to see this eternal competition being fought at its keenest pitch. It is, however, important to stress that developments in artillery and castle design did not move at a uniform pace across Europe, and that 'old-fashioned' medieval castles were to be found being besieged as late as the mid-seventeenth century.

The Artillery of Charles VIII

An important date in relation to the development of siege artillery is the French King Charles VIII's invasion of Italy in 1494.[3] As noted in the previous chapter, Charles took a modern artillery train along with him, and one notable feature was the easier mobility of the arm compared to previous efforts at transporting siege guns. For the whole of the campaign the guns kept up with the rest of the army, even when the disgraced Swiss had to drag them over the Cisa pass, and some towns surrendered at the mere sight of them. One commentator, Francesco Guicciardini of Florence, was so impressed that he wrote the following passage, comparing the pre-1494 situation with the new age of warfare that Charles VIII had brought with him:

> The French brought a much handier engine of brass, called a cannon, which they charged with heavy iron balls, smaller without comparison than those of stone made use of heretofore, and drove them on carriages with horse, not with oxen, as was the custom in Italy.[4]

He concludes with a passage that may be exaggerated yet expresses very well what was to become reality in not too many years time:

> . . . as much execution was done in a few hours, as formerly, in Italy, in the like number of days. These, more diabolical than human instruments, were used not only in sieges but also in the field, and were mixed with others of a smaller size. Such artillery rendered Charles's army very formidable to all Italy.[5]

A note of caution is needed here. Charles VIII may have possessed the most modern artillery train in Europe, but they were far from being 'galloping gunners'. Siege pieces continued to be very large, very slow and limited in numbers until late into the sixteenth century. Yet whatever their limitations in terms of size, number and mobility, cannon were here to stay. The sieges of Constantinople and

Málaga were made particularly dramatic because they were conducted using the latest technology against old-fashioned military architecture, and the latter part of the fifteenth century was to see a period of experimentation as military architects began to wrestle with the new challenge.

One early response was to pile up earth behind walls to make them thicker and more absorbent of cannon shot. Some medieval towers were simply filled with earth, but this had one serious disadvantage: when an enemy concentrated his guns on a small section the resulting earth and rubble that spilled out into the moat made an excellent assault ramp. Towers that were not just thick and absorbent but also solid were needed, and some ingenious modifications were tried. At Imola in 1472 the existing medieval rectangular corner towers were completely encased within the round towers in the solid *rocca* style that replaced them (*see* plate 12), and it is possible to walk round the inner tower within the outer one.

It was, however, in the use and deployment of defensive artillery that most clearly distinguished the new designs of fortresses from the old ones, and it was this consideration above all that led first to the abandonment of the tall, thin medieval tower for the solid *rocca*. The first point concerned the strength of floors. It was noted earlier at Constantinople in 1453 that concern was expressed about greater damage being done to the structural fabric of the old medieval towers when the cannon were fired from them than was caused by the Ottoman bombardment itself. This meant that new artillery towers had to be able to support a considerable weight.

Another requirement recognised from very early on was that castles should be built in such a way that cannon could be moved easily from one section to another. The medieval pattern of high towers that overlooked lower and narrow curtain walls did not facilitate this, so towers were lowered and were made contiguous with the walls, or were at least connected one with another by means of stout ramps. This meant that cannon could now be hauled into position much more quickly. Towers and walls were also built to be much wider, thus providing room for recoil as well as sufficient space for rolling guns along the ramparts. The result was that many town walls and castles began to take on a squat appearance. This feature also allowed better protection from an enemy's artillery mounted on the far edge of the moat, because if a town's walls were lower than the far edge of the encircling moat then the enemy's guns would have to be depressed so much that cannon could not be fired effectively – and the cannonballs might even fall out of the barrels!

Experiments were also carried out by placing cannon inside towers to fire out through portholes. In 1480 the Duke of Brittany's artillery tower at Fougères was designed to allow six tiers of guns to fire from one building. Such fifteenth-century designs look surprisingly modern, but the noise and smoke in such an enclosed space must have been dreadful. Better artillery towers were designed and built with clever ventilation systems or were left open to the elements at the rear, which had the advantage of being of no use to an enemy if a tower was captured. In spite of all these disadvantages, however, the artillery tower was probably the most common solution to the problem of putting gun emplacements on castle walls until the angle bastion came along, a development that will be discussed in a later chapter. For now, we will use one epic siege to illustrate the effectiveness of the transitional phases in castle design described above. The 'laboratory of siege warfare' where these new ideas were tested to destruction was the Second Siege of Rhodes in 1522.

The Fortifications of Rhodes

Rhodes, the island fortress of the Knights Hospitaller of St John of Jerusalem, was no stranger to siege warfare. An unsuccessful attempt to capture it had been made as recently as 1480 by Mehmet the Conqueror. In the forty years that had passed, the international brotherhood that was the Knights of St John had drawn on their vast reserves of European-wide experience to incorporate the latest in military thinking into defending Rhodes against the time when the Ottomans would return. The most interesting factor from our point of view is that the re-building of Rhodes did not involve a wholesale demolition and a fresh start, but instead a piecemeal solution, which was all the Knights could afford. It resulted in several very different forms of military architecture coming together in one place, ready for Mehmet the Conqueror's great-grandson, Suleiman the Magnificent, to transform it into a test-bed of siege warfare.[6]

The principle behind the post-1480 modernisation scheme was that artillery would play a major role in any new siege, so first of all the harbour-side Tower of St Nicholas, which had given good service in 1480, received an additional out-er artillery wall, thus giving it the overall appearance it retains today. The main towers round the town walls were strengthened and lowered to the level of the curtain wall, which was itself thickened and widened so that guns could be ma-noeuvred easily into position anywhere along its length. Traditionally, the walls of Rhodes were divided into different-named sections or 'Tongues', according to the nationality of the knights who defended the particular spot. So the 'Tower of Italy', which had seen fierce fighting in 1480, was utterly transformed under Grand Master de Carretto (1513–21), by whose name it is now known. The original tower, already reduced from its original height for the 1480 siege, was now encircled by a smooth, round and very thick wall fitted with artillery embrasures. A similar but

Suleiman the Magnificent, one of the greatest military leaders that the Ottoman Empire ever produced

simpler design was applied to the 'Tower of Spain', making these towers just two examples of the process noted earlier of encasing old towers within new ones.

By contrast the Tower of St George, which had originally been just a tall square medieval tower dating from 1421 to cover a gateway out of the city, received revolutionary treatment (see plate 13). In 1496 Grand Master d'Aubusson blocked up the gateway. In 1521, only a year before the Ottomans returned, the final reconstruction work was finished to give Rhodes something that was very unusual in Europe: a pentagonal bastion that projected majestically out into the moat, almost hiding from view the old tower left within it. It was designed by the renowned engineer Basilio dalla Scuola, and was transferred from paper to stone under the direction of the enthusiastic Grand Master Philip de L'Isle Adam (1521–34), the man who was shortly to face the new Ottoman threat.

The Tower of St George, otherwise known as the Bastion of Auvergne, has sometimes been regarded as the world's first example of the next major development in fortress design – the angle bastion.[7] But, although massive in size and of regular polygonal design, it could not quite deliver the flanking fire of the more sophisticated later designs. We may therefore regard it as an important stage in

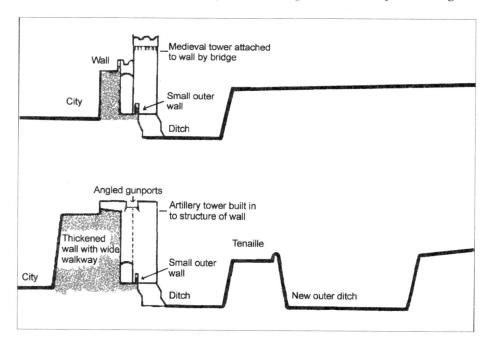

A diagram of the modifications made to the defences of Rhodes between 1480 and 1522

the progress towards the true angle bastion, which was not to be found in Rhodes at this time. Nonetheless, what it had in common with the later angle bastions was its sheer size. It totally dominated the area of the moat where it was located, and it was probably because of the strength of St George that the moat here was left at its original width.

Wider moats and ditches elsewhere gave better protection against bombardment, mining and assault, so on two other sections between the Tower of Spain and St John's Gate an extra wide, dry moat was added. The defences terminated in a high counterscarp (the far side of the ditch) and a sloping glacis beyond. Extending the moat was a considerable engineering effort, because it involved cutting down into the bedrock. In places between the old and new moats the exposed bedrock was retained, and an additional isolated wall called a *tenaille* was raised, faced all round with neat sloping stonework. In 1480 much fighting had taken place in the moat, and now for almost half the wall's length this dramatic addition allowed the defenders to cover attacks through or along the moat from every direction. It also screened the base of the curtain wall from artillery fire. The material left over was used to increase the thickness of the inner walls still further. The gates to the town also benefited from the addition of round or polygonal bastions around or beside them. Crucial among these were the bastions covering the St Athanasios Gate, the Tower of the Virgin and the Gate of St John, where curved parapet battlements gave the gunners the finest modern gatehouse protection.

Just north of the d'Amboise Gate, in the post of the Tongue of Germany, was a sharp corner. Here another innovation was tried with the construction of a *caponier* (casemate) projecting outwards into the ditch. This unique building, reminiscent of a modern-machine gun emplacement, dates from 1514 and was probably the first example of its kind in the world. It was pierced with gun ports, which enabled flanking fire to be laid along the moat in each direction. Finally, the area of the wall under the care of the Tongue of Italy, which had proved vulnerable in 1480, now boasted rebuilt walls that were inclined at an angle to one another to provide flanking fire – another precursor of the angle bastion.

The Siege of Rhodes

The trial by combat of these walls began when an advance party of ten thousand Ottoman troops landed on Rhodes on 25 June 1522. On 28 June Suleiman the Magnificent pitched his tent on Mount St Stephen and looked down towards the defiant walls just over a mile away. So much appeared to be going in his favour. The defences of Rhodes may have been strengthened since his great-grandfather's time, but the contemporary political situation in Europe indicated that the new generation of the Knights of Rhodes were far more isolated from potential support than their predecessors had ever been. Italy was a battleground between the armies of Francis I and Charles V, while other possible allies were either unable to make the journey to Rhodes across war-torn Europe or too preoccupied with their own affairs. Venice was in alliance with the Ottoman Empire, an agreement profitable to both sides, so, unlike his predecessor, Suleiman gave less attention to capturing the harbour area. With the political climate in Europe as it was, few reinforcements were expected.

Although the 1522 attacks on Rhodes were every bit as fierce as 1480, and delivered with the support of guns even bigger than those used then, the siege proved to be very different from what had been expected. In part this was because operations were conducted as much under the ground as above it. Fortunately for the garrison, some prisoners captured during a raid on an Ottoman ship just before the invasion revealed that Suleiman had recruited many miners from his conquered territories. This information persuaded the Grand Master to bring into his service a renowned military engineer called Gabriele Tadini, formerly in the service of Venice, who was placed in charge of all countermining operations.

The probable reason that the Ottomans chose mining as a principal means of attack was because of the knowledge they had acquired about the layout of Rhodes, which was built upon the foundations of an older, Greek city. The Greek town plan was based on a grid pattern, and under the streets there was an extensive network of culverts for sewage and fresh water. The walls of the Knights' defences followed the lines of some of these culverts, affording the possibility that these tremendous walls, although built upon solid rock, were already undermined for most of their length by old tunnels. The Ottoman plan was to drive mines under the moat to connect with these ancient passages where sites could be selected for explosive mines.

The Ottoman assault began, however, with the installation of cannon batteries opposite the fronts of Auvergne, Aragon, England and Provence, for what was to prove a sustained and very long bombardment. The Tongue of Germany, protected to the north by the Palace and its deep moat and anchored to the south by the formidable new bastion of St George, saw less action. Instead, the arc from the Tower of Spain round to the Tower of Italy became the Ottomans' prime artillery objective, but the garrison was ready for them. In preparation for the siege, the defenders had surveyed the land beyond the glacis, and were able to range their own guns on to the Ottoman positions in a very short time. As bands of Ottoman pioneers approached to dig trenches and build gun emplacements a hail of fire fell among them, to be followed by sudden sallies from inside the walls to cut them down in hand-to-hand fighting. Yet in spite of huge losses among the engineers, most of whom were the conscripted and therefore disposable survivors of countries captured by the Ottomans, some strong gun batteries were established. Fourteen batteries of three guns each now began to pound the curtain walls of the Tongues of Aragon and England, while seventeen worked against those of Auvergne and Italy. Most fire was concentrated on the curtain wall. The Ottomans clearly believed that to create a breach into the city at a point as remote as possible from possible flanking fire from the towers far outweighed the cost in men's lives of taking not one moat but two.

By now Gabriele Tadini had begun his countermining operations. The first was by cutting a long tunnel or trench parallel to the walls that would meet any Ottoman tunnels being driven forward. The second was the installation of a primitive listening device consisting of bells attached to taut drum skins, a simple machine designed to pick up any underground disturbances while the cannon fire continued above it. One direct hit smashed the tower of the church of St John, which had been a useful observation post. Attempts were also made against the Tower

A woodblock print of sixteenth-century gunners in action

of St Nicholas on the harbour, but its defensive firepower was as good as its new walls, so the Ottoman guns were removed and taken elsewhere. The curtain wall stood up to the bombardment better than had been anticipated, but soon the first breaches appeared. As expected, rubble cascaded into the moat to form a mound between the breach and the *tenaille*, but repair work was undertaken by night so that before dawn broke the breach had disappeared. Counterbattery fire was also fierce, and during the artillery duel on the Spanish front the Ottomans' Master Gunner lost both his legs.

By now the Ottoman miners were very busy tunnelling opposite a breach in the curtain wall of Italy. As more breaches began appearing elsewhere, other tunnels spread beneath the moat while Tadini hurriedly extended his countermines and stationed marksmen on the shattered walls to spot any Ottoman troops emerging from the ground. By early September it was estimated that the assault tunnels under the moat covered five-sixths of the wall's length, but most had foundered on meeting Tadini's own defence line. One or two, however, remained undetected, and on 4 September the besiegers managed to ignite a terrific explosion underneath the Tongue of England. Unlike an artillery bombardment, where the process was a long one and any concentration on a particular point of the wall was obvious to the defender, who could repair the damage in between shots, the blast from a hitherto unknown mine was a huge and unpleasant surprise. The resulting breach in the English section was thirty-six feet wide, and the Ottoman soldiers leaped from their trenches and poured across the moat on to the huge pile of rubble. Realising that a decisive attack was now taking place, the Grand Master de L'Isle Adam took the banner of the Crucifixion, which had been presented in 1480, and led two hours of fierce hand-to-hand fighting, which eventually succeeded in driving back the enemy horde.

On 9 September three further mines exploded, but they caused damage only to the curtain walls or the *tenailles*. The formidable reinforcements built round the gates were hardly touched, an eloquent testimony to the strength of their designs, although the bastion of St George still shows a vertical crack to this day. The Order's gunners were therefore able to continue firing into the Ottoman lines with little interruption. On one occasion the guns on St John's Gate destroyed an entire Ottoman trench line, burying the occupants.

Only one tower suffered temporary loss during the siege. This was the Tower of Spain, which was almost completely flattened by artillery fire, but a tremendous effort recaptured it for the Knights. A few days later, during a larger Ottoman assault, the Tower of Spain was lost again. This time a counterattack was led by Jacques de Bourbon. He entered the tower from below through a countermining tunnel and led a group of men-at-arms up on to the ruined walls to find Ottoman flags flying but only three Turkish soldiers left alive. The rest had already been killed by flanking artillery fire delivered from the bastion of St George. The effects seemed to confirm the wisdom behind the new designs, but it was also found that the angle and distance of the defenders' shots threatened casualties from 'friendly fire'. This was a design fault that would be corrected in the later angle bastions.

There were now breaches in every wall and *tenaille* from the Tongue of Aragon round to that of Italy, and only the artillery fire from the damaged but still unsilenced artillery towers prevented the decisive enemy assault from being launched. The Tower of Spain was so badly damaged that Tadini even recommended its demolition so that the materials could be used for the temporary entrenchments he was building inside the city in anticipation of an attack over the walls. On 11 October, as the nights were beginning to grow cold, the heroic Tadini was shot in the right eye by a sniper. The ball passed through the side of his head and went out beside his ear. Amazingly, the frightful wound was not fatal, but it put this military genius out of action for two weeks.

The Fall of Rhodes

In mid October a handful of reinforcements arrived safely into the harbour on a series of ships, but an inventory of weapons and powder made gloomy reading. De L'Isle Adam ordered that no weapons were to be fired against the enemy without a specific order from a senior officer. This was only partly to conserve stocks, because rumours were beginning to circulate of messages being fired into the Ottoman lines, and fingers were being pointed at suspected 'fifth columnists'. It was now winter. Reinforcements and supplies continued to arrive in dribs and drabs while the now-familiar pattern of mining and countermining, assaults on the breaches and bloody hand-to-hand fighting continued as it had since the summer. By the beginning of December the new tunnels added to the ancient culverts had created such a honeycomb beneath the walls that it is surprising that they stood up at all. One observer noted how thousands of Ottomans raided the town almost every night by means of this labyrinth. They were invariably driven out again before dawn, and as the stalemate continued the sultan began to send out cautious approaches offering negotiations. At first the brave messengers were driven off by arquebus fire, but at length the Grand Master was persuaded to call a general council of the Order.

For the first time in months a sober review of their position was possible, and the reports from his subordinates were not encouraging. Slave labour was now exhausted; supplies of powder and shot were almost gone; and there was no likelihood of relief arriving. De L'Isle Adam then began to hear suggestions about what should be done. He was confronted by the citizens of Rhodes, who felt that their own views about the fate of their city had been disregarded. Perhaps sensing the mood in the town, or even being accurately informed of it by his spies, Suleiman the Magnificent made a generous offer. In return for the city's surrender the Knights would be permitted to leave the island unharmed, and the citizens of Rhodes would be allowed to live as Christians within the Ottoman Empire. A truce was declared while the matter was being considered. It was soon broken, but the resulting conflict from both sides was feeble compared to the ferocity that had gone before. The citizens of Rhodes were now in open revolt, and were beginning to think of themselves as virtual hostages of these proud Knights of St John, but diplomatic moves were developing rapidly in the background.

Three individual meetings were held between Suleiman the Magnificent and de L'Isle Adam, during which an amicable settlement was negotiated. The personal trust that bound the eventual agreement between the two deadly enemies is quite remarkable and has an air of chivalry about it that is only fitting in this bizarre and anachronistic encounter. When Suleiman the Magnificent finally rode in triumph into the city through the Gate of St John he dismissed his guards, saying, 'My safety is guaranteed by the word of a Grand Master of the Hospitallers, which is more sure than all the armies in the world'.

The fall of Rhodes, which had come about only after the firing of eight thousand cannonballs and the digging of fifty-four tunnels, marked the end of Christian power in the Aegean. Between 1523 and 1530 the Order found temporary homes while they still dreamed of Rhodes and its recapture, but in 1530 Emperor Charles V, who had commented about Rhodes that 'nothing had ever been so well lost', made the Knights of St John a gift of the island of Malta. It seemed to be a bare and rocky outcrop compared with their lush island of Rhodes, but the offer was accepted, and a further stage in the Order's long history began. But Suleiman the Magnificent's chivalric action in letting the knights go away unharmed had its price, because among the survivors who had sailed away with the Grand Master on 1 January 1523 was a young knight called Jean de la Vallette. He had been blooded during the Siege of Rhodes, and forty-two years later he was to earn a glorious name when, as the new Grand Master of the Knights Hospitallers of St John of Malta, he faced another siege against the Ottomans. Once more Europe was to watch in amazement as this strange living anachronism of an institution, which somehow combined an outdated and romantic medieval chivalry with some hard-headed Renaissance technology, tested itself and its fortifications in the harsh laboratory of contemporary siege warfare.

Chapter 6

'God gave the sea to the infidels . . .'

The Granada War of 1481–92 meant that the conflict between Christian and Muslim extended right along the Mediterranean Sea. This area of water has the longest history of organised naval warfare in the world, and the war on the seas is the theme of this chapter. The struggle, fought primarily from the decks of armed galleys, was ultimately so disadvantageous for the Ottoman Empire that an Ottoman writer early in the seventeenth century could, by way of justification, make the comment that provides the heading not only to this chapter but also to the one that follows: 'God gave the sea to the infidels, and the land to the Muslims'.[1]

To the infidels, and Spanish and Portuguese ones in particular, 'the sea' had long been divided into two contrasting theatres of operation: the Mediterranean and the Atlantic. As early as 1415 the Portuguese had captured Ceuta, the North African port located across the Strait of Gibraltar from the Iberian Peninsula. The beginning of Portuguese seaborne imperialism is commonly dated from this event, but to some extent the taking of Ceuta was a false start, because subsequent Portuguese inroads into Africa involved sea voyages round the Atlantic Ocean rather than treks overland. One reason for this was the development of the caravel, a new kind of sailing ship that allowed Portuguese traders to outflank the well-established camel trains from the Islamic world. By 1444 the ocean route to the gold and slave areas of West Africa was well established, and in 1488 Bartolomeu Diaz rounded the Cape of Good Hope. Four years later, Columbus discovered the New World.

However, the sailing ships that changed the world out on the Atlantic had to wait another century before claiming a similar domination in the Mediterranean, where the oared galley still reigned supreme. Galleys were the workhorses of Mediterranean warfare, and by the end of the sixteenth century these ancient vessels had evolved as far as their inherent limitations would allow to become the floating equivalent of the artillery fortress. Naval warfare using such ships had been conducted in the Mediterranean for centuries, and the oared vessel's easier manoeuvrability in calm and shallow water and its ability to beach often gave it an edge over the superior firepower of the caravel. However, the larger cargo-carrying capacity of the sailing ship relative to the numbers of its crew, and its ability to work all year round instead of needing winter quarters, were to give it an eventual victory on commercial grounds, even if the military honours were more even for many years to come.[2]

The oared galley was so well suited to the Mediterranean that its overall design changed little over two millennia. It possessed two lateen (triangular-shaped) sails, but because calm weather bedevilled sea travel it was the vessel's oars that always provided the main means of propulsion. Between twenty-five and thirty oars lay on either side, each one of which was pulled by three or four oarsmen seated on, and sometimes chained to, their benches with a narrow walkway in between. This arrangement allowed a greater speed compared to the ancient triremes, where the oars had been in banks and each was operated by one man, so that a typical galley might contain as many as four hundred men, of whom two hundred and fifty would be oarsmen, with fighting men crammed into every other square inch of the ship.

The supply of oarsmen was always the single greatest logistical headache for an admiral. In Venice, service on the galleys was theoretically a duty of all free men and had considerable social advantages: time spent on the galleys, but not actually rowing them, was a popular choice among daring young noblemen, who regarded the position of 'bowman of the quarterdeck on a floating castle' as an entertaining alternative to manning a static one. One outstanding example of this is Miguel de Cervantes, the future author of *Don Quixote*, who was wounded on board a Venetian galley during the Battle of Lepanto in 1571.

The life of an oarsman was considerably less attractive than merely serving on board, and in 1522 we read of a recruiting drive by the Venetian Senate to raise six thousand men for the galleys. The inducements offered were considerable: freedom for life from personal taxation, training in firearms, permission to wear personal arms (a coveted privilege), and freedom from prosecution for debt during galley service and for six months afterwards. But even this did not always provide sufficient compensation for the death and discomfort that could well attend such service. By the mid-sixteenth century, the Venetians still used a majority of free oarsmen, but in all other fleets most oarsmen were prisoners. Galley fleets could also be hired, a service at which the Genoese excelled, and at the Battle of Lepanto in 1571 about one in ten of the Christian galleys had been rented from Genoa.

Overcrowding on board brought its own problems in terms of the spread of disease and the large amount of provisions and equipment that were needed. Cannonballs fired at sea could not be retrieved and used again, so adequate supplies of heavy shot had to be squeezed on board. Frequent stops also had to be made for fresh water, and this vital necessity, together with the galley's inability to operate in bad weather, made a galley fleet highly dependent upon its bases. The arrival of a hundred galleys in port meant feeding forty thousand men at short notice, a number that exceeded many contemporary armies. For many years, only Barcelona, Venice and Constantinople had the resources to support whole navies, while smaller places such as Malta and Genoa acted as important staging posts. Many of the actions to be described in the pages that follow had the simple objective of capturing suitable bases: a more useful outcome of a naval operation than merely sinking an enemy's ships.

Galley Warfare

Every man on a Venetian galley was potentially a fighting man, so all its occupants were issued with weapons and were expected to use them. Arquebuses were the only weapons that oarsmen would have difficulty in handling, so the inboard member of a threesome could have a short pike, the middle man could wield a bow, while the outer man, hampered in the constricted space, could at least throw stones. A chained man might have his shackles released when battle threatened and would be promised his freedom in return for loyal service. Others stayed chained up but could still handle weapons; unlike those who fought unfettered they could not jump overboard when the situation was too threatening.

The banks of oars down each side of a galley meant that galley warfare was conducted from the bow rather than the ship's

A Venetian galley, as used during the Battle of Lepanto in 1571

sides. In ancient times galleys had attacked each other by ramming or boarding, but by the middle of the fifteenth century Christian ships were beginning to receive extra offensive armament in the shape of breech-loading cannon mounted at the bow or the stern. Philip the Good's crusader fleet of 1445 would have been armed in this way, but after the fall of Constantinople Ottoman armed galleys began to be seen in large numbers as well. By the mid-sixteenth century, larger guns were to be found on board, including heavy cannon on sleds that could only be aimed by lining up the ship itself, rather like a fighter plane. Arquebuses and heavy muskets added to the galley's resemblance to a floating artillery fort.

The preferred tactic was to catch the enemy fleet while it was still unsuspecting and proceeding in an open order. Galleys would then close in, one against one. There would be an exchange of fire, but nothing resembling a broadside, and then a hand-to-hand fight would take place when the galleys joined. A round shot striking the side of a ship may not have produced a hole sufficient to sink the vessel, but it would invariably result in a hail of wood splinter shrapnel into the ship's interior, with devastating effects on a gun crew. Similar shots delivered against an overcrowded galley might even cripple the ship solely from the effects on its crew, and when the vessels closed arquebus fire and pikes would come into action in the maritime equivalent of the terrible 'push of pike'. This was the reality of sixteenth-century Mediterranean naval warfare, and one of the best descriptions of the sheer horror of it comes from a certain Pantero Pantera, who wrote of:

> . . . the havoc wrought among human limbs now by iron now by fire (which is not so terrifying in land battles), the sight of this man torn to shreds and in the same moment another burned up, another drowned, another pierced by an arquebus ball, yet another split into wretched pieces by the artillery. On top of this there is the terror caused by the sight of a vessel swallowed up by the sea with all hands without the remotest possibility of rescue, to see the crew half alive, half burned, sink miserably to the bottom while the sea changes colour and turns red with human blood, covered the while with arms and scraps and fragments of broken ships.[3]

Such destruction could be even worse when a galley was targeted not by another ship but by the guns of a coastal fort. The Venetian Admiral Sebastian Venier had direct experience of this when he tried to destroy an Ottoman fort at Cattaro in 1572. The Ottoman gunners were faced with a small, moving and distant target, which was to the Venetians' advantage, but the Venetian fire was also ineffective:

> . . . because, being in movement, they shoot awry, and when they do score a hit it is on a stone bastion or a thick and stout earthwork, whereas shots from the land strike thin, vulnerable wood or human flesh.[4]

Landing parties would be needed to reduce such forts. These operations often confronted the galley crews with another great danger – that of fighting in desert conditions, another difficult and unpleasant experience, which will be illustrated in the pages that follow.

The Barbary Coast

While their most Catholic majesties Ferdinand and Isabella were actively preparing in Spain for their final assault on Granada, the Ottoman Empire's Sultan Bayezid II began to show an interest in the fate of his fellow Muslims of the Iberian peninsula. Because the Strait of Gibraltar was many miles distant from Constantinople his first act was to send a reconnaissance mission under Kemal Reis, the corsair, and somewhere off the south-eastern coast of Spain Reis made the first direct contact between the Ottoman Empire and the Muslims of Granada.[5]

Some successful raiding of Christian ports followed, which led to the corsairs establishing themselves in bases on the North African coast, such as Bougie and the island of Djerba, a centrally located place between Tripoli and Tunis. Reis finally returned to Constantinople in 1495, leaving local pirates to continue the harassment of Spanish possessions. The Spanish response to these raids consisted of sporadic attacks on individual pirate lairs, but many of these operations were

The castle of Djerba, the target of an unsuccessful Spanish expedition to the Barbary coast during 1510

highly successful. One such raid in 1509 captured Bougie and Tripoli, and the following year another expedition set out for Djerba. The Spanish army arrived during August, when the intense heat destroyed both the physical health and the judgement of even these experienced warriors. The Moors of Djerba cleverly allowed the expedition to land and made a stand several miles inland at the nearest oasis. The Spanish army unerringly followed their lead, and four thousand Spaniards were killed in the resultant ambush.

In the summer of 1514 the Muslim forces made an attempt to recapture Bougie. The assault was led by the brothers Barbarossa, who were originally from the Greek island of Mytilene and operated out of La Goletta in Tunisia. Bougie was bombarded with artillery, but the attempt was called off when the elder Barbarossa brother, Oruc, was wounded in the arm. Realising that they needed much more in the way of military technology the brothers sent Piri Reis, the nephew of Kemal Reis, as an envoy to Constantinople. These efforts were rewarded by the supply of ships and equipment, and, most important of all, a strengthening of the religious and military ties which now linked one end of the Mediterranean to the other. Further religious solidarity occurred when the corsairs helped fellow Muslims to escape from Granada to North Africa.

Khereddin Barbarossa, who captured Algiers in 1529

Over the next few years the initiative swung from one side to the other. In 1529 Khereddin Barbarossa took the Spanish fort at Algiers, the one remaining seat of opposition in that vital area. Finally, in 1534 he deposed the bey (ruler) of Tunis, Muley Hassan, thereby completing his dominance of the coast from Morocco to Djerba. A response was clearly needed, and a plan for the recapture of Tunis began to form in the mind of Emperor Charles V. It was a risky operation, because to send a sizeable army over to Africa was almost to invite a French descent on the Spanish possessions in Italy, but the scheme went ahead in the capable hands of the young Duke of Alba, a man whose name we shall encounter in the future when he fights German Protestants and Dutch rebels.

Alba's first objective was the fortified town of La Goletta, which commanded the entrance to the harbour of Tunis. Alba's father had been killed during the ambush at the oasis at Djerba in 1510, and Alba almost suffered the same fate when he went foraging in the vicinity of the ruins of Carthage and was set upon by a force of Moorish cavalry. Alba had wisely left a means of retreat and lived to fight another day, but further challenges from heat and thirst were not long in coming.

When La Goletta fell the Spanish army began a march round the bay to attack Tunis itself. There were five miles of desolate scrub before the first waterhole was reached, and, just as at Djerba, their enemies were waiting for them with arquebuses and cannon. Some of the Spaniards' horses were already dropping dead from the heat when their tired and thirsty army drew up its ranks. Charles V, in the very centre of the action, had his horse shot from under him, while the Duke of Alba led a spirited cavalry charge against the encircling Moorish light horsemen. If the Spaniards' resulting victory, which drove Barbarossa back to Tunis, was a surprise, then their capture of Tunis, which followed, was nothing short of miraculous.[6]

Charles V's subsequent sack of Tunis was both unnecessary and unwise, and only the looters did well out of it (although such fortunes were often dissipated as quickly as they had been acquired). A certain Ferry de Guyon, a soldier with Charles V, hoped to retire on the fortune he had made during the pillaging of Tunis, but did not remain rich for very long. He wrote:

> I spent the winter in the village of Casafriol near Capua without so much as a coin to play heads or tails with since I had gambled and lost every cent of the money and loot I won at Tunis. So to amuse myself, I went hunting every day.[7]

Andrea Doria – Admiral of Spain

In 1537, Barbarossa counterattacked with raids on Spain and the Balearic islands. Meanwhile Suleiman the Magnificent produced yet another of those dramatic military gestures that caused periodic panic in western Europe. This time he marched a large army to the coast of Albania then landed an army in Italy near Otranto, just as Mehmet the Conqueror had done in 1480. Eight thousand irregular horsemen raided inland, and although Otranto and Brindisi held out this produced much terror. The sultan eventually withdrew all his troops from Italy and chose instead to besiege Corfu. A hastily put together alliance between Spain, Venice and the pope then sent Charles V's admiral, the Genoese Andrea Doria, in pursuit of the Ottoman fleet.

Andrea Doria is a most interesting character. He had begun his military career as a *condottiere* in Italy, and in 1512 he turned his attentions to the sea. Thereafter, as an admiral of France, the papacy and finally Spain, he developed great skills in galley warfare. Doria initially commanded two galleys, but by 1537 he led a joint fleet of forty-five Spanish, eighty Venetian and twenty-six papal galleys against the Ottomans. His approach made Suleiman the Magnificent abandon the siege and return to Constantinople, leaving Khaireddin

Andrea Doria, who fought the Battle of Prevesa in 1538

Barbarossa in charge at Prevesa, the nearest Ottoman base to Corfu.

The following year Doria caught up with him at Prevesa, but held back from fighting a decisive battle with Barbarossa when the corsair came out on to the open sea. Doria was much criticised for this, particularly by the Venetians, who were forced to sue for peace to protect their distant possessions. Barbarossa, too, was recorded as being disappointed that the two major fleets of the rival powers had not come to grips. Given that this was more than thirty years before the famous Battle of Lepanto, it is fascinating to speculate what might have happened had Prevesa developed into a full-scale battle. However, what little combat that took place is nonetheless very interesting to study. An isolated Venetian galleon (a sailing ship with no oar propulsion) lay becalmed some distance from friendly

The abortive Siege of Algiers by Emperor Charles V in 1541

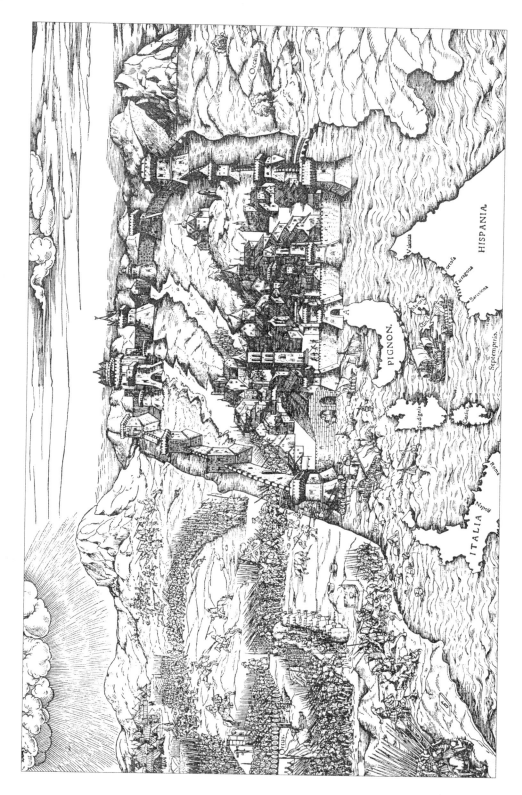

Occlus.

PIGNON.

HISPANIA

Valéria

Tortosa

Taracona

Sarcilona

Septemptrio.

ITALIA

Nipoli

Roma

galleys. The static vessel was then attacked by Ottoman galleys, but it managed to drive them off using superior broadside gunnery and took no damage from ramming. Doria's caution appeared justified, although the credit must go to the weather rather than to his seamanship, as the pursuing corsair fleet was caught in a storm and many ships were wrecked off the coast of Albania. Finally Doria laid siege to the fortress of Castel Nuovo near Cattaro on the coast of Croatia, bombarding its walls from the sea and sending in a landing party. When it was captured a Spanish garrison was put in charge, but it was retained only for one year.

Following this fine demonstration of his naval capability Charles V turned his attentions once again to North Africa and tried to capture Algiers in 1541. His fleet gathered in the Balearic islands in October, hoping that the choice of month would be too late for an Ottoman counterattack and too soon for the gales of winter. But the latter gamble was the first to be lost: heavy rain pelted the besiegers as they surrounded Algiers, soaking their gunpowder and giving their enemies a chance to hit back. Most seriously of all, about one hundred and forty ships were wrecked or damaged as they lay at anchor, so Charles ordered a withdrawal. Dissenting voices, from such people as Hernando Cortés, the conqueror of Mexico, were overruled in favour of an honourable retreat.

When the news spread that Charles was an emperor without a fleet, his enemies gleefully took advantage of the situation. In 1543 the sultan launched another campaign against Hungary, the French resumed the Habsburg–Valois Wars and Kheiriddin Barbarossa started to create fresh havoc in the western Mediterranean, secure in the knowledge that the French would not interfere, because the ebb and flow of Mediterranean politics had in fact thrown up a Franco–Ottoman alliance. In fact, Barbarossa joined the French in an attack on Spanish-held Nice, and actually wintered his fleet at Toulon!

Barbarossa's death in 1546 caused little respite for his enemies, because his successor, Dragut, went on to seize Tripoli in 1551 and terrorised Italy, Corsica, Catalonia and the Balearic islands. The balance of power only began to shift when Charles's successor, Philip II, concluded the Treaty of Cateau-Cambresis with France in 1559. The Habsburg–Valois struggle with France was now over, so Philip could turn his attentions elsewhere. It was not long before Suleiman the Magnificent gave Philip the opportunity for a decisive showdown by mounting an expedition against the island of Malta in 1565.

The Great Siege of Malta

When the Knights of Rhodes moved to Malta they did more than merely occupy another island base – they shifted the centre of gravity from the eastern Mediterranean to the west. Both geographically and conceptually, Malta lay in a region that had been a contested sphere of influence since the Granada War, and it was one of the Barbary corsairs, Dragut, who was to provide the naval arm of the Ottoman operation against the island. As a strategic base Malta had much to recommend it. With the same foresight and energy with which they had given Rhodes the finest fortifications they could afford, the Order had once more moved with the times and converted the rocky island into a formidable galley port where Spanish fleets could rest and re-arm.

The 1565 operation against Malta is often regarded as the sixteenth-century siege *par excellence*, and it certainly holds a warm place in European hearts, if only because the other two Mediterranean island sieges – Rhodes in 1522 and Cyprus in 1571 – were defeats. Those sieges, however, were essentially land-based operations against differing types of fortifications and saw comparatively little naval involvement. Malta, by contrast, exhibits certain features of being an amphibious operation similar to other attacks on coastal castles in North Africa described above, and it was as a fortress to command the sea, rather than land, that Malta had evolved.

Although financial resources did not stretch towards fortifying the area where Valletta now stands, Grand Master Jean de La Vallette, after whom the capital would one day be named, had erected a fine star-shaped fort called St Elmo to guard the harbour approaches. For this reason the Ottoman attack did not originally come from the sea. Instead the army came ashore on the west coast of the island and directed its first efforts against St Elmo. This initial operation went on for a full month. St Elmo was contested under the circumstances of a curious reversal in the physical positions of the two armies, because the Ottomans attacked by land while the Knights of Malta reinforced and supplied the place by sea. This convenient arrangement ended when Dragut arrived and placed guns at a strategic position to cut off any ships crossing the harbour mouth even by night. The resultant capture of St Elmo was expensive for the Ottomans, who lost eight thousand men compared to the six hundred killed among the defenders. Dragut was killed during the attack, and the commander of the Ottoman fleet was badly injured by a ricocheting shot.

With St Elmo out of action Mustafa Pasha was able to bring his whole force round to the harbour of Marsa Muscetto immediately to the north of the Grand Harbour. The inner defences of Malta were now subjected to seven weeks of attack in the second phase of the operation, but the system of walls kept any breaches to a minimum, and the discipline and fighting skills of the soldiers held any breaches that were created.

Early in July, a new method of attack was tried. Hassan, Pasha of Algiers, who was the son of the great Khaireddin Barbarossa, led an attack mounted in small boats on the weak points of Malta's seaward defences while a land assault went on. Both attacks failed, the waterborne one disastrously so when it was found that the so-called weak points had been covered by a boom just under the water's surface. In desperation, the leader of the unit thrust his boats against the rocky point of the spur and some of his men even got a footing, but they were driven out and exterminated when their boats were sunk in the crossfire.

This was the only attempt at an assault on Malta by sea. Otherwise the siege was the usual pattern of mining and bombardment to create breaches and desperate struggles for the gaps thus created, but by the end of August the Ottomans had had enough, and the arrival of a reinforcing fleet served only to confirm them in the decision to withdraw. Malta therefore survived to deny the Ottomans the control of the North African coast that they had sought. It was a major setback for Suleiman the Magnificent.

Galleys at Lepanto

We will close this chapter on naval warfare with an account of the most famous Mediterranean galley battle of all – the great Battle of Lepanto in 1571 (see plate 14). It was fought by a fleet that was intended to save the island of Cyprus, which was then under siege by the Ottomans. In this it failed in its primary purpose, as we shall see in a later chapter, but the way the fleet failed and then succeeded elsewhere sheds light on the methods of galley fighting used during the sixteenth century, and also shows up the political climate that could so easily stifle any military initiative.[8]

The relief operation for Cyprus was mounted in 1570 in spite of a severe fire at the Venice arsenal that caused more alarm than actual damage. Money was raised by various means such as selling high offices, and new galleys were laid down as rapidly as possible. Yet such urgency was not reflected in the actions of Venice's potential allies. Spain's Cardinal Granvelle stated openly that Venice deserved no support, because history had shown that she helped others only when it was in her own interests so to do, as if that were not the general rule governing all alliances in contemporary Europe. Eventually the Spanish came round, but not without a squabble over who should be in command of the relieving fleet. Their own contingent was to be led by Gian Andrea Doria, the nephew of Andrea Doria, who set sail with secret instructions that commanded him to place the security of the Spanish ships above all other considerations – a far from encouraging start to an allied naval operation.

To the Spanish ships were added those of the pope, while other potential allies were less than enthusiastic. The Emperor of Austria and the King of Poland did not wish to offend the Ottomans. The young King of Portugal promised seventeen ships 'next year', and a letter was written in vain to Tsar Ivan the Terrible suggesting that he should attack the Ottomans in the rear. The most cutting comment came from the Knights of Malta. If it was up to them, they said, the Ottomans could take ten islands from the unhelpful Venetians, not just one. Nevertheless, and perhaps prompted by a fear of being totally isolated in the Mediterranean, the Order sent five ships.

While the Venetian fleet waited for the orders to move, disease spread through the galleys because of the cramped and unhygienic conditions aboard. Then instead of sailing immediately for Cyprus much time was wasted attacking Ottoman possessions in the Adriatic and on the island of Corfu. By 22 September the fleet had arrived in Crete, where the news was received that Nicosia had fallen and that Piale, the Ottoman admiral, had left a small force off Cyprus and had come to Rhodes to pick up reinforcements. The allied commander, Zani, therefore concluded that he was outnumbered by an enemy much nearer than Cyprus. Famagusta would have to hold out until a large relieving force had been assembled. The Christian navy therefore turned about, the Venetian galleys returning to Corfu, the Spanish to Messina.

When the sad news of the fall of Famagusta reached Messina it was accompanied by the additional intelligence that a large Ottoman fleet had assembled and was ravaging Christian lands while waiting for the approach of the relieving force. Their location was reported to be the mouth of the Gulf of Corinth at a place called Lepanto. With such a large navy assembled and with its prime objective lost, it would have been difficult to resist the opportunity for revenge, so Don John (John) of Austria, the illegitimate son of Emperor Charles V who had overall command of the fleet, sailed into the attack.

The Christian fleet went into battle in a wide crescent, the main line consisting of galleys ranked close together with a reserve squadron half a mile to the rear. Don John also had a secret weapon in the form of the galleass; these were not sailing ships – only two vessels of that type being present at Lepanto even though their potential had been shown at Prevesa – but galleys of double the usual size, higher built and with overhead protection for their oarsmen, and larger and more numerous guns in their bows. Six galleasses fought at Lepanto, and were placed in pairs ahead of the main line of galleys so that their size and firepower could have more impact. The right wing of the fleet was under Gian Andrea Doria with the left wing under the command of the Venetian Agostino Barbarigo. There was a gap of only three galleys' width between the two flanks and their centre section under Don John of Austria himself.

This was to be a galley battle in the grand style, because every ship was crammed with soldiers and the tactics were to be those of a land battle. The wind was westerly and blew in the Christians' favour, although they were outnumbered by the Ottoman galleys, apparently by two hundred and seventy ships against two hundred and twenty. There is little in the way of naval manoeuvring to be discerned from the fighting that took place

Don John of Austria, the victor at the Battle of Lepanto in 1571

once two came to expected, the leasses broke the line, but each one was the sides grips. As mighty gal-Ottoman front immediately surrounded by five or six enemy galleys. Don John's flagship galley rammed the flagship of the Ottoman commander, Ali Mouezinzade, with such violence that the prows of both ships were broken off from the impact, leaving the two vessels stuck together. Don John's troops then boarded the enemy flagship and fierce hand-to-hand fighting took place until Mouezinzade was shot through the head. Someone stuck it on a pike as a trophy.

Similar encounters took place all along the line as individual galleys locked together. It was a scene of utter confusion, but it soon became clear that the Christian soldiers, who were more generously supplied with firearms and better protected with body armour, were gaining the upper hand. Fifteen thousand Christian galley slaves were liberated from their chains, and in the end only six Ottoman ships escaped. The Muslim casualties were enormous, running into scores of thousands, while Christian losses totalled fifteen galleys sunk and 7,566 dead.

The Battle of Lepanto was immediately hailed as the salvation of Christendom. This was something of an exaggeration: not only did Lepanto come too late to save Cyprus but it also failed to cripple the Ottoman war effort as much as contemporaries liked to think. But Lepanto, being a victory, was to remain vivid and celebrated in European memory alongside the Great Siege of Malta. On the Ottoman side Mustafa Pasha, who had captured Cyprus, returned in triumph to Constantinople to find the city in a depressed mood because the news of the defeat at Lepanto had preceded him. But so vast were the sultan's resources that he had rebuilt his fleet by 1573, and time was to justify the Ottoman leader in his boast against the Republic of Venice that on Cyprus he had cut off one of her arms, whereas at Lepanto, the last great galley battle in the Mediterranean, the Christians had only shorn his beard.

It was to be many years more before this optimistic note subsided and the Ottoman Empire realised that it had become outflanked by the Portuguese in the Indian Ocean. The Ottomans then hurried to invest in sailing ships and comforted themselves with the thought that God may have given the sea to the infidel, but on land the position was reversed. How this was achieved will be the theme of the next chapter.

Chapter 7
'. . . and the land to the Muslims'

The expression 'a decisive battle' is one that is often misused. Most military historians like the campaigns they are describing to have had some measurable outcome, but it is only rarely that a conflict can be regarded, justifiably, as having had a decisive effect on a country's history. The Battle of Mohacs, which was fought on 29 August 1526 between the kingdom of Hungary and the Ottoman Empire of Suleiman the Magnificent, is one outstanding example of the genuine article. It resulted in the death of Hungary's king and the land being split into three parts. The kingdom that had been a front-line state of Christian Europe for more than two centuries was effectively going to cease to exist for a century and a half, and the whole engagement took only two hours to fight – an extremely decisive action indeed.[1]

Hungary on the Front Line
During the latter part of the fifteenth century, Hungary had enjoyed something of a golden age under the cultivated King Matthias Corvinus. His death without an heir in 1490 did not lead to any apparent cultural extinction, but the weakness of the kings who succeeded him was very marked. Hungary began to slip into a political and military vacuum, and its enemies sought to take advantage. The new king of Hungary was the Pole Wladislaw II Jagiello. He was king of Bohemia as well as Hungary, which should have promised great military and political strength, but unfortunately for both countries he was regarded as a stranger in two lands. Faction fighting was endemic, and when Wladislaw II died in 1516 the joint throne was inherited by his ten-year-old son Louis (Lajos) II. The monarch's tender age caused problems for both his kingdoms, but more so in Hungary, where there was an emerging feeling in favour of a native Hungarian king instead of a foreigner. This faction's candidate was John Szapolyai, a Transylvanian nobleman of great ambition and few scruples, but by far the greatest threat to the increasingly divided kingdom came from the Ottoman Empire.

John Szapolyai, the Ottoman nominee for the throne of Hungary following the Battle of Mohacs in 1526

Previous chapters have referred to the military skills of Suleiman the Magnificent, who became sultan in 1520.[2] His father, Selim I, had busied himself almost exclusively with Asia and Africa, thereby leaving undisturbed a situation of peace between the Ottomans and Hungary that had lasted for fifty-seven years. In accordance with the established Ottoman custom of revoking all former international agreements upon the accession of a new ruler, Suleiman sent envoys to Buda to start negotiations over the renewal of the peace accord. The Hungarian king reacted by detaining the envoy against his will, an act that caused consternation in diplomatic circles. European leaders found it difficult to understand such a provocative political act being carried out by a kingdom that appeared to lack any military strength with which to back it up.

When the Ottomans responded to this incident in a suitably aggrieved manner the Hungarians appealed for help to Emperor Charles V. Their plea was delivered in a robust manner when a Hungarian envoy addressed the Diet with a stirring reminder of the historic role that Hungary had played on Europe's front line. 'For who prevented the unbridled madness of the Ottomans from raging farther? The Hungarians! Who checked their fury that overwhelmed like the swiftest current? The Hungarians! Who warded off the Ottoman darts from the throats of the commonwealth of Christendom? The Hungarians!'[3]

There was much more in this vein, but the envoy could not have addressed the emperor at a worse time. Charles V had just sent a letter to Francis I of France that amounted to a declaration of war. There was also the matter of Martin Luther, who opposed the proclamation of a crusade with the words, 'to fight against the Ottomans is to resist the Lord, who visits our sins with such rods'. Divine punishment notwithstanding, it was obvious to Luther that any success in a campaign that was sanctified with the anachronistic title of a crusade would benefit the papacy. Luther's comments were condemned in a papal bull of Leo X but were widely circulated among Protestants, who took them literally in the light of scriptural references to scourges being sent from the Almighty to chastise his wayward people.

The emperor's conclusion was that if the King of Hungary was unable to defend himself then he should renew the truce with the sultan, because no military support was possible. Hungary, therefore, stood alone against what was to prove to be the most serious Ottoman advance against Europe in almost a century. But to the Ottomans, as much as to the Hungarians, the twenty-five-year-old Suleiman was still an unknown quantity. History now remembers him as perhaps the greatest sultan of his line, a man who fully justified the two epithets he was given – 'the Magnificent' to Europeans and 'the Lawgiver' in his native land – but in 1521 his greatness was merely the greatness of his potential.

The Road to Mohacs

The key to any advance into Hungary was the city of Belgrade, which lies on the southern bank of the River Danube at its confluence with the Sava. It had remained out of Ottoman hands in spite of the vigorous siege in 1456 and the capitulation of much of the rest of the Balkans. Suleiman set out to capture Belgrade on 16 February 1521. His army was followed up the Danube by a supply convoy of forty boats and on reaching Nis in Serbia the force divided. One part, commanded by Ahmed Pasha, the *beylerbey* of Rumelia, moved against Szabacs, followed a few days later by Suleiman himself. The second main body, under the Grand Vizier Piri Pasha, headed for Belgrade, while the *akinji* (irregular cavalry) were also separated into two bodies – the first to act as scouts, the second to raid into the Carpathian Mountains of Transylvania. Szabacs defended itself with fruitless heroism, and the heads of the slain were displayed on pikes.

Suleiman then proceeded to build a bridge across the Sava, but severe flooding rendered it useless. He was able to transfer his army across the river by using boats, and then it was marched downstream along the northern bank towards Belgrade. His arrival on the enemy side of the Sava was greeted by loud cheers from his army, which had already begun to besiege the city from the south. An initial assault was repulsed, so Suleiman began bombarding the walls from an island in the middle of the Danube, and five hundred janissaries were ordered to go up the Danube in boats so as to intercept any possible relieving force. On 8 August an attack was launched which caused the defenders to abandon the town, burn it and retire to the castle, where they held out for a further three weeks. Belgrade only surrendered after a main tower had been destroyed by a mine.

An immediate move against Hungary was now expected, but in fact no advance materialised for another five years. In 1522 Suleiman was busy capturing Rhodes, and he was further distracted by revolts in Egypt and a mutiny among the janissaries in Constantinople, so it was not until the winter of 1525 that Suleiman found himself free enough to continue his advance. The Hungarians had not been idle. Raiding and skirmishing had continued since 1521, and in 1524 some fifteen thousand *akinji* were defeated by Pal Tomori, the warlike Archbishop of Kalosca, who had been given the task of defending his country's southern borders with the most slender of resources. On this occasion the severed head of the Ottoman commander was sent back to Buda amidst great rejoicing. Yet these successes did little to conceal the huge political divisions that existed within the Hungarian court and nobility, of which the rivalry between the supporters of the young king and those supporting John Szapolyai was merely the most visible. As for foreign help, little had changed since the rhetoric of 1521. Charles V was now riding high since his victory at Pavia, but his aims and those of his brother Ferdinand, Archduke of Austria, were chiefly concerned with eliminating heresy on the one side and the French on the other before they could consider committing forces to the defence of Hungary against the Ottomans.

Thus it was that, on 23 April 1526, Suleiman the Magnificent left Constantinople at the head of an army of perhaps a hundred thousand men and three hundred cannon to advance against a kingdom that was divided against itself and almost abandoned by its allies. The long march lasted eighty days before contact was established with the enemy. Dreadful weather added to the Ottoman difficulties, and torrential rain increased the current of the Danube so much that the fleet of eight hundred supply vessels had great difficulty keeping up with the army. Nevertheless strict discipline was maintained. Soldiers were executed for treading down young crops or even letting their horses graze on them, and in spite of his slow progress Suleiman was able to take heart from two things. The first was the constant arrival of reinforcements to his standard. The second was the exemplary efficiency demonstrated by his grand vizier Ibrahim Pasha, who had been promoted following the retirement in 1523 of Piri Pasha, the besieger of Belgrade. Uniquely among men of this rank, Ibrahim Pasha was considered worthy to have been granted the unprecedented honour of a standard of six horse tails, only one less than the sultan himself.

When the sultan arrived in Belgrade, Ibrahim Pasha was sent on ahead once again to capture the fortress of Petrovaradin, which lies on the southern bank of the Danube about midway between the Sava and the Drava. Two mines opened up a breach in the walls, and the citadel fell to the Ottomans with a loss to the besiegers of only twenty-five men. All this time the Ottoman advance had been shadowed and monitored by Archbishop Pal Tomori, who had finally been forced to withdraw across the Danube at Petrovaradin. An Ottoman force then compelled Tomori to move still further to the west.

The time it was taking the Ottoman army to advance, and the reliable intelligence regularly fed back to the Hungarian court by the energetic archbishop, should have allowed plenty of time for King Louis II to make sufficient defensive preparations. He was no longer a child, but a man of twenty years, yet the factional fighting and rivalry which had dogged his reign was now to spiral out of control in a disastrous and tragic manner. After much discussion, it was decided that on 2 July the whole force of the Hungarian realm should rendezvous at Tolna on the Danube, about fifty miles south of Buda. Urgent messages were sent to Prague asking the government there to send Bohemian and Moravian contingents with all haste. This was almost four weeks before the fall of Petrovaradin, yet by the time

Grand Vizier Ibrahim Pasha, who was considered worthy to be granted the unprecedented honour of a standard of six horse tails, only one less than the sultan himself

Archbishop Tomori was to be found staring helplessly across the Danube at that captured castle, not one Hungarian soldier had arrived at the agreed muster point far to the north.

It was obvious to Suleiman and his grand vizier that the most likely place for their advance to be challenged was the River Drava, the only river barrier that now remained between the sultan and Hungary since the fall of Belgrade. The Drava joins the Danube just below Osijek in Croatia and for much of its length forms the present-day border with Hungary. On their way to Hungary the Ottomans captured Illok on 8 August, in spite of being delayed again by wet weather, and it was not until 14 August that the sultan reached the junction of the Danube and the Drava, where he expected to find a huge Hungarian army sitting on the Drava's northern bank. But there was no enemy in sight.

Christian Disunity

Louis II had reached Tolna on 2 August, and at last some of the expected contingents began to join him. There were armies from Hungary and Poland, including mercenary armies of foot-soldiers, but none yet from Croatia, Moravia or Bohemia. The bishops of the Hungarian sees of Varad (the present-day Oradea in Romania) and Gyor arrived, as did Gyorgi Szapolyai, the brother of John, the rival for the throne of Hungary. As for John Szapolyai, the decision had been made that he should be invited to invade Wallachia from Transylvania and thus distract the Ottomans on their right flank.

It was to King Louis's great credit that he appreciated as much as did Suleiman the tremendous strategic importance of the line of the Drava. It was very late in the day for it to be secured, but by 8 August there was still time to reach it from Tolna, so the young king ordered Count Palatine Stephen Bathory, who held a position equivalent to prime minister, to occupy Osijek and defend the Drava. But a majority of the Hungarian nobles who were ordered to march with him refused to move. They would only serve under their king, they declared, not his mere deputy. Bathory tried to set them an example of loyalty, even though a bad attack of gout made it difficult for him to mount his horse. But the plan had to be abandoned, and instead of sending a vanguard to the Drava the whole army marched on to a point midway between Tolna and Osijek, near the little riverside hamlet of Mohacs.

At Mohacs Archbishop Tomori crossed the Danube from the east to join his king. The Hungarian army was now complete, but completion did not imply unity. In total contrast to their previous statement that they would fight under their king and none other, the nobles began a contentious and unruly council of war at which they voted to have two joint commanders – Archbishop Tomori and Gyorgi Szapolyai. The decision was a victory for the Szapolyai faction over the royalists, but such dissension during the few days prior to a battle was a very regrettable development. With the matter of the command structure settled, discussion then passed to the question of what to do while the Ottoman army approached.

Some urged waiting or even withdrawing until other allies appeared. The Croatians were known to be on their way. John Szapolyai and his Transylvanians had been summoned from their previous duties to come and aid the king directly, but they were no nearer than Szeged, a hundred miles to the east, and the Bohemian vanguard had not even passed Bratislava. A more belligerent argument was put forward by Archbishop Pal Tomori, who argued that it would be a disgrace to withdraw, even if the army was incomplete.

The slow but steady arrival of reinforcements over the next few days strengthened this viewpoint considerably. First the king's artillery train landed by boat from Buda, then came three thousand Croatians and more Hungarian 'warrior bishops'. Large numbers of fortified wagons also arrived, but when one Polish mercenary captain advised the Hungarians to use the wagons to create a defensive line he was scorned for his pains. In the event a *laager* of sorts was built at the rear, but it played little part in the subsequent battle. As the numbers swelled, the decision to stand and fight at Mohacs became almost inevitable, although there were still some dissenting voices. Ferenc Perenyi, the Bishop of Varad, made a comment that turned out to be more prophetic than humorous, when he counselled that Hungary would have twenty thousand martyrs the day after the battle, so the pope had better be ready to canonise them all.

Meanwhile, Suleiman had dealt with the undefended line of the Drava in a manner that was militarily effective and profoundly symbolic. He gave orders for a bridge of boats to be thrown across the river, a task his enthusiastic followers completed in five days, according to Suleiman's diary. When all his army were safely across he burned Osijek and then destroyed the bridge itself. There was to be no turning back.

The Reckoning at Mohacs

The battlefield of Mohacs is located south of the present-day town of Mohacs, along the road to Croatia, and most of the actual fighting probably took place in an area between four and seven miles distant from Mohacs. The site is very well preserved to this day, although communication across its southern part is made difficult as it is bisected from north to south towards the village of Udvar by the wire fence that marks the boundary between Hungary and Croatia.

In 1526 most of the land to the east of the present road, including the section now
inside Croatia, was swampy woodland. It was made much worse and more extensive than normal by the heavy rain that had dogged the campaign up to that point,
and the little river called the Borza, which eventually empties into the Danube,
that had disappeared into the morass. West of the present road the ground grew
gradually firmer and began to slope up towards a prominent wooded ridge – still
identifiable today – that dominated the battlefield to the south and west. In 1526
the forest also continued round to the south, and the combination of woods and
ridges shielded the Ottoman advance from the eyes of the Hungarians. It was on
this gently sloping grassland west of the modern road, which fell from west to east
into marshland and the Danube, that the most decisive battle in Hungarian history took place.

Louis II set up his standard at a point just over half-way between Mohacs town
and the Borza. Archbishop Tomori's headquarters was established to his rear. The
main forces of the Hungarian army arranged themselves somewhere near the Borza. Authorities differ as to whether they crossed it or not, but the river was certainly not large enough to pose any obstacle. The front rank was divided into two
sections: on the right was the division of Ferenc Batthany of Croatia and on the
left was Peter Perenyi, brother to the Bishop of Varad. Behind them was the main
body in one line, while on the right wing there was a separate detachment under
Gabor Raskay, whose orders were to guard against any possible flank attack by the
Ottoman troops believed to be concealed beyond the village of Majs at the foot of
the south-western ridge. No equivalent guard was placed on the left wing, because
the lines of both armies on the eastern side of the battlefield stretched as far as
they dared towards the virtually impassable mixture of swamp and flooded forest.

The sultan, who was aware of the potential striking power of the Hungarian knights, arranged his defences in depth. A thin screen of dispensable *azaps*
(conscripted light horsemen) stood out in front. The Rumelian and Anatolian
horsemen, supported by some artillery, constituted the first two major lines,
under Grand Vizier Ibrahim Pasha and Behrem Pasha respectively. The third line
consisted of the heavy artillery, fifteen thousand janissaries and the *sipahis* on the
flanks, under the personal command of the sultan himself. Squadrons of cavalry lay
to the rear in support, while far over on the left wing, and much advanced towards
the Hungarians, stood the force of *akinji* under Bali Bey and Korsev Bey, which the
Hungarian detached force had been posted to watch.

The Battle of Mohacs began with a salvo from the Hungarian artillery, and
a tremendous charge of Hungarian knights took place across the firm grassland.
At first all went well. The shock of the knights' charge broke the Rumelian and

Anatolian horsemen, and they advanced towards the third line. Meanwhile, Gabor Raskay had advanced against the *akinji* near the village of Majs and broken their formation too, but he failed either to pursue or annihilate them.

Archbishop Tomori's knights continued their advance into the Ottoman ranks and looked as though they were about to make contact with the sultan himself when suddenly they were brought to a violent halt by the fire from the line of Ottoman guns, which were chained together along the line of a depression. The failure to identify this Ottoman artillery was a major intelligence blunder on the part of the Hungarians. The guns may have caused little physical damage because of the elevation at which they were being fired, but the psychological effects at such a short range, and so unexpectedly, proved to be a crucial turning-point in the battle. The Ottoman chronicler Kemal Pasha explained the advance of the Hungarians into the mouth of the guns as being the result of a clever feint by the Grand Vizier Ibrahim Pasha. 'The young lion', he declares, 'no matter how brave, should remember the wisdom and experience of the old wolf.'[4]

Part of the Hungarian left wing gave way and retired to the marshy ground, and when the Ottomans launched their counterattack the main body of the Hungarian knights was driven straight back towards the king's camp, where the men found to their dismay that some Ottoman light horsemen had already got there and were slaughtering the camp followers. Kemal Pasha gets quite poetic at this stage when he writes of:

> . . . all these murderous swords stretched out to lay hold on the garment of life, the plain seemed like a fiend with a thousand arms; with all these pointed lances, eager to catch the bird of life in the midst of slaughter, the battlefield resembled a dragon with a thousand heads.[5]

Meanwhile the detached Ottoman units of *akinji* under Bali Bey and Korsev Bey, whom Gabor Raskay had so regrettably allowed to regroup, advanced from Majs in two sections, one against the flanks of the mêlée, which was now indicating a full Hungarian retreat, and the other on towards the king's position at the rear. The slaughter must have continued back as far as Mohacs, with most of the killing happening around the area of the modern memorial to the battle. Here in 1960 were discovered three mass graves, their location strongly suggesting that the bodies of the ordinary soldiers had been buried where they fell.

The battle was finished by 6 p.m., after only two hours of actual fighting. Of the king's estimated thirteen thousand foot-soldiers only three thousand got away. Many of the dead must have perished as they struggled through the swampy edge

of the Danube, but the most serious loss in terms of Hungary's political future was the decimation of its most senior officials from crown and church. Brave Archbishop Pal Tomori of Kalocsa was killed, along with the chancellor Laszlo Szalkai, Archbishop of Gran (Esztergom). Of the next rank down there perished Bishop Ferenc Perenyi of Varad, Bishop Balazs Paksi of Gyor, Bishop Ferenc Csaholyi of Csanad, Bishop Fulop More of Pecs and Bishop Gyorgy Palinay of Bosnia. Among the allies of Hungary fell Count Frangipani of Croatia and Count Stephen of Schlik, the only Bohemian leader to have arrived for the battle.

Louis II of Hungary completely disappeared. He had fled from the battlefield, but when his horse tried to climb the steep bank of a small stream it fell and landed on top of him, crushing him to death (see plate 15). His body was only found and identified two months later when the floods of the Danube had subsided (see plate 16). A number of prisoners were taken, but the sultan had them all beheaded the next day as his ancestor Bayezid the Thunderbolt had done at Nicopolis in 1396. He saved only five prisoners for ransoming. The heads were piled high, and that of Archbishop Tomori was displayed on a pike. The sultan's diary expresses the matter very laconically:

> 31 August – The emperor, seated on a golden throne, receives the homage of the viziers and the beys; massacre of two thousand prisoners; the rain fell in torrents . . .
> 2 September – Rest at Mohacs; twenty thousand Hungarian infantry and four thousand of their cavalry are buried.[6]

The Dismemberment of Hungary

Of the Hungarian leaders at Mohacs very few escaped with their lives to begin rebuilding the country. Their number included Deputy Chancellor Istvan Brodarics, Bishop of Szerem, who survived to write an important eyewitness account of the battle. Apart from him only Count Palatine Stephen Bathory, the bishops of Agram and Nitria, and the Ban of Croatia escaped, together with a good many of the light cavalry who disgraced themselves by plundering on their way home.

John Szapolyai was still in Transylvania, and his hand had yet to be played. The earlier decision to send him off raiding, and then withdraw him hurriedly, was a grave mistake, because not only did it tie up important troops from eastern Hungary but it also allowed Louis's greatest rival to avoid immolation in the bloodbath

Ferdinand Habsburg, the brother of Emperor Charles V, who became the rival king of Hungary in 1526

that was to come. He eventually arrived at Mohacs the day following the catastrophe, and hurriedly withdrew when the sight of destruction met his eyes.

After three days rest Suleiman the Magnificent continued unopposed to Buda, burning the cathedral city of Pecs on the way. On entering Buda on 10 September he ordered the place to be spared, but it was burned and looted anyway and many treasures were carted off to Constantinople while the irregular horsemen raided throughout Hungary. The widowed Queen Mary fled to the safety of Bratislava and then Vienna, the seat of her brother, Archduke Ferdinand of Habsburg. On 26 October the exiled parties elected him King of Hungary. His wife Anne, the sister of the late King Louis II, became queen.

Suleiman the Magnificent, of course, had other ideas. He had already decided to make Hungary into a tributary principality, and he intended to do it speedily. He was helped by the ambitions of John Szapolyai, who sent envoys to the sultan at Buda to offer his services, which were accepted.[7] So on 10 November 1526 the Ottoman nominee John Szapolyai was crowned King of Hungary by the Bishop of Nitria, one of the few prelates who had escaped the disaster of Mohacs. Thus to add to the massacre at Mohacs and the Ottoman subjugation, Hungary now had to suffer the problem of rival kings, and two centuries of war and disunion were to follow as a result of one of the world's most genuinely decisive battles.

The Siege of Vienna
The close linkage that existed in Ottoman society between military success and political power ensured that as a result of the victory at Mohacs Suleiman was regarded as being more magnificent than ever. All Europe expected him to return to the Danube in 1527 to continue where he had left off, but his Ottoman Empire stretched into distant domains of which few Europeans were aware, and these other territories were to occupy him for some time to come.

His Balkan governors nonetheless served to demoralise Hungary still further by capturing Jaicze and Banja Luka in Bosnia in 1527. But Hungary hardly needed any external pressure to be demoralised, because a civil war between its two monarchs was already performing that task very successfully. That same year King Ferdinand, with the help of Bohemian troops, drove John Szapolyai's armies out of Buda, captured a string of castles along the line of the Danube and also took Szekesfehervar. Szapolyai, naturally, appealed to the sultan for support, but help did not come in 1527, nor did it come in 1528. Instead, Szapolyai became a footnote in the next great Ottoman advance against Europe, where the aim was not merely the reconquest of that part of Hungary unfortunately lost to Suleiman's pliant vassal but also the most ambitious campaign of the sultan's reign. It was also one that would be seen as threatening the heart of Christendom in a way that an attack on the buffer state of Hungary could never do: Suleiman the Magnificent was going to attack Vienna.

The sultan left Constantinople on 10 May 1529 and reached Osijek on 6 August, with an army of perhaps one hundred and twenty thousand men. He met up with Szapolyai on 18 August, on the ill-fated field of Mohacs, whither Szapolyai had brought six thousand troops from Transylvania to join the Ottoman host. With the Hungarian king leading the way, the army of invasion proceeded north. Buda capitulated on 8 September, and Szapolyai gratefully installed himself within it while the rest of the army continued on along the Danube. To the dismay of the Austrians, several of the fortresses they had recently captured from Szapolyai now surrendered in his name, and the only place that put up any sort of defence was Bratislava, from where the accompanying Ottoman fleet was bombarded as it sailed up river. But on 27 September Suleiman the Magnificent arrived safely at the gates of Vienna.

Unfortunately for King Ferdinand, his brother, Emperor Charles V, was too embroiled in his French wars to help him. As for other potential supporters, in spite of Ferdinand's warning that if Austria fell then Germany would be next, many among their number still saw Lutheranism as a greater danger than the Turk. Yet they need not have worried long about Protestant support, because Martin Luther, who had opposed a crusade against the Ottomans in 1521, had thoroughly eaten his words by 1529. Times had changed, and any Protestants of a pacifist nature who might welcome a further Ottoman advance could now have their resistance stiffened by a tub-thumping new publication from Martin Luther entitled *On the War against the Turks*.

Ferdinand's garrison at Vienna was more than sixteen thousand strong, but these men defended medieval walls from which modern artillery bastions and the like were conspicuous only by their absence, and the wall that surrounded the city was in many places no more than six feet thick. There is little left today to remind us of the epic siege of 1529, but one German printmaker obligingly recorded the layout of city and siege lines in an enormous multi-section print based on his own sketches made from the spire of St Stephen's church, a vantage point that also served the defenders well. We also know from accounts of the siege that the usual precautions were taken of levelling the houses just inside the walls and building an inner earthen wall from which a counterattack might be launched.

In spite of the weak state of the old-fashioned walls, the majority of the garrison were professional soldiers fighting under Count Nicholas von Salm, who had recently distinguished himself at Pavia. One of his sorties out from the walls, designed to disrupt the digging of sap trenches (which it did successfully), also came within a hair's breadth of capturing Suleiman's illustrious 'six horse tailed' Grand Vizier Ibrahim Pasha. Otherwise the siege was the time-honoured sequence of bombardment and mining, although the former was greatly reduced, because much of the Ottoman heavy artillery had been left behind due to the foul weather, and the latter technique was vigorously countered by sheer bravery. Several Ottoman mine heads were blown in, and on 6 October eight thousand men of the city took part in an attack designed to clear the ground behind the Ottoman front line, where mines were started. Immense damage was done, although the congestion on the army's return meant that the rear companies were badly cut up.

After a number of attacks had been repelled, an Ottoman council of war on 12 October began to consider the possibility of a retreat. Winter was fast approaching, so Suleiman decided that one final effort should be made. His men were spurred on by the promise of a rich reward to the first man to climb over the wall. But even this could not guarantee victory, and at midnight on 14 October screams were heard coming from the Ottoman camp as their prisoners were massacred in preparation for a withdrawal. The retreat was disastrous. On land, the army struggled through early snow, and on the Danube the ships came under fire from the cannons of Bratislava. In Buda, Szapolyai came out to congratulate his suzerain on a great victory, but the contrast with the confident army that had marched north was very noticeable.

The Siege of Güns

It is testimony to the immense resources of the Ottoman Empire that Suleiman was back in Hungary in 1532 for a second try at Vienna with an even larger army than he had brought with him in 1529. This time he needed it, because ready and waiting for him in Vienna was Ferdinand's brother Charles V with some of the finest soldiers in Europe. He had collected what may have been the largest army that western Europe had seen up to that time. The result was to make Suleiman change his plans. Instead of heading for Vienna, he turned westwards into the narrow strip of Hungarian territory towards the Austrian border that was still in Ferdinand's possession. After taking a few minor places he then headed even further west and laid siege to the castle that was then, as it is today, the last fortress in Hungarian territory. The town is now called Koszeg, but in 1532 the Austrians called it Güns.

The Siege of Güns holds an affectionate place in Hungarian hearts. It was a tiny place, defended by only seven hundred men, yet it held out against the Ottomans for almost as long as mighty Vienna in 1529. Its commander was one Miklos Jurisics, a Croatian by birth and a captain of great resolution and integrity. His seven hundred men had been intended for the general muster at Vienna, but stayed behind when they realised the Ottomans' immediate intentions. They had no cannon, few arquebuses and little powder.

The siege was started by the capable Grand Vizier Ibrahim Pasha, who was in blissful ignorance of these facts. Suleiman came to join him shortly afterwards. The layout of Güns's walls made mining a feasible strategy, but even though several mines succeeded in blowing respectable-sized holes in the fortifications, every subsequent assault was beaten off. A wooden bulwark was erected near the walls from which the castle was bombarded with the Ottomans' heaviest guns, but on 28 August Jurisics replied to a summons to surrender with a defiant refusal. After this performance had been repeated twice, another attempt was made to storm the castle, this time with such fury that the assailants succeeded in gaining control of the breach. This set up such a dreadful howl from the civilian population, who thought they were about to be massacred, that the Ottomans thought reinforcements had arrived, and withdrew hastily. Three hours later, Jurisics was summoned to a parley in the tent of Ibrahim Pasha to receive his proposals for an extraordinary deal. Suleiman the Magnificent, who still did not realise how small the force was that had delayed him for so long, offered to spare the garrison and march away if Jurisics would offer him a nominal surrender. The only Ottomans who would be allowed to enter the castle would be a token force which would raise the Ottoman flag and keep their comrades out before withdrawing for good. Jurisics was acutely aware of the desperate straits his tiny garrison was in, and agreed to this unprecedented proposal.

Bulls' Blood

The most important result of the sultan's second invasion of Austria was an unexpected peace treaty concluded with King Ferdinand. It confirmed the right of Szapolyai to be king of all Hungary, but recognised Ferdinand's possession of his existing territories. A breathing space was therefore given to all sides, and it would be nine years before Suleiman the Magnificent resumed his land war against Hungary and Austria, a time during which his military and political resources would be tested acutely against equally formidable foes in Persia, Armenia and Moldavia, as well as the naval campaigns described in the previous chapter.

It took the death of Szapolyai in 1540 to change the situation. His heir was but a few weeks old, so Queen Isabella hurried to have him crowned in his cradle as news of a rapid advance on Buda by Ferdinand began to reach her ears. When the border fortresses on the Danube began to surrender to Ferdinand, the queen sent desperate appeals for help to Constantinople. Suleiman responded the following year, helped immeasurably by the fact that Charles V was preoccupied far away with his plans for Algiers, and more locally by the incompetence of Ferdinand's commander, Rogendorf, whose advance had stalled at Buda. The queen welcomed the new Ottoman presence, but became suspicious when the sultan asked for the baby king to be brought to his tent. No harm was done to the child, whom Suleiman swore solemnly to protect. The catch was that, in the sultan's opinion, this protection would better be exercised if the child and his mother were moved to the safety of Transylvania until the infant, now named John Sigismund, was of age, while Ottoman forces occupied Buda. All that remained of Habsburg-owned Hungary was now a strip of borderland. It looked as though just one mighty push could take the sultan again to Vienna, but a further peace agreement allowed young John Sigismund Szapolyai to attain the age of eleven years and be recognised as Prince of Transylvania.

When the Ottomans returned to Hungarian territory in 1552 a further reverse awaited them at Erlau (now called Eger), which lay almost at the north-western extremity of Ferdinand's remnant of Hungary. It was to provide the second of three instances in which small Hungarian fortresses defied Suleiman the Magnificent. Güns had held out for twenty days. In 1552 Erlau repulsed the Ottomans for thirty-eight days.

In command of Erlau was Istvan (Stephen) Dobo, whose garrison was sustained by large quantities of the local red wine. Someone who saw the wine dripping from the whiskers of the defenders during the siege claimed that they were fortified by bulls' blood, an appellation that has stuck for the local vintage to this day. At Erlau the women of the town played a gallant part by keeping their menfolk supplied with powder, ball and of course flagons of 'bulls' blood', while emptying cauldrons of boiling water over the Ottoman siege ladders (see plate 17). The result was a second humiliation for another numerically overwhelming Ottoman army.

The defeat at Erlau marked the beginning of a troubled few years for Suleiman. His woes included very serious dissension within his own house, largely over the question of who would become the next sultan. This added to the gloom that arose from the military blow delivered to his prestige by the repulse of his armies during the Siege of Malta in 1565. The one thing that might satisfy him was victory in battle, so in January 1566 Suleiman went to war for what was to prove the last time. He was seventy-two years old, and suffered so badly from gout that he had to be carried in a litter, yet his 1566 campaign was the thirteenth military expedition he had conducted in person. By comparison, his great enemy Emperor Charles V had retired from active service at the age of fifty-six. The new invasion was also Suleiman's seventh campaign against Hungary.

On 1 May 1566, Suleiman left Constantinople at the head of one of the largest armies he had ever commanded – perhaps as many as two hundred thousand men. His weakened state meant that the host proceeded slowly, and only reached Belgrade after forty-nine days marching. From the Belgrade area Suleiman made ready to move to the northern border area and Erlau, where he intended to reverse the result of 1552 before moving against Vienna. But he had hardly started on his way when news came of the defeat of one of his favourite generals, Mohammed of Trikala, at the castle of Siklos, in southern Hungary. The reversal had been brought about by one Miklos Zrinyi, who had fought the Ottomans during the Siege of Vienna more than thirty years previously. Although a Croat by origin, Zrinyi had been accepted by the Hungarians as one of their own and had strengthened his position by marriage and the inheritance of vast estates in Hungary. Loyal to a fault towards the Habsburg claim on the Hungarian throne, Zrinyi had been a thorn in the Ottoman flesh for many years.

The End at Szigeth
In 1566 Zrinyi compounded the Ottoman embarrassment by basing himself at Szigeth (Szigetvar), another fortress near the Hungarian–Croatian border. Szigeth was off Suleiman's planned line of advance, and involved marching away from the army the emperor was known to have assembled near Vienna, but the angry sultan nevertheless gave orders for a diversion to the west and an attack. He was clearly in a bad mood. When his representative in Buda, Mohammed the Lion, ventured into his presence to report that he had lost Tata and Veszprem to Austrian attacks, Suleiman had him strangled in his tent without even the vestige of a proper examination into his conduct.[8]

On 5 August 1566 the Ottoman army took up its positions around Szigeth for a siege that was to become the equivalent of Malta on dry land, although the combination of rivers, moats and marshes around Szigeth made Zrinyi's castle look very much like an island fortress. The water defences were fed by the River Almas, a tributary of the nearby Drava, and had been cunningly utilised to surround what was an unusual design of castle. Szigeth fell into three sections, each of which was linked to the other by bridges and causeways. Although it was not built on particularly high ground the inner bailey, which occupied much the same area as the castle site does today, was surprisingly inaccessible, because two other baileys had to be taken and secured before a final assault could be launched.

The first of the three sections was the old town and its medieval walls. The second was the so-called 'new town', which lay in the drained area now occupied by the modern town of Szigetvar. Only then came the citadel with its up-to-date angle bastions, and it was from one of these that Zrinyi fired a warning shot when the sultan's army appeared in sight. Ottoman morale was high. At Szigeth Suleiman was motivated by thoughts of revenge as well as conquest, and spurred his men on with readings from the Koran. Fierce fighting ensued during the next two weeks. A spell of dry weather favoured the besiegers by reducing the water level in the moats, and by 19 August both the old and new towns were in Ottoman hands. While a fierce counterbattery bombardment went on, with both sides giving as good as they received, the Ottomans began to throw material into the moat of the inner fortress to create a causeway across. Meanwhile, Suleiman offered terms to Zrinyi and tried to undermine the resolution of the defence by arrow-letters written in Hungarian and German. When these were contemptuously rejected, a tremendous assault began. The defenders repulsed it, but Suleiman had high hopes of taking the castle in a second attack that was delivered on the auspicious anniversary of the Battle of Mohacs. But still the castle held out.

However, for the past two weeks Suleiman's engineers had been digging a mine under one of Szigeth's principal bastions. This was a very hazardous undertaking against a fortress that was surrounded by water fed from a river. They managed to reach beneath the wall without detection and fired the mine on 5 September. The resulting explosion was more than anyone had dared hope for. An enormous hole now existed at the corner of Szigeth, and flames had spread to the buildings inside. The fall of the castle was inevitable, but the Ottoman high command hesitated for a moment, for on that very same day Suleiman the Magnificent died in his tent behind the siege lines.

No doubt the immense strain of the current campaign had contributed towards this most unwelcome event, but at all costs it had to be kept secret. Only the sultan's innermost circle knew of his demise, and the courier despatched from the camp with a message for Selim, Suleiman's successor, may not even have known the content of the message he delivered to distant Asia Minor within a mere eight days. Zrinyi certainly did not know of the momentous development. He was now in command of a battered fortress with only three sides left standing. An assault across the breach could come at any moment, so Zrinyi decided to resolve the issue by leading his men in one last suicidal sortie. He had only six hundred able-bodied soldiers left, and with Zrinyi at their head they charged across the bridge into the Ottoman host who were preparing for the final advance. Zrinyi died almost instantly when two bullets hit him in the chest, and very few of the 'gallant six hundred' survived their absorption into the hostile Ottoman ranks. The Ottoman army then surged forwards into the remains of Szigeth, only to be met by a colossal booby trap when the castle's magazine exploded among them.

Miklos Zrinyi, who defended the castle of Szigeth in 1566 against Suleiman the Magnificent

Szigeth had fallen, and with admirable presence of mind the grand vizier forged bulletins of victory in the sultan's name. These announced to the people that their lord regretted that his current state of health unfortunately prevented him from continuing with the hitherto successful campaign. His lifeless corpse was borne back to Constantinople while those officials in the know pretended to keep up communication with him. Ottoman sources state that the pretence was maintained for three weeks, and that even the sultan's personal physician was strangled as a precaution. A local tradition states that Suleiman's body was laid to rest at Szigetvar and a mosque raised over the site which is now occupied by a church, but his corpse cannot have stayed there for long.

Thus died two remarkable commanders, whose effigies now appear side by side on the site of Suleiman's camp a few miles north of Szigetvar, where a Hungarian–Turkish friendship park has recently been established. But Zrinyi, for all his bravery, was a minor general by comparison to the man whose military and political achievements had raised Ottoman prestige to its greatest height. With the possible exception of Mehmet the Conqueror, Suleiman the Magnificent was easily the greatest of his line, and thirteen military campaigns led personally by a ruler is a phenomenal record. History would show that never again, not even at the celebrated Siege of Vienna in 1683, would Christian Europe ever be in quite the peril from the Ottomans as Suleiman had placed it in the years between 1521 and 1566. When Ottoman fortunes eventually declined and scholars lamented for the fact that God had given the seas to the infidel, the Ottomans were able to take comfort from the fact that, through the instrument of His will that was Sultan Suleiman the Magnificent, God had given the land to the Muslims.

The final sally from Szigeth by Zrinyi and his men, who charged to their deaths, not knowing that their besieger, Suleiman the Magnificent, had died in his camp

Chapter 8
The Bastion Wars

If prizes were ever awarded for the world's oddest-looking castle then the Italian fortress of Sarzanello would be a serious contender for first place. It occupies a dramatic position on top of a hill to the north of the town of Sarzana, from whose walls may be gained the first inkling of Sarzanello's curious design (*see* plate 18). From this angle Sarzanello looks like two fortresses joined by a narrow bridge, but it is only through close inspection that its true nature is revealed. One half, dating from 1493, is an almost perfectly equilateral triangular fortress with huge round towers at each vertex, while the other is a strange construction covering a similar-sized area that looks like a gigantic flat iron or the bows of an ocean liner turned to stone. This section, added in 1497, is the world's first ravelin (*see* plate 19), an architectural feature that sought to convert a more conventional castle into a modern artillery fortress by adding a detached angle bastion, a new concept in war as important to the story of Renaissance warfare as the Swiss pike.

The Development of the Angle Bastion
No fortress or fortress system has ever existed in a vacuum. There is a purpose to their creation, a reason why a commissioning monarch or a city's fathers have decided to spend so much time and money on them, even though it is sometimes difficult to identify a truly defensive purpose lying behind expensive and time-consuming endeavours. The walls of Lucca, for example, took 150 years to built. This was forty years longer than it took to built St Peter's Basilica in Rome, and 'each of the estimated six million hand-made bricks . . . could very easily represent a pang of well-founded fear or a sleepless night for the Lucchese citizens'.[1]

The classic example is the Great Wall of China, where some of the sections created by the Ming that ride snakelike along the crests of mountains have actually been built in the worst possible defensive positions, yet awed enemies and visitors alike by their appearance.[2] In such cases we see fortresses making an essentially political statement about the prince who has created them. They define spheres of influence, establish borders and proclaim the wealth of a monarch in no uncertain terms.

Beyond such political considerations the military purposes for which fortifications may be created are many and varied. On the smallest scale there may be the straightforward and simple goal of defending the space enclosed by the walls, whether that be a castle, a city or a town. Beyond this microcosm there may be an overall strategy of using a network of such fortresses to defend a territory or a particular border of that territory. Both of these objectives may be stated in defensive terms, but there can also be a considerable aggressive aspect to fortress building. Fortresses allow a leader to extend his conquests by providing a secure base and a jumping-off point for the next objective. Fortresses also intimidate, particularly when they take the form of a citadel within a city.

The great test, of course, for any fortress or fortification system occurs when the place is put under a state of siege. No matter how good its walls, supplies, lives and determination were always finite commodities, so that we read time and again of a garrison placing less faith in the strength of its walls than in the expectation of the arrival of a friendly army to relieve it. In other words, a policy of fortifying a territory could only succeed when used in conjunction with field armies who were able to relieve the garrisons under siege.[3] An early example is provided in Brittany in 1480, when the Breton defeat at the Battle of St Aubin de Cormier was followed by the surrender of St Malo.[4]

Yet fortresses were rarely expected to hold out for ever, so we must look for more subtle objectives in their creation, and these objectives may be located largely in the dimension of time. At the very least the mere existence of fixed fortresses would delay an enemy, interrupt his advance and ultimately confound his strategy. A well-designed defensive system could therefore hold up and obstruct an invader while allowing free passage to an ally. It also provided secure storage space, and served as a potent symbol of a ruler's power – at least until he lost it. Even though a fortress might ultimately fall, it could have done immense damage to the enemy in the process by tying down huge numbers of an enemy and could inflict a huge casualty list upon him.[5]

The conduct of a siege was a hugely expensive undertaking in terms of supplies, consuming tons of food, gunpowder and shot.[6] When an army was engaged upon a siege it was unable to threaten anywhere else, and also became vulnerable to outside attack. This situation is exemplified for ever by the comical situation at the Siege of Turin in 1640. The French in the citadel were besieged by the Spanish in the city who were in turn besieged by a French army outside the city walls who were also besieged by a Spanish army in siege lines![7]

The fifteenth-century experience of sieges involving artillery taught the world
of the Renaissance many lessons about the effects of siege warfare on a range of
fortification options. Rhodes provides an example of a response, but throughout
Europe architects and theoreticians had long attempted, with ruler and compass,
to calculate fields of fire, blind-spot areas of towers and the angles of walls in the
fifteenth- and sixteenth-century equivalent of computer modelling.[8]

The results were as varied as they were impressive. As early as 1433 the re-
builders of the walls of Pisa had experimented with flanking fire.[9] This was a new
possibility brought about by lighter, more mobile cannon mounted on the wider
ramparts of modern fortifications, and the first casualty of such deliberations was
the round tower, which allowed too much dead ground. In many cases round towers had already become less round when it was found that increasing the height
of the scarped sections of a tower to as much as two-thirds of the tower's overall
height provided a better glancing surface for cannonballs than did round surfaces.
Extended scarping, however, made vertical defence less practical, because dropped
projectiles tended to roll harmlessly down the sloping surfaces instead of bouncing
off at a sharp angle, so medieval machicolations were gradually dispensed with.

The new concentration of effort focussed on flanking fire. As the experience of
heavy guns inside towers had not been a happy one, a lower, highly scarped platform that projected from the walls and enabled shots along them was the natural
progression, thus the angle bastion finally emerged. The tower, which was essentially a defensive feature, had given way to the bastion, which was also virtually
an offensive weapon. Old towers were replaced by angle bastions, and sometimes
even buried deep within them.

Built out of brick, stone or earth to a design as thick and as massive as contemporary architecture could make them, the angle bastion's distinctive arrowhead
shape meant that artillery fire could be delivered not only across a ditch but also
along the line of the walls as flanking fire. The most sophisticated versions were
constructed with such geometrical precision that each bastion covered another
and produced a fortress with no blind spots. One authority on military architecture has called the angle bastion 'the most radically effective architectural element since the arch'.[10] It revolutionised castle design both by resisting offensive
artillery and by providing a secure platform for defensive fire. From the Spanish
Netherlands, where the bastions were of earth, to Famagusta, where they were of
stone, this common theme of new military architecture 'in the Italian style' (*trace
italienne*) changed the appearance of towns and cities wherever it appeared, and
siege warfare was never quite the same again. Fortifications may still have had a finite 'best by' date when placed under siege, but a system of angle bastions ensured

that the besiegers lines would have to be that much longer, and his supplies that much more numerous, giving the defenders that extra modicum of time wherein a friendly army might ride to their assistance.

Needless to say, the hugely expensive angle bastion system did not appear overnight. When Ferrara's walls were built between 1500 and 1506 its towers were round, but when they were restructured between 1512 and 1518 three angle bastions were added. Michele Sanmichele's work at Verona using angle bastions did not begin until 1530. By 1534 the only arguments aired during the rebuilding of the walls of Rome (apart from the huge cost implications) concerned the actual siting of the defences and the lengths of the walls. That the city's defence would rely on angle bastions was never doubted for one moment. The style spread far and wide over the following decades, and by 1560 the inhabitants of the fortress of Narva could glare across the river at Muscovy's resolutely medieval Ivangorod from within the protection of three angle bastions.[11] Narva was, however, an exception in northern Europe. In places like Pskov and Smolensk, where resources to build such constructions were scarce, and wide-ranging cavalry operations took the role of siege lines, and sieges resembled more the operations of the Middle Ages. Curtain walls and solid round towers, defended by artillery, still held out against long siege efforts (see plate 20). Nothing was ever completely predictable.

The Bastions of Cyprus

The wars of the latter half of the sixteenth century provided many opportunities for the angle bastion and its alternatives to be tested in battle. As a vivid case study, we will examine the Ottoman operations against Cyprus, which possessed two splendid fortress systems. The Ottomans attacked both of them, while architects looked on from a safe distance as the siege was conducted using techniques that anticipated the classic methods of the seventeenth century.

Unlike Rhodes, Cyprus was ruled not by an anachronistic order of chivalry but by the ruthless and hard-headed Republic of Venice, whose image, in modern European opinion, embodies all that is good. It is the Serenissima, the romantic queen of the Adriatic and the treasure house of art and religion. But this was not how Venice was always regarded. To the people of Cyprus in the sixteenth century the 'pearl of the Adriatic' was seen as an oppressive interloper, and a visitor in 1508 stated baldly in his report that 'all the inhabitants of Cyprus are slaves to the Venetians'. The Republic was to them an alien ruler who forced them to build fortifications for fear of a greater threat from the Ottoman Empire.[12]

The walls of Nicosia had been described by an enthusiastic visitor in 1509 in the words, 'methinks I never saw so fine and complete a wall', but he was not a military man, and when proper surveys were done during the 1560s the reports listed decay, weaknesses and worrying gaps. Count Julius Savorgnano was therefore sent to Cyprus, where he worked for ten months on the walls of Nicosia. The Venetian nobles on Cyprus provided the money, and the ordinary Cypriots supplied the muscle power. His plan was for a round and symmetrical angle bastioned *enceinte* based on earthworks that were revetted for half their height in stone. The use of earth speeded up the process considerably, and by the end of 1565 eleven obtuse-angled artillery bastions protruded from the walls of Nicosia – 'the very first European town to be surrounded by a geometrically perfect perimeter of text book bastions'.[13]

The Venetians had also been remodelling their other base at Famagusta, and the date of 1492 above the doorway to the so-called 'Othello Tower'

A plan of the walls of Nicosia, which, in 1565, became the first European town to be encircled by a geometrically perfect set of bastions

marks the beginning of a process that was intended to transform a medieval fortress into a masterpiece of Renaissance military engineering. But in 1498 there were complaints that funds were insufficient, and in 1500 it was noted not only that there were too few artillerymen but also that the only competent one among them was suffering from gout. Nevertheless, over the next thirty years visitors to Cyprus expressed their astonishment at the impressive walls of Famagusta and stated to a man that they thought the defences were impregnable. There were some worries that the two rocky reefs out in the harbour could provide gun emplacements for an enemy, as well as that there might be an even more serious and recurrent problem over the strength of the garrison. However, a knowledgeable German observer in 1521 estimated that Famagusta could hold out for a year against the Turk 'or even the King of Spain' should that ever be required.

By the time the Ottomans attacked, eighty years of work had gone into Famagusta's defences. The great Land Gate with its impressive ravelin was added in 1544, and a decade later the further development of the defences was entrusted to Count Hercules Martinengo. His plans included adding a series of *cavaliers* (gun platforms) high enough for their artillery to command the country outside. He also strengthened the north-west corner by adding an angle bastion in the Italian style. It was begun in 1558, and was named after him as the Martinengo bastion.

This was the scene that met the eyes of Savorgnano when his surveying exercise moved to Famagusta, but the hard-headed Venetian was not totally impressed. The walls were about two miles in extent, but the nearby swamps made it an unhealthy place to live and the harbour could take only about ten galleys. The old towers would be unlikely to withstand many cannon shots, and the new Martinengo bastion, although it looked very solid, was still incomplete. In Savorgnano's opinion it was too small and situated so close to the line of the walls that proper enfilading fire could not be delivered along the curtain. In addition the moat was too narrow and the scarp too low, and the walls also needed another six bastions, all of which would take an additional sixty years to build! There was neither time nor money for this, but before the Ottomans arrived nine more *cavaliers* were hastily erected, the ditches were widened and the area around burned and scoured to give a clear field of fire.

The Siege of Nicosia

When Suleiman the Magnificent died in 1566 he was succeeded by his son Selim II, who, even before his accession, is said to have openly announced his intentions of conquering Cyprus. Popular legend ascribes his enthusiasm to his preference for Cypriot wine over all other varieties.

In 1568 the Ottoman war in Hungary concluded with a peace treaty that left Selim free to achieve his objective. He selected two men to lead the operation. Lala Mustafa Pasha was appointed general in command of his land army, and Piale Pasha, who was of Croatian origin, took charge of the Ottoman fleet. The invasion force of about three hundred and fifty ships sailed for Cyprus on 27 June 1570 and landed without opposition on the southern coast of the island on 3 July.

The military operations of the Ottoman conquest of Cyprus fall into two distinct episodes. The first was the seven-week-long Siege of Nicosia, which lasted from 22 July to 9 September 1570. This was followed by the much longer Siege of Famagusta, which held out for eleven months between 15 September 1570 and 1 August 1571. An allied fleet for the relief of Cyprus assembled at Messina only on 25 September 1571, a full eight weeks after Famagusta had fallen. The victory gained at Lepanto was to be won by this fleet, but at the price of the loss of Cyprus.

Just as the approach of the allied fleet was plagued by infighting and delay, so did the command of Cyprus's capital unfortunately fall into the hands of Nicolas Dandolo, a man whom contemporaries described as poor-spirited, stupid and irascible. There were two excellent military men on the island. One was the captain of Famagusta, Mark Antony Bragadino, whose duties required him to be based there, and the other was Astorre Baglione, who was sent from Nicosia to Famagusta because that was expected to be the Ottomans' first objective. Under Dandolo's command in Nicosia were about twenty thousand fighting men, of whom only about half were 'effectives' due to the ravages of disease and their lack of training.

The city, with its fine new angle bastions, had supplies and munitions for a two-year siege, but these were badly administered. For some unaccountable reason nine hundred heavy arquebuses were sent out of the city to be used in the mountains, and the rest, which were correctly placed on the walls, were largely unused because 'the soldiers did not know how to discharge them without setting fire to their beards'. The rivalry that existed between Nicosia and Famagusta also played its own part in compounding the tragedy, because there was actually a dispute over who should cut and store the crops that lay midway between the two cities. The result was that much of this precious food reserve was left for the Ottomans.

Lala Mustafa advanced on Nicosia from the south-east, and took up positions opposite the bastions of Tripoli, D'Avila, Constanza and Podocataro. The Ottomans also sunk new wells in the belief that the existing ones would have been poisoned. Mustafa then sent cavalry detachments around the walls to entice the defenders out into the open. Dandolo was reluctant to engage them, and when he was finally persuaded to allow a few sallies out the defeat of his troops and the beheading of one of their captains amply confirmed his misgivings.

On 30 July Mustafa began the construction of earthworks for artillery emplacements as close to the walls as he dared. This was accomplished in spite of fierce cannon fire from Savorgnano's angle bastions. The resultant Ottoman fire from their laboriously constructed temporary forts did little damage, because most of the sixty-pound shots simply buried themselves in the soft earth of the turf-covered slopes that formed the upper part of Savorgnano's bastions. From the de- fenders' point of view the only disadvantage to this remarkable absorbency factor was that any earth that was dislodged tended to fall into the ditch and thus gradually built up a ramp, which would make the Ottomans' assault that much easier when it eventually came.

In order to prepare for this event, Mustafa began sapping forward in long zig-zags which went through the counterscarp and into the ditch, throwing out earth and making traverses, which were stiffened by wood fascines brought up by horses. This was a remarkable operation that anticipates the methods ascribed to the great Vauban a century later. From the trenches the Ottoman arquebusiers, who were regularly relieved by fresh troops, kept up a constant fire so that no defender dared show his head above the parapet. Venetian countermeasures proved to be of little avail. A *cavalier* built within the walls to look down on the enemy forts outside was never used after the first person to ascend it was shot dead.

Dandolo added to his men's problems by providing them with too little gun-powder out of his stores, and ordering them to fire at the Ottomans only when they presented in groups of at least ten. It is no wonder that many of the garrison suspected him of treason. The mounds of earth that had piled up after spilling down the faces of the bastions made a successful attack look more likely with every day that passed, so the Venetian defenders prepared a line of entrenchments from which a counterattack could be delivered inside the four most vulnerable bastions. The Ottomans, for their part, gradually developed their approaches towards the damaged bastions, throwing bags of incendiary material over the walls, and using fire arrows to set light to the bales of cotton with which the Venetians had packed their inner defences. The unbroken volleys of arquebus balls against the walls fur-ther demoralised the garrison who were unable either to see their enemies or to hit back at them. The labourers working on the entrenchments deserted their posts. Disease spread, food was short and inadequately distributed, so everywhere morale and discipline began to crumble as fast as the earthen bastions.

On 9 September the forty-fifth and largest attack on the walls of Nicosia was delivered. The points of assault were the four bastions that had been battered for months. So fierce was the attack that the prepared entrenchments filled up with the corpses of the defenders. The defending gunners were still starved of powder,

and it was only when an artilleryman on the Caraffa bastion made a personal pro-
test that an attempt was made to get further supplies to them. The man's words
were recorded by an eyewitness, and serve as an epitaph for Nicosia's angle bastions that were capable of devastating flanking fire only if that fire were available:

> Why have we no powder to drive them off? While I had powder to flank
> them they could not gain ground. What the devil! Have we eaten the pow-
> der? Have we swallowed the balls? Your saving it for St Mark, I doubt not,
> will mean the loss of all.[14]

The lack of ammunition allowed the Ottomans entry. As panic spread through
Nicosia the northern Kyrenia Gate was opened, and many tried to escape, only to
be cut down by the Ottomans. Realising that all was now lost, Dandolo dressed
himself in his finest robe so that he would be recognised and spared. The first aim
was achieved but not the second, and Dandolo was beheaded, the most senior of
the twenty thousand to lose their lives in the sack that followed.

The Siege of Famagusta

Careful lest a relieving force might arrive at their moment of victory, Lala Mustafa
Pasha rapidly consolidated his position and ordered the repair of Nicosia and an
advance to the north. The arrival outside the gates of nearby Kyrenia of a captured
Venetian officer, chained to a horse and with two severed heads dangling from his
saddle, was warning enough of what was likely to come their way too, so the castle
soon surrendered. The defenders of Famagusta, however, were made of sterner
stuff, even though the demand to surrender was accompanied by a basin containing Dandolo's head. They would fight on until the relieving fleet arrived.

An advance guard of Ottoman cavalry arrived before Famagusta on 15 September. The situation which faced Mustafa was very different from the challenge
he had overcome in Nicosia. Instead of eleven modern angle bastions built half
from earth he was confronted by only one angle bastion set within otherwise old-
fashioned medieval walls of stone. But these walls were very thick and the ditch
outside them was cut out of the rock, so there would be no falling earth to provide
a ramp. The strongest points lay at the south-western corner, where stood the
Land Gate with a huge ravelin outside it, and in the north-west corner the massive
Martinengo bastion was to be found, from whose modern walls the Venetian guns
had the range of several Ottoman encampments. The weak links were the minor
towers, which dated from pre-artillery times and had neither the strength nor the
space to hold modern cannon. Some sections of the walls were suitable for heavy

artillery, notably the spur that projected into the harbour to the tower, which held the chain that closed it off. Guns here provided flanking fire along the sea wall.

More than two hundred thousand may have been present outside Famagusta, and the comment was made that so many soldiers were ready for the assault that 'they could have filled the ditch by each throwing one of his shoes into it'. Losses in action were steadily replenished by further troops shipped over from the mainland, and as many as 145 guns finally joined in the bombardment, including four huge cannons firing shot of up to two hundred pounds in weight. They assisted in depositing an estimated one hundred and twenty thousand iron shot and forty-three thousand stone rounds into the city during the course of the operation (see plate 21). On the defenders' side were probably about eight thousand five hundred men with ninety artillery pieces. They were well used and on one occasion a sixty-pound shot fired over a distance of three miles scattered a review of troops that Mustafa was carrying out in person.

Another means of defence was the use of incendiaries known as wildfire, which consisted of a mixture of 'Spanish pitch, black pitch, saltpetre, sulphur, camphor, turpentine, rock-oil and ardent spirit', compounded together with heat and put into containers of metal, glass or pottery. They appear to have acted by means of an explosion that distributed the incendiary material like a primitive napalm bomb. Other varieties of bomb were larger, and relied more on the explosive element to produce an anti-personnel effect, as their iron casings burst to release chips of stone or arquebus balls. Bombs that worked exclusively through their explosive properties, such as pottery grenades, also existed.

The Ottomans set up an artillery battery on the rocky spur out in the harbour. Other guns from different locations joined in the bombardment and an extensive programme of sapping began. Both sides used mines with considerable effect. On one occasion a distant mine was placed under an Ottoman observation post and fired remotely using a cord attached to the trigger of a wheel lock.

The most noticeable difference between Nicosia and Famagusta in terms of defence was in the infinitely superior leadership and organisation shown in the latter siege. Bragadino and Baglione were both admired and popular, yet maintained strict discipline. Unlike Dandolo, they also encouraged sorties against the enemy, which were largely successful. To prevent the enemy from approaching the walls on foot caltrops were scattered, which caused the besiegers many problems when they ventured out for the numerous personal combats that took place in grand chivalric fashion.

One far from chivalrous aspect of the siege was the parading round the walls of the severed heads of the defenders of Nicosia mounted on spears. This may have been upsetting, but the potentially more serious effects of saps and artillery do not seem to have been anything like as effective as they were at Nicosia.

In January 1571 the defenders were greatly heartened by the arrival of reinforcements in the harbour under the command of Mark Antony Quirini. The force consisted of sixteen hundred soldiers and many supplies, and were joyfully received. Quirini also managed to capture an Ottoman transport and destroyed several enemy shore positions off Famagusta. If his dash and skill had been emulated in even a small part by the rest of the Christian fleet that was so laboriously assembling then the history of the next few months might have been very different. As it was, Quirini's expedition was a bold gesture, but little more.

The lack of control that the Ottomans had over the approaches to Famagusta was illustrated once again when the defenders were able to construct two casemates on the inner side of the counterscarp from which flanking fire could be delivered along the line of the moat. Each casemate was connected to the walls by a ditch, and protected by a covered way. The Ottoman response was to lay down an enormous system of trenches using their forty thousand Armenian sappers and local peasants. The result was that for a distance of three miles south of the fortress a maze of zigzagging trenches capable of sheltering the entire Ottoman army covered the landscape, each excavated so deeply that when mounted men rode along them only the tips of their lances were visible. At the point where the saps came within artillery range of the city two forts were erected from beams and fascines packed with earth and bales of cotton.

Ten forts were made like this, and the close-range bombardment from them started on 12 May. Heavy arquebus fire also began with an aim of keeping the defenders' heads down — the tactic that had worked so well at Nicosia — and two hours before dawn on 19 May the fiercest artillery duel of all commenced. From the Ottoman side seventy-four cannon, and the four great cannon, firing from the new forts, battered the southern walls from the great Land Gate to the Arsenal Tower, as well as causing great damage within the city itself. In reply the Venetian artillery knocked out several Ottoman cannon and destroyed their gun emplacements. However, such were the besiegers' excellent resources that the earthworks were rebuilt overnight.

Soon a simple shortage of powder led to a dramatic curtailment of the counter-battery work and Famagusta's gunners were ordered to fire only thirty shots a day from thirty guns. By 24 May the Ottomans had secured the edge of the counterscarp close to the outer ravelin by the front gate, which they then attempted to capture. The defenders replied by exploding a mine underneath the ravelin itself, so any gain was nullified.

On 3 June the Ottomans tried a new form of attack in the ditch, which consisted of filling it in along a section and then cutting traverses so that they were sapping across the moat. The height of the traverses extended to the walls, so there was little that the defenders could do except throw incendiaries blindly into the passages. In this way the Ottomans gradually clawed the way towards the breaches of Famagusta, tearing down the defenders' entrenchments as they came to them and laying mines. Bragadino's men countermined as best they could, but a successful explosion under the Tower of the Arsenal on 21 June carried away all the face and the parapet of both flanks, the entire platform in front of the entrenchments and eight feet to its side. Dazed by the explosion, the company in charge of the Arsenal Tower could offer little immediate resistance to the attack which rapidly followed, but other units came to their aid and those Ottomans down in the entrenchments were deluged with incendiaries. Unfortunately an accidental discharge of the wildfire mixture set off a load as it was being delivered to the front line, and caused five hundred casualties among the defenders. After five hours of bitter fighting, during which Baglione himself played a personal role, the Ottomans were driven off with the loss of about six hundred dead.

The breach at the Arsenal was repaired during the night of 21 June. The following day another Venetian frigate came to the harbour, and this time the garrison was assured of succour within eight days. But before that promise could be tested another assault was carried out. The explosion of a mine under the damaged ravelin of the Land Gate, which not only blew the ravelin to smithereens but also conveniently filled the ditch nearby with the debris, announced the start of the fresh assault. Once again the Ottomans sapped across the results of their labours while guns strafed the area of destruction so that the defenders could not make repairs. The attack was eventually driven off, but not without considerable casualties among the defenders.

By 28 July all the garrison's meat had been eaten, along with all the city's horses, donkeys and cats. The following day the strongest assault seen up to that point was delivered to the accompaniment of several exploding mines. Although they were deafened by the noise of the guns and choked by the dust from the ruins, the garrison held the breaches in spite of a loss of two-thirds of their strength. During the night a mine at the Arsenal Tower brought down much of what remained of it, and such was the shortage of building materials that breaches were now being repaired using soldiers' clothing filled with earth. The following two days were to see the final Ottoman attacks on Famagusta carried out as a series of episodes of hand-to-hand fighting over the heaps of rubble that had once been the city walls. In one incident an Ottoman hero called Canbulat charged the Arsenal Tower. Here the defenders had apparently rigged up a contraption that spun round a number of sword blades on a wheel to cut down any attacker entering the narrow passage. Canbulat was cut to pieces but destroyed the machine in the process. He lies buried in the former Arsenal Tower, which now bears his name.

Few arquebuses were fired to meet the Ottomans' advance because powder was running so low, and an inventory taken on 31 July revealed that only seven barrels of powder of any variety was left. Food was every bit as scarce, so, with still no sign of the relieving fleet, the garrison surrendered on 1 August 1571. Unlike Nicosia, where the white flag had not been raised and the Ottomans had fought every inch of their way in, there was no immediate massacre. Instead Mustafa's fury was first released against Bragadino himself, whose ears and nose were cut off. Leaving him to ponder on his future fate a slaughter began of the prisoners. Baglione then had his head cut off and paraded triumphantly in front of the Ottoman army, while hundreds more of the survivors were cut down.

Thus ended the second of the two great sieges on Cyprus. The angle bastions had delivered flanking fire and withstood bombardment just as their designers had intended, but, in the absence of relief, even the strongest fortress always has to surrender at some time. At Nicosia this factor of time was made more acute by deficiencies in leadership, which showed beyond any shadow of doubt that modern fortifications such as angle bastions were only as good as the men who defended them. The theories behind flanking fire and geometrical models were fine so long as a garrison had powder with which to fire.

Nevertheless, the Ottomans had besieged well. Their system of angled sap trenches and approaches anticipated the methods to be associated with the name of Vauban a century later. As even the comparatively primitive walls of Famagusta held out for nearly a year, the indication was certainly given that, when a well-supplied and modern design of fortress was defended by a skilled commander who enjoyed the confidence of his followers, then siege warfare was likely to take a very long time. It may have been the case that nothing was infinitely impregnable, but angle bastions gave a defender advantages of time in addition to the more obvious advantages of solidity. As one modern commentator puts it:

> From the last third of the sixteenth century a cordon of rampart- and bastion-defended fortifications effectively blocked Ottoman expansion westward. And that, at the time, was revolution indeed. Fortifications were Europe's trump card in the sixteenth-century confrontation with the Turk.[15]

Chapter 9
Knights Old and New

The constant theme throughout this book is one of change, as the ideals, the behaviour, the environment and the weaponry of war become transformed in response to advances in tactics, armaments and defensive warfare. Previous chapters have traced such 'revolutionary' changes in terms of castle design, galley warfare and the pike square. We will now examine the mounted warrior of the Renaissance in terms of his evolution from knight to cavalryman.

Knighthood, wrote the great military historian Hans Delbrück, was based on 'qualified individual warriors', whereas cavalry consisted of 'tactical bodies composed of horsemen'.[1] This need for a sharper distinction between types of mounted men arose from the use of light cavalry. For example, du Bellay, in his *Discipline Militaire* of 1548, identified four types of mounted men: knights (*gendarmes* or men-at-arms), light horsemen (*chevaux legers*), stradiots (*estradiots* or *ginetes*) and harquebusiers.[2]

This fundamental shift will be analysed by reference to campaigns and battles, but we will also take a more personal look at the knight himself by examining the lives of three individuals whose chivalric careers cover almost the whole time span of this book. The names of the trio are: Pierre Tenaille, known as Bayard, who was born in about 1476 and died the year before Pavia; Blaise de Monluc, who fought at Bicocca and Pavia; and François de la Noue, who died in 1591. Their overlapping careers illustrate in microcosm the great changes in warfare that were taking place all around them. Not the least of these were developments in firearms, which affected all of them in a very personal way. Bayard and la Noue were both shot dead by arquebus balls, while de Monluc was severely wounded by one in the battle that ended his active military career.

The *Chevalier* Bayard
Through the reputation he acquired as '*chevalier sans peur et sans reproche*', Bayard took the chivalric ideal of knighthood into the sixteenth century. His real name

was Pierre Tenaille. He was born some time between 1473 and 1476 and sprang from a remarkable pedigree. His great-great grandfather had been killed at Poitiers in 1356, his great-grandfather had died at Agincourt in 1415 and his grandfather had been killed fighting the Duke of Burgundy at Montlhéry. Finally, his father had retired wounded from the Battle of Guinegatte in 1479. It was quite an act to follow! The duchy of Savoy provided Bayard with his initial military education, and from there he moved on to serve under the Duke of Lorraine.

The first we hear of Bayard in action is during Louis XII's campaign in southern Italy fighting 'El Gran Capitán'. Shortly before the Battle of Cerignola in 1503, when entrenched arquebusiers broke the French advance, Bayard was engaged in a wonderfully old-fashioned knightly encounter at the Siege of Barletta. A truce had been agreed between de Córdoba and the Duc de Nemours, the commanders of the two sides. Having nothing better to do, two picked units of French and Spanish knights engaged in a tournament-cum-battle called 'Battle of the Thirteen'. Unfortunately for the combatants, the Battle of the Thirteen got slightly out of hand. This is not to say that nasty things like pikes or arquebuses were used, of course, but the Spanish, instead of attacking the French knights, concentrated instead on their horses, bringing to earth all but two *chevaliers*. This was considered unfair, and, when the angry and unhorsed Frenchmen responded by lining up behind a rampart of dead horses in an uncanny premonition of the ditch and stakes that would destroy them at Cerignola, all vestiges of gallantry seemed to have disappeared. The Battle of the Thirteen therefore marked another milestone along the road towards the decline in the ideals of knightly chivalry.

As the Bayard story continues its Italian episode we are presented with a further example of individual knightly gallantry that seems somehow bizarre when set in the overall context of what is known to have happened. It was noted in an earlier chapter that a crucial point in the Battle of the Garigliano in 1503 was the crossing of the river using a concealed bridge at Molo de Gaeta, which brought the Spanish into a close encounter with the French. Bayard is described as holding the bridge single-handedly against two hundred Spanish knights before being reinforced. It is a glorious episode, but there is nothing in the lines that follow to tell us how the army was subsequently routed by sheer weight of numbers, and then surrendered the position in return for safe conduct.

Bayard is next found in action during the French war against Venice that resulted from the formation of the League of Cambrai: an alliance created in December 1508 between the French, Emperor Maximilian and the pope. During the Siege of Padua in August 1509 the emperor asked the French commander for some knights

The French knight Bayard, who was almost the last medieval knight

to lead his *landsknechts* on foot, a request which provoked the haughty reply from Bayard that:

> ... the king has no soldiers in his ordinance companies who are not gentle-men. To mix them with the foot-soldiers, who are of a lower social status, would be treating them unworthily.

Bayard suggested instead that the emperor should use his own 'counts, lords and gentlemen' for the purpose, but when the order to dismount was passed on to them the German knights replied in similar vein that it was not at all their duty to advance on foot or to enter a breach and that their real task was to fight on horseback like gentlemen.

The year 1510 was to find Bayard participating in the defence of Ferrara against the army of Pope Julius II, the warrior pope who led his army into battle in a unique variation on the conventional papal role. In 1512 Bayard was involved in the capture of Brescia and was wounded for his pains, only managing to return to the French army just in time for the Battle of Ravenna. At Ravenna, Bayard's role ap-pears to have been that of the classic mounted knight, and he was much involved in the pursuit of the Spanish cavalrymen, although Bayard kept a cooler head than his commander, Gaston de Foix. They had galloped for six miles in the chase, and Bayard begged de Foix to halt and rally his men, 'which he promised to do', says the narrative, but failed to keep his word, and 'evil befell him in consequence'.

The actual evil happened a little later, when the battle was as good as won and de Foix was watching the routed Spanish infantry from a safe distance. Some French crossbowmen drew his attention to a column of retreating Spaniards who were attempting to reach Ravenna by making a long circling movement to the French rear. Forgetting Bayard's earlier pleas, de Foix set off in pursuit of them, but these men were both tough and desperate, and with admirable self-discipline they arranged themselves in a defensive formation. A few arquebus shots were fired at the French knights, and the edged-weapon men then charged home against them with levelled pikes.

Not one of the French knights escaped. De Foix's own charger was hamstrung, and when he rose from the ground he was cut down by deadly wounds to his head. A few miles further on the same Spanish soldiers met Bayard and his fel-low knights returning from their pursuit. Being ignorant of the fact that these men had just killed his commander-in-chief, Bayard responded positively to the Spanish captain's call that they should not fight but let each other pass in safety, 'because you know', said the captain, 'that you have won the battle'.[3]

The Field of the Cloth of Gold

The next we read of Bayard is when he is in action in the second Battle of Guin-egatte in 1513, an encounter that is interesting for several reasons. It was almost a purely cavalry battle, so that it is usually referred to as the 'Battle of the Spurs'. Guinegatte also provides the only example of a battle in which King Henry VIII of England led his men personally into battle and took part in the fighting. As the French camp at Guinegatte was set up near the site of the Battle of Agincourt the association with the example of Henry V is quite considerable, but it will first be necessary to explain how an English army came to be fighting in France in 1513. Popular imagination has it that Henry V invaded France and fought a battle, while Henry VIII invaded France and had a meeting. This was the famous 'Field of the Cloth of Gold' in 1520, the great tournament-cum-peace conference that not only showed how much things had changed since Agincourt but also demonstrated how terribly civilised the peace-loving English were compared to their European neighbours. The reality, as always, is considerably more complicated than myth would have us believe.[4]

Henry VIII succeeded to the throne of England in 1509 following the death of his father Henry VII, a man who had managed to keep England out of any major involvement in continental wars. The English longbow, and the myths surrounding the victories it had won, still held a cherished position in English hearts, and had even been strengthened by the battle the weapon dominated at Stoke Field in 1487, when Lambert Simnel's rebellion had been crushed. Simnel had hired German *landsknecht* for his army, who came to England with the long pikes that were the latest thing in infantry weaponry. Unfortunately for them they did not also bring body armour with them, and the English cloth yard arrows felled them by the score.[5]

Henry VIII, who was no mean archer himself, was not blind to the superiority of pikes over the traditional English bill when used against cavalry, and when he invaded France in 1513 he hired *landsknecht* of his own because native English pikemen were still in very short supply. But also in short supply were English knights, because the majority of these had given up fighting on horseback during the previous century. He had enough light cavalrymen, who appear in the muster roles as 'javelins' (or 'northern horse') and 'demi-lances' (who wore half-armour with unbarded horses), but few knights with full equipment (*see* plates 22 and 23). So Henry VIII went recruiting in the Low Countries for so-called 'Burgundian knights', the spiritual descendants of the knights of Charles the Bold.

After crossing over to Calais Henry first laid siege to Therouanne. His timing was perfect because the main forces of the French were still in Italy, having lost the catastrophic Battle of Novara against the Swiss pikemen a few weeks earlier. The French nevertheless managed to maintain constant pressure against Henry's invasion force by means of raiding and harassment, but the fortified town of Therouanne was in desperate straits.

The Duc de Vendome thereupon thought up an elaborate strategy for attacking the English siege lines and keeping them so thoroughly occupied that a relief column might be slipped into Therouanne through some weak point. Two demonstrations were planned, one on the siege lines to the west and the other to the south. It was to be a rapid operation by cavalry alone, so the French foot-soldiers were to be kept well back while the relief supplies were to be conveyed by mounted mercenaries, Albanian *stradiots*, each of whom was to carry a side of bacon and a sack of gunpowder.

Vigilant English scouts soon reported 'a great plump of spears' behind the church tower of Guinegatte. Henry VIII accordingly sent out an army against them with a considerable mounted vanguard, and was joined by his ally Emperor Maximilian. As the French had planned their operation to be a surprise attack, the sight of the approaching English army made their commander reconsider his plans. But the *stradiots* were already into their part of the operation, and some French knights had begun skirmishing with their English counterparts. Some lances were broken, but the main body of the English knights, who knew that they had considerable infantry support behind them, simply sat and waited to be attacked. Meanwhile, mounted archers left their horses and poured arrows into the French lines in gleeful homage to nearby Agincourt. At this point the French commander gave orders for a retreat: a wise decision but one that was made too late, because the English knights saw their opportunity and charged.[6]

Unfortunately for the French the bacon-carrying *stradiots* had been driven off from the supposed weak points in the siege lines by cannon shot, and at the precise moment when the English charged in front they arrived back on the French flank and made the confusion and disorder that much greater. The 'Burgundian knights' then charged in on to their flanks, so the whole body of French knights galloped off in the direction of their camp, discarding lances and banners and even cutting off the bardings from their horses to lighten the load. Henry VIII had missed the initial excitement, but now came riding up to join in the vigorous pursuit until the French knights reached the comparative safety of their foot-soldiers. Had Henry then pressed home his attack with his own infantry, a French commander reckoned that he would have annihilated the entire French army. Instead, the French escaped remarkably lightly, with few casualties but many prisoners, among whom was the *chevalier* Bayard.

Plate 1 *A largely unrestored section of the Theodosian walls of Constantinople between the Belgrade Gate and the Golden Gate*

Plate 2 *The medieval walls of Belgrade, as seen from across the River Sava*

Plate 3 *The army of the Swiss confederacy kneels to pray prior to the Battle of Mürten in 1476 (From a painting in the Hotel Weisses Kreuz, Mürten)*

Plate 4 *Pay day for mercenaries as depicted in the Sercambi chronicle of Lucca. The Battle of Mürten began while Charles the Bold's mercenaries were still drawing their pay*

Plate 5 The walls of the church of San Juan de los Reyes in Toledo bear the chains from Christian prisoners liberated at the fall of Granada in 1492

Plate 6 Boabdil, defeated at Granada, hands over the keys to King Ferdinand and Queen Isabella on 2 January 1492 (Painting by Pradilla in the Palacio del Senado, Madrid)

Plate 7 Gonzalo Fernández de Córdoba – El Gran Capitán – the victor of the battles of Cerignola and the Garigliano, who learnt his trade during the Granada campaign. He is depicted here in the church of the Convent of San Jeronimo, Granada

Plate 8 Gaston de Foix, the French commander who was killed at the Battle of Ravenna in 1512, from his tomb in Milan

Plate 9 *The Battle of Marignano in 1515, as depicted on the side of the tomb of Francis I in the cathedral of St Denis, Paris*

Plate 10 *Emperor Charles V, as depicted in a statue in Toledo*

Plate 11 The superb life-sized diorama of the Battle of Pavia in 1525 in the Royal Armouries Museum, Leeds. The colours are deliberately muted to give the impression of the misty conditions when the great battle was fought

Plate 12 The rocca of Imola in Italy. In 1472 the existing rectangular corner towers were completely encased within the round towers in the rocca style that replaced them, and it is possible to walk round the inner tower within the outer one. This was a typical response to the challenge made by artillery to medieval fortification styles

Plate 13 *The Tower of St George in Rhodes, an early example of a pentagonal bastion that anticipated the angle bastion form. A near-vertical crack may be noted down the side. This was caused by a Turkish mine during the siege of 1522*

Plate 14 *The Battle of Lepanto in 1571, the famous naval encounter where the Christians took revenge for Cyprus, from a painting in the cathedral at Montagnana, Italy*

Plate 15 *The death of King Louis of Hungary at the Battle of Mohacs in 1526*

Plate 16 *The recovery of King Louis's body after the Battle of Mohacs*

Plate 17 *The heroism of the women of Erlau*
during the siege by the Ottomans in 1552.
They are attacking the enemy in addition to
supplying their menfolk with 'bulls' blood'

Plate 18 The castle of Sarzanello as viewed from the town of Sarzana, showing its two parts: the main triangular-shaped fortress, and the world's first ravelin, which was added in 1497

Plate 19 The ravelin at Sarzanello

Plate 20 *Three stages in the development of fortifications are shown in this view of the castle of Kuressaare, which lies on the island of Saaremaa in Estonia. To the left rear we have the very solid and tall medieval castle of the Livonian Order. To the right rear is a circular artillery tower dating from the late fifteenth century. The photograph is taken from one edge of a series of angle bastions that enclose the fortress*

Plate 21 *The church of St George of the Greeks at Famagusta in Cyprus bears artillery damage from the siege of 1571*

Plate 22 *The armour of King Henry VIII of England, made in Greenwich about 1520. It is designed to cover the wearer from head to foot, leaving no area unprotected*

Plate 23 *A three-quarter field armour, probably French, of about 1600, owned by Henry Wriothesley, 3rd Earl of Southampton. Each plate of the armour is decorated by being etched with a design of animals and flowers*

Plate 24 *A knight with a wheel-lock pistol, as shown by a light field armour of Sir John Smythe. Its origin is German (Augsburg) and English (Greenwich) from about 1585*

Plate 25 *A* reiter *in action with his pistol, from a painting of a cavalry battle by Jan van Huchtenburg (1647–1733)*

Plate 26 The snow and ice of winter show to great effect the shape and layout of a detached earthwork ravelin in the middle of the moat of Kuressaare Castle in Estonia. Contemporary Dutch examples are very similar in appearance

Plate 27 The sack of Naarden, as depicted on the front of the 'Spanish House' at Naarden

Plate 28 *The governor of Leiden offers himself as food for the citizens during the siege of 1574*

Plate 29 *The relief of Leiden, as the ships surmount their final obstacle*

Plate 30 *The walls of the Pskov Kremlin, as viewed from the frozen river during the winter of 2004–5*

Plate 31 *The icon of Pskov, painted to commemorate the defeat of Stefan Bathory's army in 1581. In this detail we see the Virgin Mary appearing above the tower named after her*

Plate 32 Hetman *Zolkiewski, the victor of the Battle of Klushino, shown here during the*
Battle of Cecora in 1620, when he was killed

Plate 33 *The relief of the Kremlin by Russian forces in 1612, the end of the 'Time*
of Troubles'

Plate 34 *The Battle of Kerestes in 1596. This was a notable Ottoman victory over the forces of the Austrian Habsburgs*

Plate 35 *The Siege of Kanicsa in 1600 saw the service of Captain John Smith, who wrote about it in his memoirs. This scene from the operation appears on a ceiling painting in Sarvar Castle, Hungary*

The story of Bayard's capture is a colourful one. According to his biographer, Bayard approached an English knight and held his dagger to the unfortunate man's throat, only to inform the astonished soldier that the great Bayard was actually surrendering to him, not capturing him. Both Henry VIII and Emperor Maximilian desired to meet their distinguished prisoner, who was given the nominal freedom dependent on his promise to tour Flanders for six weeks while taking part in no fighting. The garrison of Therouanne surrendered shortly afterwards, but neither this nor the successful Siege of Tournai that followed could quite equal the feeling of glory that Henry VIII had obtained from the Battle of the Spurs.

In 1514 Bayard was again involved with Henry VIII but in a very different situation, because one of the terms of the resulting peace treaty between England and France was the marriage of Louis XII to Henry's daughter Princess Mary Tudor, and Bayard was invited to the wedding. Louis, however, had less than a year to live, and when his successor, Francis I, reasserted his claims to French territory in Italy it was Bayard who led the advance through the Alps under the benign gaze of the ever-obliging Duke of Savoy, and surprised the Spanish commander Prosper Colonna at dinner.

The epic struggle at Marignano found Bayard in the field in grand style. Francis I was in armour when the approach of the Swiss was announced and bade Bayard knight him there and then, which the veteran warrior did with great dignity. The approach of battle then plunged both of them into the thick of the fighting, and one incident from Bayard's experience that day will serve to illustrate how confusing a sixteenth-century battle could be. Having charged through a mass of Swiss soldiers, Bayard had blundered in the dark into a vine trellis, which forced him to dismount. He took off his helmet and greaves and scuttled on all fours along a ditch towards the French positions. By chance he came upon a friendly unit under the Duke of Lorraine, who lent him a helmet and a horse (his third that day) and he re-entered the battle.

In 1523 Bayard served Francis I in a further Italian campaign under the command of Admiral Bonnivet. Francis's domestic problems, arising from the revolt of Charles of Bourbon, kept him from personal participation. Bonnivet soon showed that he was not up to the task by failing at the Siege of Milan and even being attacked in his winter quarters. He tried to withdraw in good order, but was pursued and defeated at La Sesia in April 1524. At La Sesia Bayard led a hopeless charge against the pursuing Spaniards, but an arquebus ball caught him, and he fell, dying, from his horse. So passed away the last of the great French knights of chivalry, a man whose life had spanned the first glorious years of pike warfare and the bitter lessons of Cerignola and Marignano. A gentleman knight to the very last, Bayard

The death of Bayard at La Sesia in 1524

fought from horseback whenever possible but was more than willing to dismount when circumstances demanded. He was eternally loyal to the French monarch, and the arquebus ball that mortally wounded him at La Sesia at least ensured that he never lived to see the sad defeat and capture of his king at Pavia.

Blaise de Monluc

When Bayard was serving as knight in the company of the Duke of Lorraine, the second member of our trio became one of his 'archers', the curious appellation given to the light horsemen who served the French knights as squires. Gascon Blaise de Monluc was born in 1501, and, like the Gascons of fiction such as D'Artagnan and Cyrano de Bergerac, he set off at the age of fifteen to seek his fortune. Bayard was clearly a hero in the army and the ideal to which young de Monluc aspired. The glory of Marignano was still fresh in everyone's mind, and it was only the question of expense that prevented de Monluc from following his idol as a mounted knight. Instead, his comparatively impoverished state made him accept a position as an officer of foot, and it was through commanding infantry that de Monluc was to make his military reputation. His literary reputation as a writer of memoirs was to follow much later in life. Unlike Bayard, whose *'loyal serviteur'* produced his biography in the style of Froissart's chronicles, de Monluc's life has come down to us in the autobiography he produced after his retirement. It is a lively work, and paints in vivid detail the reality of knightly life in the mid-sixteenth century.[7]

De Monluc's first experiences of battle proved to be far from encouraging in view of the glorious future he desired. His initial encounter was Bicocca in 1522, where he shared in the humiliation sustained by the Swiss pikemen in French service. Worse was to come at Pavia, where de Monluc followed his king into captivity, only to be speedily released because he was not worth trying to ransom!

The great Bayard had now passed away, and when in 1527 Francis I renewed the war against the Habsburgs the result was a complete disaster and a peace treaty that meant almost seven years of enforced idleness for Blaise de Monluc. This at least gave him time to recover from a dreadful wound to his arm sustained at the Battle of Forcha di Penne in February 1528, an incident that serves to illustrate just how tough knights had to be in those days. De Monluc's memoirs record vividly how the enemy:

> . . . peppered me in the meantime with an infinite number of arquebus shot, one of which pierced my target and shot my arm quite through . . . and another battered the bone at the joint of my arm and shoulder that I lost all manner of feeling.[8]

His comrades dragged him to safety, but not very carefully, because:

> . . . they made me tumble head over heels . . . wherein rolling over the ruins
> of the stones I again broke my already wounded arm in two places. As soon
> as my men had picked me up, I told them that I thought I had left my arm
> behind me in the town, when one of my soldiers, lifting it up from where it
> hung like a scarf, dangling upon my buttocks, and laying it over the other,
> put me into a little heart.[9]

De Monluc was so determined to continue his military career that he refused to
have his arm amputated. This was, in any case, a surgical procedure that threatened either death or lifelong poverty, so he chose instead to lie on his back for
two months, experiencing a physical pain that he regarded as nothing compared
to the torment he was enduring by missing the subsequent campaigns. Amazingly,
he was back in action by August of the same year with his arm bound to his side
over a cushion.

De Monluc returned to the military scene in 1536 when a further phase of the
Habsburg–Valois Wars began. Francis I had noted his rival Charles V's preoccupation with the Danube front against the Ottomans. The emperor had then had to
shift his attentions hundreds of miles away for the capture of Tunis. With so many
distractions it was time for the French king to strike again, and once more his
target was the old French obsession of Milan.

Full of confidence, the French army crossed the Alps, expecting the usual warm
welcome in Turin, but the traditional cosy arrangement had fallen apart. Duke
Charles III of Savoy, who was in fact Francis's nephew, refused the French king
a passage over his lands. His obstinacy proved to be a minor setback, because by
1536 the French armies had long experience of the Alpine passages and swept on
unopposed. They brushed the Savoyards to one side and deprived them of Turin
before Charles of Savoy's new ally Charles V could raise a finger to help him. The
ultimate aim of the campaign, the recovery of Milan, was not achieved during the
operation, but the French annexation of Turin was a disaster for the House of Savoy. From 1536 until 1559 the French made sure that they never lost control of Turin
or the Alpine passes, and it was only through events many hundreds of miles away
that the dignity and possessions of Savoy were eventually restored.

De Monluc saw some action in this phase of the war when Charles V retaliated
against Francis I by invading Provence and laying siege to Marseilles. More anx-
ious than ever to win honour, de Monluc volunteered for the hazardous operation
of destroying some mills close to the imperialist positions near Aix en Provence,

Blaise de Monluc, the renowned Gascon commander who was also a man of letters

which were supplying the invaders with flour. He was brilliantly successful, but received no recognition for this feat of arms. Nor was he any more fortunate in the campaign in Picardy, and when the Truce of Nice brought the war to an end in 1538 de Monluc felt that he had been badly served.

After another long truce, de Monluc returned to northern Italy in 1543 for the campaign that ended with the victory of Ceresole. Here he took part in several glorious episodes such as ambushing the governor of Fossano and destroying the bridge over the Po at Carignano, all stories which de Monluc recounts in his memoirs with all the enthusiasm of a ripping yarn. His participation at the great Battle of Ceresole is equally larger than life. It was at Ceresole that de Monluc placed arquebusiers within the pike square, thus anticipating the development that was soon to become universal, but his account of it is somewhat restrained in its self-congratulation, when he writes:

Upon my faith I have never seen nor heard of the like before and thought myself to be the first inventor of it; but we found that they were as crafty as we, for they had also done the same thing, who never shot no more than ours till they came within a pike's length, and there was a very great slaughter, not a shot being fired but it wrought its effect.[10]

De Monluc was knighted on the battlefield of Ceresole and later in the year, in a parallel to the career of his hero Bayard, de Monluc found himself back in France and fighting Henry VIII of England at Boulogne.

The Camisade de Boulogne

By 1544 Henry VIII was no longer the dashing young knight of Guinegatte but a man diminished by ill health who nevertheless thought that his presence on a battlefield could achieve marvels. An expedition led to France by his brother-in-law Charles Brandon in 1523 had ended with famine and mutiny, and in fact the 1544 enterprise fared little better. Boulogne fell after a siege of a few months, only for the Peace of Crépy to threaten its return. But Henry was as determined that it should stay in English hands as the French were for its reversion, and the Dauphin (the future Henry II) took advantage of the confusion to recapture the place in an expedition that is known as the Camisade de Boulogne.[11]

De Monluc was in the attacking army. At midnight the French troops, supported to the rear by some Swiss pikemen, made an entry into the town through some weakly guarded points and inflicted much slaughter. De Monluc claimed a personal kill of two hundred Englishmen. But overconfidence set in, and the triumphant French turned to looting because there was much to pillage. The English counterattacked in force and drove out the French, while the Swiss stayed in reserve and were never ordered into battle.

It was during this confusing encounter in the dark amid pouring rain that de Monluc had his first and last encounter with English archers. He was wearing a coat of mail and a morion helmet and carrying a shield. Finding himself in retreat:

... they bestowed some arrows upon me and shot three arrows into the target and another through a sleeve of mail I wore upon my right arm, which for my part of the booty I carried home to my quarters.

In his subsequent writings, de Monluc despises bows and arrows for their short range and lack of hitting power compared to an arquebus ball, and there can be few people in history who have suffered an arrow in one arm and a bullet in the other and lived to compare the consequences. He also despised the English. He had been brought up on the tales of Crécy and Agincourt, but his experience of the English at Boulogne led him to dismiss the great English medieval victories on the grounds that, as the English then ruled Gascony, the French had been fighting half-Gascons, so that was why they had won. De Monluc of course was a Gascon himself, so he should know.

As for the overall picture, the possession of Boulogne was temporarily settled in England's favour through a treaty in 1546. By this time the French navy was active in the Channel and Henry's mind had shifted from continental adventures to constructing the famous line of forts along the south coast that remain as the most noticeable military memorial of his life and times. When both Henry VIII and Francis I died in 1547 de Monluc continued to serve the new French monarch Henry II, who, as Dauphin, had observed de Monluc's qualities. Like his father before him, Henry II took advantage of Emperor Charles V's preoccupation with the threats from the Ottomans on one side and German Protestants on the other to reopen hostilities against him in 1551, capturing Metz, Toul and Verdun in 1552.

The Siege of Siena

In 1554 the loyal and able de Monluc received his most celebrated command when he took over the defence of the city of Siena and showed that he had a talent for siege warfare equal to that he had demonstrated on the battlefield. The eighteen-month-long siege was probably the last expression of the old Italian city-state patriotism demonstrated for so long by such places as Florence. Even though it made a hero of de Monluc, the French could not sustain indefinitely an outpost so far across the Mediterranean where the emperor's galleys dominated. Nevertheless, de Monluc's energy was astounding, and his matter-of-fact account, although perhaps embellished with the benefit of hindsight, shows an acute grasp of such concepts as the use of the 'half moon' in defensive warfare that would not have been out of place at Rhodes or Güns:

> Now I had even determined that if ever the enemy should come to assault us with artillery to entrench myself a good distance from the wall where this battery should be made, to let them enter at pleasure, and made account to shut up the two ends of the trench, and at either end to plant four or five pieces of great cannon loaded with great chains, nails and pieces of iron.[12]

After this close-range bombardment the defenders would rush in with halberds and swords. The scheme was put into operation during the siege, as were many other efforts, which de Monluc urged. Peasants went out to listen for enemy movements by night, and brave women carried baskets of earth on their heads to repair the breaches.

But de Monluc was also forced to make some very unpleasant decisions, and the section in his memoirs where he described the expulsion from the city of the *bouches inutiles* ('useless mouths'), who spent eight days starving in no-man's land because the besiegers tried to drive them back, produces the most moving writing in all his work. 'God has need to be merciful to men of our trade,' he writes, 'who commit so many sins and cause so many miseries and mischiefs.'[13]

The French Wars of Religion

So the last phase of the Habsburg–Valois Wars dragged on towards a conclusion, both in Italy and in France, and when a bitterly disappointed Emperor Charles V failed to recapture Metz in 1555 he promptly abdicated. The domains of the house of Habsburg in Germany and Austria, together with the imperial crown, passed to his brother Ferdinand, leaving Charles's heir King Philip II of Spain to concentrate on his own inheritance, which included the Low Countries – a poisoned chalice indeed. Philip II's marriage to the late Louis XII's widow Queen Mary Tudor of England ensured English help for his cause, so there was a sizeable English contingent in the army which Philip deployed against Henry II in 1557.

De Monluc was back in action in France and consolidating his reputation for siege work in the opposite direction when he captured Thionville in 1558. This was the high point of his career, and the overall French commander obviously trusted him enough to delegate considerable powers to him. As de Monluc puts it so quaintly, 'he gave me leave to make the trenches according to my own fancy', which he did with some thought for counterattacking against an enemy sortie, adding at every twenty paces:

> . . . a back corner, or return, winding sometimes to the left hand and sometimes to the right, which I made so large that there was room for twelve or fifteen soldiers with their arquebuses and halberds.[14]

Thionville was the last major action of the Habsburg–Valois Wars, which were settled by the Treaty of Cateau-Cambresis. This put an end to military adventures for many soldiers. De Monluc was one of them, and he complained bitterly that France had given up much that she had fought for during the past twenty years. Then his good master, King Henry II, was killed in a tournament accident, and the new king, Francis II, lived for only one year. France gradually slipped into chaos as the disgruntled nobles of France began to identify with the two religious factions of Roman Catholic or Huguenot Protestant, which were beginning to divide the country. The result was a terrible series of conflicts that became known as the French Wars of Religion.[15]

De Monluc flirted for a while with the Protestant cause, but was given the job of keeping the peace in Guienne on behalf of the royal party, a business that was certainly not without bloodshed. Here he showed the same necessary ruthlessness that he led him to expel the *bouches inutiles* from Siena. Much against his own better judgement, de Monluc became 'the hammer of the Huguenots', working on the principle that 'one hanged man is worth a hundred killed in battle'.[16] When war began in 1562 de Monluc returned to active service as much as his masters would allow, because his diplomatic skills were also in great demand. There were battles nonetheless, and in July 1570 he was to be found leading an assault on the small but well-fortified Navarre castle of Rabastens. De Monluc was by then at least sixty-nine years old, but still retained the enthusiasm of his youth. However:

> I had caused three or four ladders to be brought to the edge of the moat, and as I turned about to call for two of them to be brought to me, an arquebus shot clapped into my face from the corner of a barricade.[17]

With blood pouring from his mouth de Monluc ordered his men to continue the assault while he withdrew to the rear. It was soon discovered that the bullet had removed half his face. He eventually recovered from the wound, but was horribly disfigured and chose to wear a mask for the last few years of his life.

A lonely and embittered old man, he began to write his memoirs, and achieved through his books the recognition for his military insights that he felt he had otherwise been denied. His comments are always to the point, and never is he more scathing than in his condemnation of the weapon that had put him so brutally on the retired list:

> Would to heaven that this accursed engine had never been invented. I had not then received those wounds which I now languish under, neither had so many valiant men been slain for the most part by the most pitiful fellows, and the greatest cowards; poltroons that had not dared to look those men in the face at hand, which at distance they lay dead with their confounded bullets.[18]

When the Duke of Anjou, to whom de Monluc dedicated the work, became King Henry III further rewards were heaped upon him and Blaise de Monluc became Marshal of France in 1574. He died three years later, having finally received the recognition that he had always regarded as his due. King Henry IV of France was later to refer to de Monluc's work as 'the soldier's bible'. In place of Bayard's *loyal serviteur* we have de Monluc's own words to provide his hagiography, which shows him to be a transitional figure between the medieval Bayard and a different form of warfare that followed, in which de Monluc was not ashamed to take part.

François de la Noue

The last of the three warriors to be considered in this chapter knew of Marignano and Pavia only from history books, and was just able to see some action in the Habsburg–Valois Wars in the years immediately preceding the Treaty of Cateau–Cambresis in 1559. François de la Noue was born in 1531 in Brittany, and, like Bayard and de Monluc, served as a nobleman's page, in his case in the royal court of King Henry II. When the religious issue replaced hatred of the Habsburgs, la Noue took the opposite route to Blaise de Monluc and converted to Protestantism. For some time, at least, this in no way diminished the trust in which he was held by the influential Duc de Guise, who sent la Noue to Scotland in 1560 to accompany the return home of Mary Queen of Scots, the widow of Francis II.

When the French Wars of Religion began, la Noue became heavily involved on the Huguenot side. Like de Monluc, la Noue was also a man of letters, and his detailed accounts of the Huguenot armies illustrate both their religious fanaticism, which equalled that of the men who would shortly be leading the Dutch Revolt,

The Battle of Dreux in 1562

Der Marschallt von
S. Andreas

and the deplorable tendency in any army to plunder, steal and vandalise. 'Our infantry lost its virginity', he writes, 'and allied itself to Mademoiselle pillage.' But la Noue was also a considerable military theoretician, and his conclusions about weaponry and tactics, an example of which will be discussed in detail in a later chapter, were to prove essential reading for decades to come.[19]

In the first of these wars, la Noue fought at the Battle of Dreux in 1562. He survived to write an account in which he expressed surprise at its unusually long duration – five hours – and the remarkable fact that both commanders were taken prisoner. He also praises the Swiss for their resilience. Elsewhere the Landgrave of Hesse had commented that for his pay the warrior would attack once; for his country he would attack twice; and for his religion he would attack three times. At the bitter Battle of Dreux the Protestant horsemen attacked four times for the French Huguenots.[20]

La Noue then took part in the Battle of St Denis in 1567 during the second war and Jarnac (1569) in the third war, where he was taken prisoner. The same thing happened again during the Battle of Montcontour in 1569, but at the Siege of Fontenay his whole world was turned upside down. A severe wound required his left arm to be amputated, to which la Noue agreed in spite of all the risks from surgery and the possible penury that had encouraged de Monluc in the opposite decision. His arm was replaced by an artificial one made of iron, so that his nickname became *bras de fer*. This naturally restricted his fighting role, but his skills as a negotiator for the Protestant cause soon provided a different outlet for his talents.

In spite of all the chivalric glory of Jarnac and Montcontour, set-piece battles and ransom negotiations are not the things for which the French Wars of Religion are best remembered. In August 1572 it was hoped that the rift between the king and his Protestant subjects would be healed by the marriage of the young King of Navarre and Margaret de Valois, King Charles's sister. But a botched assassination attempt precipitated the notorious St Bartholomew's Day Massacre. Thousands of Protestants were killed, depriving the Huguenot command of much of its leadership, and driving a wedge between the two faiths that was to last for decades. Many Huguenots fled the country or sought refuge in the one fortress that provided them with a place of safety – La Rochelle. When hostilities began again this formidable stronghold on the west coast became the focus of all the royalist efforts.[21]

The Siege of La Rochelle in 1573 ranks with Famagusta as one of the epic sieges of the age. Its progress was nothing out of the ordinary, just the usual business of approach trenches, bombardment and assault on the customary large scale, but it is interesting to note the influence behind the scenes of both Blaise de Monluc and François de la Noue. The royalist de Monluc had been involved with an earlier plan to take La Rochelle in 1567 and had subsequently written a long memorial concerning its strength and strategic importance. The year 1573 found him in an advisory position supporting the efforts of the besieging Duke of Anjou, while the respected Huguenot François de la Noue 'of the iron arm' became involved in negotiations for an honourable surrender as Anjou grew increasingly desperate. Any excuse for him to dismantle his siege lines and march away would have been seized upon with glee. Then, out of the blue, such an opportunity arose when a message arrived informing the Duke of Anjou that he had just been elected King of Poland.

In 1578 la Noue was presented with a new prospect of action when the Duke of Alençon responded to a request for help against the Spanish from William of Orange. He sent la Noue into the Spanish Netherlands at the head of three thousand French and Scottish troops. It was to prove a personal disaster for la Noue, because in 1580 he was taken prisoner for the third time. On this occasion there was to be no speedy release from admiring captors who were Frenchmen first and Catholics second, because la Noue was now in foreign hands. He was confined to the uncomfortable castle of Limbourg (in present-day Belgium) for a captivity that was to last for five years, and, just as de Monluc had employed his declining years to write his memoirs, so la Noue used his enforced idleness in jail to produce his influential *Discours Politiques et Militaires*. It was a work that covered every aspect of military life, from cavalry charges to wheel-lock pistols. It was translated into English as early as 1587, and became essential reading for military men.[22]

After being freed in 1585, la Noue watched from the sidelines as the French Wars of Religion reached their climax. When Henry of Navarre ascended the French throne as Henry IV, la Noue was given a position in the army that was sent to Picardy, but he arrived too late to take part in the Battle of Arques in 1589. The following year he was wounded at the Battle of Belleville, and in 1591 he was sent to his native Brittany, where he laid siege to Lamballe. Wishing to examine the nature of the breach his guns had created, he climbed up on to the parapet where a bullet laid him low. He died fifteen days later at the age of sixty, honoured by all who knew him or knew of him.

As the next chapter will reveal, François de la Noue's military thinking encompassed new ideas of knightly behaviour that took account of the impact of innovative developments in weaponry and posed questions about the influence these would have on knightly behaviour. With la Noue, whose mind was ever on cavalry, just as de Monluc's had been on infantry, we see the final evolution of the sixteenth-century knight, and his passage into uncharted territory.

Chapter 10
Black Knights and Devilish Weapons

As the previous chapter noted, the veteran Huguenot commander François de la Noue was also a man of letters, and among other matters discussed in his influential *Discours Politiques et Militaires* he devotes several pages to a recent and formidable addition to the knight's armoury. This weapon was the wheel-lock pistol, and la Noue begins his account by condemning that which he is about to describe. Just as others before him had denounced the bombard and the arquebus, so la Noue calls the pistol a 'devilish' weapon, which, he reckons, 'was invented in some mischievous shop to turn whole realms . . . into desolation and replenish the graves with dead carcases. Howbeit,' he adds ominously, 'man's malice hath made them so necessary that they cannot be spared.'[1]

So what was it about wheel-lock pistols that made them so disgusting and yet so indispensable? Was la Noue's outburst no more than the ritualistic condemnation of innovation that would be expected from a *chevalier* – la Noue had a lifelong interest in mounted warfare – or were these new weapons really so revolutionary that they represented a genuine threat to knightly combat and the manner of waging it?

The Wheel-Lock Pistol
The wheel lock, the first weapon to be called a 'pistol' in world history, was probably a German invention, although the word 'pistol' is of Czech origin. It was essentially a small arquebus designed to be held in and fired from one hand. The major difference from the foot-soldier's arquebus, however, was not primarily one of size but in its firing mechanism. Experiments had previously been carried out with mounted arquebusiers, who were the natural successors to mounted crossbowmen, but, because they proved to be not much more effective than their forerunners had been, the pistol held the promise of a real change. In place of the arquebus's smouldering, spluttering match, which was dropped by the serpentine on to the powder chamber, the new weapon had on its side a wheel with a serrated

edge. Using a key, this wheel was wound against a spring, and when the trigger was pulled the wheel rotated and rubbed against a piece of iron pyrites (later a flint) held between two metal jaws. The result was a shower of sparks, which ignited the powder in the pan.

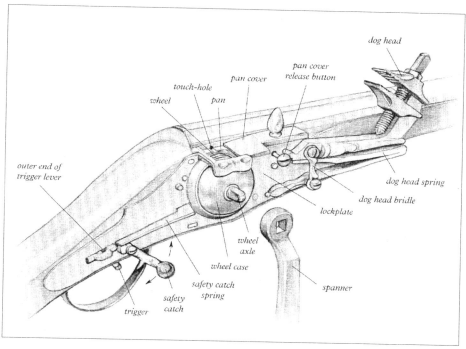

The external parts of a wheel-lock pistol

For a busy cavalryman the advantages of a pistol over an arquebus were obvious: there was no need for two hands to fire it (an important consideration for a horseman) and it did not present the serious safety concerns that the arquebus's burning fuse did. Also, given that the pistol-carrying horseman could easily be supplied with two weapons (one carried on either side of his saddle), with perhaps a third in his boot, to which more might be handed to him by a servant, the age of the firearms-using, mounted knight may be said to have finally arrived.

The wheel-lock pistol, nevertheless, had several drawbacks. The wheel mechanism itself was a delicate piece of machinery: if knocked during a charge or struck by a sword, it could easily be put out of alignment and would not work. Also, the spring was not able to store its rotational energy indefinitely, and it was found that if a spring was wound up too soon before an encounter then it might run itself down. An officer in the English Civil War made just such a discovery when the pistol he had wound up the night before refused to fire. Yet the very nature of these deficiencies made the pistol an ideal firearm for the knightly classes (*see* plate 24). The weapon was temperamental and required frequent servicing, which meant that it was just the thing for a warrior who was surrounded by servants![2]

Curiously, this view of the wheel-lock pistol as essentially an upper-class battle-field weapon was by no means the official reaction to its appearance early in the sixteenth century, when its reception was profoundly negative. It was noted then that the absence of a smouldering match meant that a pistol could be concealed on the person of an assassin or a thief, and for this reason Emperor Maximilian tried in 1518 to have them banned throughout the empire. In 1532 the city council of Nuremberg, whose workshops had rapidly become a major centre of production, complained that the ban was both ineffective and unnecessary. All that it had done was to deprive law-abiding citizens of these weapons, while criminal gangs had them in plenty – so much for gun control! But as time went by the attitude changed, and Maximilian's successor, Charles V, liked wheel locks so much that he owned several himself, and all we hear of bans from this time on is a prohibition in Venice against owning guns small enough to be concealed inside one's sleeve.

The first appearance of the wheel-lock pistol in warfare, as distinct from dark alleys in Venice, would appear to be during the 1540s. It is known that they were used against the Ottomans in Hungary in 1543 because when the fortress of Stuhl-weissenberg (now Szekesfehervar) fell to the Ottomans wheel-lock pistols were among the booty and excited great curiosity. The following year, French troops found themselves on the receiving end of wheel-lock pistol fire during a skirmish with German cavalry in Champagne. The new weapons were described then as being 'little arquebuses, with barrels only a foot long'. Some of the German cavalry units who used pistols wore black armour and called themselves *schwartzen-reiter* ('black riders'). The French called them *diables noires* ('black devils'). The term *schwartzenreiter* was eventually shortened to *reiter* (*see* plate 25), and it entered other European languages to mean a mounted man whose chief weapon was a pistol.[3]

The Pistol and the *Caracole*

The greatest drawback of the wheel lock on the battlefield was tactical. A pistol had a much shorter range than an arquebus, although this was somewhat compensated for by its greater muzzle velocity and improved accuracy. Yet to achieve its potential of tremendous hitting power, the wheel lock had to be fired at an enemy from no more than fifteen feet away, and even at this range the *reiter* could still miss his target. While this was going on, the enemy arquebuses, with their longer range, had no doubt already been fired during the horseman's approach.

One answer to the problem was provided by the development of the *caracole*, a cavalry manoeuvre whereby several ranks of *reiters* rode up in turn against the enemy lines. The first rank fired their pistols, wheeled and retired to the rear to reload. They were replaced by successive ranks that kept up a virtually constant fire. The original purpose of the *caracole* was to deal not with arquebusiers but with squares of pikemen, who had proved to be impervious to a charge with lances. As a military tactic it was nothing new – Vegetius had recommended something similar for the Roman legions. Theoretically at least, the *reiters* would pour so many bullets into the pikemen that their formation would collapse. In practice, however, in the words of Michael Roberts, it provided 'a pretext for doing nothing while seeming to do much'.[4]

The great disadvantage involved in the *caracole* was the human one of the horseman's natural reluctance to get so close to his target that he himself might first be either shot or spitted on a pike. François de la Noue was a prominent critic of the *caracole*, and wrote that men in the following ranks would hear their comrades firing in the front rank, and immediately fire themselves, usually into the air, 'Peradventure they imagine that their great noise should terrify the enemy, which perhaps it would do if they were sheep or crows.' Cowards would even refrain altogether from shooting in their turn, and would wheel back to the rear. For a *caracole* to work effectively, the *reiters*' discipline and morale had to be of the highest quality lest disorder and confusion set in. The dire effects of firing pistols before the enemy ranks had actually been reached may easily be envisaged, and equally important was a need to use men who had been so well trained that they could fire while moving without hitting either their comrades or their own horses. Also, as la Noue shrewdly observed, the withdrawing part of the manoeuvre looked suspiciously like a retreat, and could very easily become one if the targets in the enemy front line took advantage of any apparent disorder.

The *caracole*, nevertheless, had its enthusiasts. The Digges brothers, who fought in the Dutch Wars, believed that the *caracole* was a splendid tactic to use against a pike square, and was much superior to the lance. Such enthusiasm notwithstanding, the weight of military opinion was against the 'dainty' *caracole*, and when the distinguished military historian Delbrück studied the subject and dismissed it as being suitable only as a training exercise he was merely echoing the prevalent view in the sixteenth century. Indeed, so bitter was the opposition to the *caracole* that the whole notion of aristocratic knights using pistols, which was in any case tainted by the slur of class distinction, was regarded with serious suspicion.

That the baby was not thrown out along with the bathwater rested on a broader view and a different observation – that pistol-packing horsemen may have little effect against infantry, but could be very useful against fellow knights in cavalry–cavalry encounters. This was la Noue's eventual conclusion, and after his ritual condemnation of the pistol and his negative comments about the *caracole* that we noted above, he eventually hits a positive note when he waxes lyrical about the efficacy of *reiters* against knights armed with lances. La Noue's discussion begins with a consideration of the order that cavalry should adopt in formation and in action, an issue that had already been exercising military minds for half a century before the wheel-lock pistol was invented. French knights traditionally kept to a shallow formation (*en haie*) so that their lances might be used to their best effect. It was a formation that emphasised, and indeed relied on, individual bravery. In complete contrast, German knights had tended to attack using deep squadrons (*en host*). In about 1480, a certain Philip von Seldenek recommended a minimum depth of nine ranks. The examples he gives of squadrons of two hundred (fourteen ranks) and a thousand men (twenty-eight ranks), respectively, envisage a 'flying wedge' formation whereby the mass of horsemen is led by either five or seven very experienced troopers, the density increasing towards the rear until a line of twenty-one men is reached in the rear ranks.

This sounds an incredibly clumsy use of mounted knights, and in fact the first Battle of Guinegatte in 1479 (which is sometimes referred to as the last battle of the Middle Ages) saw French knights *en haie* envelop German knights *en host*, but the biggest threat to the deep squadron was from field artillery. At the Battle of Ravenna in 1512 Fabrizio Colonna's cavalry came under cannon fire while they were waiting *en host*. It was then that one cannonball tore through the ranks and took out thirty-three men and horses. The addition of pistols to the equation in the 1540s made the situation completely different, so the debate rumbled on for another generation. La Noue definitely favoured the German model:

> Herein we must say that the Germans exceed all other nations, because they seem to be not only close but even glued to each other . . . whensoever they be broken, in their retire and fight they still remain separate and joined together, which the spears do not.

He then compares the effectiveness of multiple ranks of lancers and concludes that their impact could be nullified for broadly the same reason as applied to the use of the *caracole* against infantry – the lines got tangled up and could not impact on their opponents:

. . . whereupon I will say that although the squadrons of the spears do give a gallant charge, yet it can work to no great effect, for at the outset it killeth none, yea, it is a miracle if any be slain with the spear.

By comparison, la Noue had observed that the German *reiters*:

. . . do never discharge their pistols but in joining, and striking at hand, they wound, aiming always either at the face or the thigh. The second rank also shooteth off so the forefront of the men-at-arms squadron is at the first meeting half overthrown and maimed.[5]

The secret of *reiter* success against other knights was therefore not to try a *caracole* but to break into their formation as soon as possible, because 'reiters are never so dangerous as when they be mingled with the enemy, for then be they all fire'. In summary, a *reiter* charge should be designed for shock, with pistol shots concentrated at point-blank range on the weak points of an armoured opponent, such as his face. As the examples that follow will show, the empty pistols were replaced by the *reiters'* swords as they broke into the formation. This, incidentally, was a tactical innovation credited to Gustavus Adolphus in the seventeenth century, but already used to good effect during the sixteenth. 'I am driven to avow', writes la Noue, 'that a squadron of pistols, doing their duties, shall break a squadron of spears.' To achieve this, according to the Duke of Alba, a seventeen-horse depth was needed. He based this calculation on the measurement that a squadron of close-ordered horsemen occupied three times space in depth as they did in breadth, so a front of a hundred horsemen in seventeen ranks would be twice as wide as it was deep.[6]

What *reiters* could deliver so effectively was good old-fashioned shock combined with modern firepower to produce devastating results. On the occasions when this was put into operation, it was noticed that cavalry actions tended to be of shorter duration than hitherto. Tavannes, another military commentator, noted drily, 'The large pistols make . . . close action so dangerous that everyone wants to leave, making the fight shorter.' The 'pistol revolution', if such it can be called, therefore promised great changes in knightly behaviour, but the *caracole* was a blind alley into which good generals must not blunder and by which they must not be distracted. Indeed, a *reiter* squadron performing a *caracole* would be in a worse situation than men-at-arms *en haie*, because the rows of horsemen moving to the rear with empty pistols were the perfect target for a charge, a situation that was exploited by the Polish hussars at the Battle of Klushino in 1610.[7]

Giving Up the Lance

By the 1580s, when la Noue was writing in his prison cell at Limbourg, his fellow countrymen, the French *gendarmes,* were starting to carry a pistol in a holster
along with their lances, but they were still very reluctant to abandon the lance
altogether because they regarded the shooting of wheel locks as 'a base and servile
occupation'. As noted earlier, la Noue's predecessor Blaise de Monluc displayed a
similar snobbishness about firearms, in that he regarded wheel-lock pistols as a
gentleman's weapon and the arquebus as a tool of the lower classes. His reasons
may have had much to do with the technical points enumerated earlier, but de
Monluc had a certain understandable antipathy to the arquebus because the bullet
from one had removed half his face.

The less snobbish la Noue, however, realised that *reiter* warfare required more
order and discipline in action than the average noble knight was inclined to contribute to the overall operation of a battle, whereas 'such as imagine the pistol to
be such a terrible and offensive weapon are not greatly deceived'.[8]

So how was it possible to counter the *reiters*? Duke Henry of Guise wrote in
1588 that 'to defeat the *reiters*, one must have a well-ordered troops of good musketeers and arquebusiers . . . this is the sauce with which one spoils their taste'.[9]
De Monluc also believed that it was bullets not lances that would stop them, when
he wrote that:

> We very much lose the use of our lances, either for want of good horses, of
> which methinks the race visibly decays, or because we are not so dexterous
> in that kind of fight as our predecessors were; for I see we quit them for the
> German pistols, and indeed, for fighting in gross battalions, these are much
> more ready [useful] than lances are.[10]

The *Reiter* in Battle

The debate over mounted tactics continued long after the deaths of both de Monluc and la Noue. The experience of the battles of Kircholm (1605) and Klushino
(1610) was to make an important contribution to the discussion, as a later chapter
will show. As late as 1616 Johann Jacobi von Wallhausen, the founder of Europe's
first cavalry school, could be found trying to cover all his bases by arguing that a
knight should be dressed in bullet-proof armour and be armed with pistols, sword
and lance at the same time![11] So was the age of the armoured knight and his lance
finally at an end, or was it simply a matter of a change of weapon and tactics? What
do the battles of the time tell us?

As noted above, a skirmish in Champagne in 1544 was probably the first field encounter when wheel-lock pistols were fired in anger, but the first major campaign in which *reiters* were used was the war between the Schmalkaldic League and Emperor Charles V. The Schmalkaldic League, which was founded in 1530, was an alliance of German Protestant grandees and in its organisation anticipated the revolt of the Spanish Netherlands a generation later. Its members were also in the forefront of military development. According to the report of a Venetian ambassador the Schmalkaldic horsemen were noted for their ability and good order, especially in the excellent manner they obeyed the trumpet signals.[12]

The Treaty of Crépy with France in 1544, followed in 1546 by a long truce with the sultan, left Charles V free to deal with more domestic matters. But his rivals acted first, and in July 1546 they moved against him from two directions. A large army under Philip of Hesse and John Frederic, Elector of Saxony, marched upon Charles from the north, while another approached from the south-west.[13] Charles could well have been in grave peril had it not been for two unexpected factors. First, his enemies preferred to negotiate rather than attack, which gave the emperor ample time to raise troops. Second, and more surprisingly to the Schmalkaldics, one of their most important members, Maurice the Margrave of Misnia, defected to the imperial side. Maurice was Elector John Frederic's cousin, and so opportunistic was his move that he quickly overran much of the elector's territory. Unsurprisingly, John Frederic then chose to march north with the bulk of the Protestant army to evict Maurice, leaving Philip of Hesse isolated. Charles V struck eagerly and successfully at this latter, weaker target while his foes were so conveniently divided.[14]

Meanwhile, John Frederic took his revenge on his cousin Maurice the Margrave of Misnia and ejected him from Thuringia. He then added to his triumph by annihilating an army of seven thousand men sent by Charles and put under the command of Albert of Hohenzollern–Kulmbach. Charles, however, advanced at the head of some thirty thousand men to confront him, and as John Frederic only commanded half that number he withdrew across the River Elbe at Mühlberg and broke down its bridge. John Frederic was desperately short of allies because Philip of Hesse had begun futile negotiations with Charles, the evident intention being to save his own domains.

Charles had collected a sizeable number of boats on his side of the Elbe with which to make a pontoon bridge, but a local peasant, whose farm had been destroyed by the elector's men during their withdrawal, happily disclosed to Charles's army the location of a ford. The crossing began on the very dark and foggy morning of 24 April 1547.[15] The river was wide, and thus it was that an astounded

Elector John Frederic of Saxony, who was defeated at the Battle of Mühlberg in 1547

Schmalkaldic army suddenly felt bullets whizzing round them. Their experience of firearms was with arquebuses and pistols, which they knew were of too short a range to reach across the Elbe. But the Duke of Alba, Charles V's general, was employing a new, heavier, long-range version, which was fired from a forked rest and had been given the name of 'musket'.

The tough Spanish infantry led the imperial army during its crossing. The musketeers felled the occupants of boats on the far shore and the vessels were then taken by other Spaniards who clambered on board with knives between their teeth. They were followed over the ford by the light cavalry, and then came Charles himself at the head of his *reiters*, a scene immortalised for ever in a painting by Titian. The vanguard hastily secured the far bank and began to construct the planned bridge of boats to facilitate the progress of the rest of the imperial army.

John Frederic, Elector of Saxony, was taken completely by surprise. His camp lay three miles beyond the river, and he had eaten a leisurely and hearty breakfast before learning of the disaster. Without even considering a counterattack, he gave orders for his army to retreat to the safety of Wittenberg. Once Charles realised what had happened, he sent the Duke of Alba on ahead to harass his opponent's withdrawal. The Protestant army had gone scarcely three miles when its rear was attacked. Sensing that the heavy *reiters* would soon be upon him too, John Frederic resolved to stand and fight. This gave Charles the opportunity to draw up his army in battle array, and he wasted no time in sending in squadrons of *reiters* and other cavalry units against the elector's more vulnerable mounted men on the wings. On the imperial right, Maurice the Margrave of Misnia used old-fashioned mounted arquebusiers, who softened up the Saxons sufficiently for a triumphant charge. Other imperial mounted troops completed an encirclement by bursting out of cover on the road to Wittenberg. Great was the slaughter. The elector, having defended himself with the sword, was captured and taken before his emperor. He was eventually imprisoned for life, and all his domains, together with the title of Elector of Saxony, went to Maurice the Margrave of Misnia. Thus did the Battle of Mühlberg put an end to the Schmalkaldic League through a combination of cavalry and infantry tactics, old and new. Philip of Hesse, who might have saved John Frederic, paid for his inaction by a similar sentence of imprisonment.

Yet, strange to relate, there was one more act to play: the newly promoted Maurice, Elector of Saxony, reasserted his Protestant sensibilities and made an alliance with France against Emperor Charles V. However, his delusions of grandeur came to an abrupt end at Sievershausen in 1553. The battle included a skirmish between rival squadrons of *reiters*, and an anonymous bullet from a wheel-lock pistol felled the erstwhile Margrave of Misnia. He died two days later.

The Wheel Lock in the French Wars of Religion

Accounts of the Habsburg–Valois Wars and the French Wars of Religion indicate that warriors called *reiters* appeared regularly on both sides. Henry II of France had a few wheel-lock men in his service as early as 1548, and for the next four decades *reiters* were to be found fighting against and beside lance-wielding men-at-arms. These heavily armoured mounted mercenaries put their skills into action to the usual accompaniment of pillage, mutiny and general mistrust. They were often called *cuirassiers*, because they wore the full armour and helmet of the knight, with the exception of leg armour, which they discarded in favour of long, stout leather boots – a mode of dress that was soon to become very familiar on the battlefields of western Europe.

Mercenary units of *reiters* were hired in regiments of two or three companies of three hundred men each. According to one such contract, the *reiters* were supposed to be:

> . . . good and valiant cavalrymen, men of war and service, true Germans, well mounted and armed with corselet, mail gloves, gauntlets, morion, and equipped with two pistols each, a cutlass and a mace.

The Battle of Mühlberg in 1547

A *reiter* company would also contain certain specialists, including a pistol worker, whose maintenance duties would have been vital. *Reiters* are listed in the two opposing armies at the Battle of St Quentin in 1557. At the Battle of Gravelines in 1558 the marshal, des Thermes, employed German *reiters* who had deserted from imperial service, while other *reiters* fought against him.

Good examples of *reiters* in action with wheel-lock pistols and swords are provided by two battles in particular. The first is Henry of Navarre's victory at the Battle of Coutras in 1587 using a mixture of pistols and shock tactics.[16] He was fighting Duke Anne of Joyeuse, the favourite of the Catholic king, Henry III. Henry of Navarre was a cavalry specialist who believed that a leader's place was at the head of his men, and his enthusiasm for placing himself at the front of cavalry charges caused great concern to his lieutenants. The *reiter* action, which was decisive to the outcome of the battle, took place when Joyeuse led a charge of *gendarmes* with lances against the centre of Henry's army. The *gendarmes* charged *en haie*, but so irregularly that what had been a line deteriorated into loose squadrons of faster horses and braver riders at the front while the slower and more cowardly tried to keep up. Arquebus fire from Henry of Navarre's infantry compounded their disorder, and at that precise moment Henry's six-deep squadrons of *reiters* flung their wedge-shaped formation at the ragged line and smacked clean through it, just as la Noue had prophesised.[17]

The next few minutes became a textbook illustration of the great Huguenot's military theories put into operation by a cavalry leader who possessed all the dash of a medieval knight. Joyeuse's lances were contemptuously knocked to one side as Henry's *cuirassiers* blasted the riders at point-blank range with their wheel-lock pistols. Henry enjoyed one of the best days of his life, shooting dead the first horseman that he met and capturing a standard from the second. Joyeuse surrendered to a group of Huguenots who surrounded him, shouting that he was worth a huge ransom, but one of them simply raised a pistol and blew the duke's brains out.

By the time of the Battle of Ivry in 1590, Henry of Navarre had become King Henry IV, but he still believed in leading his army into battle. 'If you miss my pennon', he announced to his commanders, 'rally round my plume'. The use of cavalry at Ivry is particularly interesting because almost every combination of mounted man and weapon discussed above is found at this one battle. Henry's Catholic opponents launched a simultaneous attack along the front with three different varieties of cavalry. On the right flank were *reiters*, who set out to perform a *caracole* that was a classic failure. Having first been shaken by a volley of arquebus fire, they discharged some of their pistols and then wheeled round prematurely, leaving their leader, Eric of Brunswick, dead on the field.

Unfortunately for their comrades, this withdrawal took them in a disorderly fashion against the left flank of their fellow horsemen in the centre, who were men-at-arms, bearing lances, drawn up *en haie*. Their commander, Charles of Mayenne, Duke of Guise, had to halt his advance to let the *reiters* ride by, which removed much of the impetus of the charge he had been setting in motion. On his left flank, the other mounted unit, which consisted of horse-arquebusiers, fared much better and managed to empty a volley into the king's ranks, killing Henry's standard-bearer. Thus it was that the king had indeed to be identified by his white plume, which was inevitably in the thick of the action.[18]

With Henry at their head, a counterattack was launched by the king's troops, who hit the disturbed line of Mayenne's lancers and broke through. With their rear ranks jammed together, the Catholic knights threw down their useless lances and drew their swords, which were apparently the only other weapon they possessed. Henry's cavalry were all wheel-lock men, and there began fifteen minutes of mayhem with close-quarter exchange of pistol shots and sword cuts. Henry IV himself drove right through the mass at the head of his 'flying wedge'. Meanwhile, out on Henry's own right wing was a regiment of mercenary *reiters* under Dietrich von Schomberg. Its target was the unit of mounted arquebusiers, and the *reiters* charged in classic German style to blast their opponents at close range with their pistols and then continued on with swords drawn.[19]

Ivry was the culmination of everything the old campaigner François de la Noue had prophesied and argued for throughout his long career. In one of his *Discours Politiques et Militaires* he had been particularly scathing of young gallants who read so many chivalric romances that they began to believe that real battles were won using 'magic arms and armour, and are backed by a fairy or a magician'. The 'black knights' with their devilish wheel-lock pistols represented reality and were the true sign of the knight's future.

Chapter 11
Fire, Ice and Flood

Military historians are seldom surprised and rarely shocked, because the re-current folly of mankind that we know as warfare tends to hold few revelations for an experienced student of the subject. Accounts of battles and sieges have so many features in common regardless of where or by whom they are carried out that reading about them breeds its own sense of *déjà vu*. Yet occasionally one comes upon a campaign that grabs one's attention simply because of its sheer unpredictability. When the war includes a number of acts of bravery that stand in a class of their own, together with a unique environment that produces severe challenges and an equally bizarre and impressive range of responses, then the result is a military operation that begs study both for its own qualities and for the feeling that here is something very different from the usual run of things. The wars that attended the birth of the Dutch Republic provide just such an example. There is heroism, appalling savagery and an astounding determination on both sides, all conducted against the background of a landscape so extreme that it often acted as a third foe, adding fire, ice and flood to mounted knights, wheel-lock pistols, cannon and pikes as foes to be overcome.[1]

The Dutch Revolt

The seventeen provinces of The Netherlands had first been united by the Duke of Burgundy, and then inherited by Emperor Charles V. Under King Philip II of Spain, the light imperial touch that had hitherto kept the inhabitants both peaceful and content was replaced by a firmer and less tolerant line. Outbreaks of Protestant anger in August 1566, when Calvinists seized churches and destroyed their Catholic images, provoked unpopular, if understandable, reaction, and paved the way for a religious rebellion that went hand-in-glove with the people's opposition to the unpopular policies of their distant ruler. In August 1567 Don Fernando Alvarez de Toledo, Duke of Alba, the captain general of the Spanish Army of Flanders, was sent to restore order. Alba was a veteran of Charles V's wars, and we noted him earlier in the warmer climes of Tunis and the decisive Battle of Mühlberg. From the time of his appointment to the Spanish Netherlands, his ruthless approach made enemies of all their inhabitants, from the simplest peasants to their aristocratic leaders such as William of Orange, who was nicknamed 'William the Silent'.

Alba's first problem in suppressing the revolt was a logistical one. Separated from the Spanish homeland by the unfriendly kingdom of France, the *tercios* had to be provided and supplied via a circuitous route that took them by ship to Italy, then by land over the Alps and then via a mixture of sympathetic and hostile lands to an area that must have seemed to the average Castilian like the ends of the earth.[2] The southern part of these distant possessions, which roughly corresponded to modern Belgium, was 'knights' country', but beyond these solid grasslands lay the two provinces of Holland and Zeeland. These formed the heart of the rebellion against Spanish rule, and their terrain was so very different: four great rivers – the Lek, Linge, Maas and Waal – came together to create a natural barrier against any army approaching from the south. Holland was crisscrossed by rivers, canals and drainage channels, and was protected from the forces of nature by ancient and carefully maintained dykes and windmills that kept the huge rivers and the unfriendly North Sea from flooding acres of reclaimed land.

Alba's harsh treatment of his opponents provoked more serious opposition, and the first battle of the Eighty Years War, as the struggle is known, was fought in 1568 at the Battle of Heiligerlee. This was a cavalry encounter that provides us with another good example of the *reiter* in action.[3] Louis of Nassau, the brother of William of Orange, was in command of a small mercenary force of German *reiters* and *landsknechts*. He was opposed by Jean de Ligne, Count of Aremberg, who led the *tercio* of Sardinia, together with more Spanish and Germans. After some fierce fighting around the peat bogs that characterised the landscape, Aremberg led a cavalry charge. During the action pistols were used in a rare display of single combat when Aremberg and Adolphus of Nassau met one-to-one and used wheel locks against each other. Aremberg received and disregarded a pistol wound from his adversary and then laid Adolphus dead at his feet with a bullet through his body. He also shot a couple of companions of Adolphus with his two remaining pistols, but then someone shot Aremberg's horse. The stricken animal was unable to carry its rider any further. The count staggered on a few paces as his own bullet wound began to take effect, but within minutes he was despatched by a sword.

Heiligerlee may have been the first battle of the Dutch Revolt, but it was to prove to be atypical. Most of the immediate armed resistance to Spanish hegemony that followed was carried out at sea by the 'Sea Beggars' – privateers operating from England. In 1572 William the Silent, accompanied by the Sea Beggars, landed

at Brielle in Zeeland to lead the revolt against Spanish control. While the Sea Beggars kept the upper hand in maritime operations, the subsequent phases of the conflict on land largely involved the capture and recapture of garrisons and towns – operations in which William the Silent was almost always unsuccessful. Mounted troops were to play only a small role in the war. Indeed, after the Battle of Gembloux in 1578, one of the few pitched battles that occurred, a sympathetic English observer consoled himself with the thought that a defeat in such circumstances was nothing compared to the challenge mounted by a fortified position, because 'one good town well defended sufficeth to ruin a mighty army'.

His observation was an acute one, because most Dutch towns were indeed well defended. They may not have sported geometrically perfect angle bastions of brick and stone, but were instead protected by a mixture of medieval walls, angle bastions and ravelins – the construction of which reflected the profound difference between the landscape of The Netherlands and the arid plains of Cyprus. The Dutch had developed to a fine art the use of water as a defence, and being short of stone had combined this element with that of earth to surround their towns with structures that had little in common with the Martinengo bastion at Famagusta other than their overall shape. Instead, many of them were built of earth, sculpted and carefully maintained to provide an absorbent surface for cannonballs at a fraction of the cost that would have been needed for equivalent walls of brick or stone (see plate 26).[4]

Nevertheless, the system had certain drawbacks. The surrounding water may have discouraged mining, but when the surface froze an attacker's job was made much easier. It was, however, possible to bring about a collapse of the earthen walls, but to do this the enemy had to get close to the town, and beyond the walls the defensive system of earth and water interlocked with the canals and dykes that it so closely resembled. Vast lakes bordered several towns, draining eventually by way of rivers into the huge complex of islands that was known as Zeeland (literally 'sea-land'). In the words of a contemporary English commentator, the area was:

. . . the great bog of Europe. There is not such another marsh in the world that's flat. They are a universal quagmire . . . indeed, it is the buttock of the world, full of veins and blood, but no bones in it.

Goes and the Weapon of the Sea

In late 1572 there occurred the first of several incidents of bravery against the elements that were to give the Dutch Revolt a unique place in military history. The

The Battle of Heiligerlee in 1568, the first battle of the Dutch Wars

River Scheldt enters the North Sea around the isles of Zeeland, and in the days before modern land reclamation changed the topography the Scheldt flowed past the island of South Beveland, which lies six miles off the coast to the west of Bergen op Zoom. On South Beveland lay the strategic fortress of Goes (or Tergoes), which the rebels were besieging. The Duke of Alba was determined that it should not fall, and he gave orders for its speedy rescue. Thus it was that three thousand Spanish troops found themselves on the mainland with the relief of Goes as their objective. No doubt most of them were expecting to be ordered into boats by their commander, Cristobal Mondragon, but it was not to be. Instead, after one of the most remarkable commands ever uttered by a military leader, the entire Spanish army was marched headfirst into the sea.[5]

The reasoning that lay behind this unexpected manoeuvre was some reliable intelligence supplied by a local official who was of unquestionable loyalty to the Spanish cause. South Beveland had not always been an island, and owed its status to a disastrous storm that had cut it off, leaving an expanse of sea called the Verdronken Land ('the drowned land'). The tide rose and fell by about ten feet. The sea bed was muddy and treacherous, and three deep and fierce channels intersected it. But given the right tidal conditions, and under the leadership of an experienced local guide, it was possible to cross the sea on foot with the expectation that the water would never be more than about five feet deep. After this dubious reassurance, and with their powder and biscuit held above their heads, three thousand men set out in complete darkness to test the proposition for six very cold and very wet hours.

Accounts of the expedition tell us that the men were only informed of the nature of the operation immediately prior to plunging into the 'drowned land', with its slimy, treacherous base. There they trudged, slipped, swam and struggled in single file almost until daybreak. The water never passed higher than their shoulders, but it also never settled lower than their chests, and just before the sun rose the vanguard emerged on to the dry land of South Beveland. Out of the three thousand men, only nine had been lost during the perilous sea crossing. After a short rest the hardy invaders pressed on for Goes, whose besiegers had already been informed that a relieving Spanish army had arisen from the depths of the ocean. Faced with such a display of superhuman determination, the siege was quickly abandoned. It is no wonder that the Spanish infantry was regarded as the best in Europe.[6]

Naarden and the Weapon of Fire

While his lieutenants had been making military history at Goes, the Duke of Alba had been engaged in an operation against towns in the north-east to isolate Holland and Zeeland from them. Very little resistance was given, because the tale quickly spread of how any opposition to the Spanish was met by fire and sack. Thus fell Mechelen, and when Zutphen attempted a feeble opposition to the entrance of the Philip II's troops Alba sent orders that not a single man should be left alive and that the whole town should be burned to the ground. The order was carried out almost to the letter, with captives being tied together in pairs and thrown into the river. The massacre was carried out so swiftly and so suddenly that friendly troops nearby, who might have attempted the town's rescue, knew nothing of what was happening. 'A wail of agony was heard above Zutphen last Sunday,' wrote Count Nieuport, 'a sound as of a mighty massacre, but we know not what has taken place.'[7]

The victorious army then headed west for friendly Amsterdam, which was the only place to remain loyal to Philip II of Spain throughout the war. Amsterdam would provide a good base for attacking the rebels in Holland and Zeeland, but en route, beside the Zuider Zee, lay the town of Naarden (see plate 27). Having heard of the fate of Zutphen, Naarden's citizens hurried to parley with the Spanish commander. After some negotiation it was agreed that the inhabitants would be spared in exchange for the keys of the city, yet no sooner was the Spanish army in possession of Naarden than it began a systematic slaughter of the populace. The town was then fired to flush out any people who had taken refuge in their homes. Alba wrote later that 'they had cut the throats of the burghers and all the garrison, and that they had not left a mother's son alive'. Adding his own voice to the comments, a fellow Spaniard claimed that the sack of Naarden was 'a punishment for having been the first of the Holland towns in which heresy built its nest.'[8]

Haarlem and the Weapon of Ice
The citizens of Haarlem were the next to fear the Spanish advance. They had good reason to be apprehensive, because tales of Spanish cruelty reached them long before any army, but one curious episode served to hearten the defenders. A little fleet of armed vessels, belonging to Holland, became frozen in ice near Amsterdam. Believing that they had them at their mercy, some Spanish troops crossed nervously over the ice to attack the stricken vessels. But the crews were ready for them, and had constructed an impromptu ice fortress. More surprising for the Spaniards was the way in which bands of Dutch musketeers left their frozen citadel to attack them, apparently gliding across the surface of the ice with the help of strange blades fastened to the soles of their boots! Hundreds of Spanish soldiers were killed, and when, after twenty-four hours of resistance, the ice castle finally melted, it had done its job and the ships escaped.[9]

The skirmish on the ice provided an unusual curtain raiser to one of the longest and bitterest sieges of the entire Dutch Revolt. Haarlem was one of the largest cities in the Spanish Netherlands, but it was also one of the weakest, with medieval walls and just one ravelin in front of its main gate. On its western side were the blustery downs and the waves of the North Sea. Ten miles to the east lay Amsterdam, the two cities being separated not by land but by a huge inland lake called the Haarlemmermeer (an area which has since been completely drained and provides part of the land for Schipol Airport). In the winter of 1572–3 the lake was frozen, and as the Duke of Alba brought up thirty thousand troops towards Haarlem's walls the icy surface witnessed an endless procession of sledges and skaters bringing last-minute supplies and ammunition to the threatened city. The inhabitants, now well armed and determined, prepared to defy Alba and his men, and to face up to his threats to visit upon them the same fate as Naarden.

The Duke of Alba was determined to dispose of Haarlem by the quickest and most efficient means possible, so he concentrated three days of fierce artillery fire on two of the city's gates, firing about fifteen hundred cannonballs in all. But as fast as breaches were made the holes were repaired with rubble, sand and earth, and even with statues contemptuously removed from former Catholic churches which had been appropriated by the Calvinist rebels. The holy images were jammed into the spaces left by the cannonballs, a practice which offended the devoutly Catholic besiegers and confirmed their opinion that in the suppression of the Dutch Revolt they were engaged in a truly noble crusade against heresy.

To Alba's astonishment, the assault force that followed the artillery barrage was driven off with heavy losses. Changing his tactics, he ordered a mine to be driven under the ravelin that protected one of the gates. Meanwhile, reinforcements from William of Orange began making their way towards Haarlem, but these unfortunates became lost in the fog and were apprehended by the Spanish, so very few got through. Their second-in-command suffered the indignity of having his severed head thrown into the city, the first act of atrocity of the Haarlem campaign. It was one to which the citizens responded with a barrel of heads of Spanish prisoners.

As the Spanish mine inched forward, Dutch countermines spread sideways to intercept it and many a fierce skirmish was fought in the bowels of the earth. In late January 1573 more supplies arrived on sledges and skates across the Haarlemmermeer. A tremendous Spanish assault then captured the ravelin, only to discover that the defenders had erected a 'half-moon' inside it from which to launch a counterattack, and once more the Spanish army was driven back. As the siege dragged on, the spectre of starvation arose and drove the citizens to take desperate measures. On one occasion a group marched out under the cover of thick fog with the intention of spiking the enemy's guns under their very noses, but all were slain at the cannon's mouth, and fell around the battery with their hammers and spikes still clutched in their hands. Prisoners taken by both sides lived only a short while before being hanged in public in full view of their comrades. As one Spanish commentator put it, both besiegers and besieged 'seemed inspired by a spirit of special and personal vengeance'.[10]

The Siege of Haarlem was still continuing in spring 1573, and Alba, who had known sixty years of warfare, wrote to Philip II of Spain that 'it was a war such as never before was seen or heard of in any land on earth'. But spring also meant that the Haarlemmermeer would no longer freeze over, so the emphasis of the siege changed to a ship-borne contest for control of the lake. In this the Spanish were victorious and the citizens of Haarlem were permanently excluded from the lake that had supplied them with such a vital lifeline.

By 1 July the food shortage was becoming so acute that Haarlem sought to negotiate, but the discussions were abruptly terminated by a tremendous artillery barrage. No assault followed because Alba was convinced that the city was on the point of surrender. He was right. A relief army sent by William of Orange from Delft was cut to pieces, and the next message the burghers of Haarlem received from their prince was one advocating a negotiated surrender. It was a bitter blow made worse by the knowledge of the fate that would surely befall the defenders when the Spanish marched in. As it happened, the English and German mercenaries who had fought in the garrison were dismissed, and then every other soldier was butchered. There was no sack, but more than two thousand executions were carried out as a dreadful revenge for resisting the Spanish for eight months.[11]

Alkmaar and the Weapon of Flood

The next town to face Spanish anger was Alkmaar, which lay towards the tip of the peninsula north of Haarlem and Amsterdam. Eight hundred soldiers and thirteen hundred citizens faced a besieging army of sixteen thousand veteran troops. Compared to Haarlem's antiquated walls, Alkmaar's eight bastions proclaimed it as a modern fortified town, and its geographical position gave additional reason for hope that had not been appropriate in the case of Haarlem.

As a last desperate resort, the burghers of Alkmaar decided to open the sluices of Zyp, which lay a few miles distant, and to break a few dykes to let the sea sweep away the Spanish army. Yet to do this would destroy land and livelihood for miles around, so a brave volunteer slipped out of Alkmaar to obtain the consent of the local inhabitants. While he was away, an attack began that equalled the Siege of

Haarlem in the ferocity with which it was both delivered and repulsed. (During the fight to protect Alkmaar, the inhabitants were helped by information obtained from a captive Spaniard. The man was later executed, in spite of offering to join the Dutch cause, but the words he used, that he was willing to 'worship the devil as they did', was an unfortunate turn of phrase to have employed when negotiating with staunch Calvinists).

The besiegers soon noticed that the ground across which they were fighting was becoming increasingly waterlogged. There had been strong support for the dykes to be cut whatever the consequences, although guards had to be placed near the sluices to prevent them being closed by dissenting farmers who would lose their lands. All that was needed was for a strong north-westerly wind to drive the sea further in, then the two great dykes would be cut and the inundation would be complete. The envoy whose negotiations had set in motion this dramatic event then headed back to Alkmaar. He successfully regained the security of the walls, but the Spanish obtained the letters he had taken with him. The besiegers now knew the reason for the rising water level and the consequences of it. Faced with the prospect of sixteen thousand men being drowned in their siege lines, the Spanish army withdrew. Alkmaar was therefore saved, but at a terrible price, because even though the operation to flood the land was only partially carried out the subsequent pumping and reclamation work that was needed to restore the situation that had existed prior to the siege was to occupy Dutch engineers for the next hundred years.[12]

Mookerheyde and the Weapon of Gold

Dutch willingness to destroy so much land in order to save the town of Alkmaar marked a further turning-point in the war. Yet beside the terror, the flooding and the valour of citizens other factors were already working against the Spanish. The capture of Haarlem had been a Pyrrhic victory for Alba, who had lost ten thousand men in the operation, and when a sack of the city was forbidden the Spanish army mutinied for the pay which it had not yet received. The Siege of Alkmaar had failed after three bitter months, and when rebel Leiden became the next Spanish target the attitude of its people reflected the determination that had sustained their compatriots:

> You hear that in our town are both dogs, cattle and horses. And if we should in the end want [for] these, there hath every one of us a left arm to eat, and reserve a right arm to beat the tyrant and the rest of you which are his bloody ministers from our walls.

The defiance emanating from within the besieged walls of Leiden showed that Alba's ruthless policies had failed both militarily and morally, and his conspicuous lack of success in winning the hearts and minds of the Dutch made it inevitable that he should go. At the end of 1573, therefore, Alba's place as captain-general was taken by Don Luis de Requescens, the former governor of Milan, a brave but exhausted veteran who had been looking forward to an early retirement.

The year 1574 therefore began with a new Spanish commander in his post and fresh crises for him to face. In January, while Leiden was still under siege, Middelburg fell to the rebels, thus delivering the strategic island of Walcheren into Orange hands. In March, the Siege of Leiden had to be temporarily abandoned to face a threat from Count Louis of Nassau, who was on the march to relieve the city. His recruitment of troops for the Orange cause was made easier by the presence just across the German border of several thousand mercenaries who were escorting France's Duke of Anjou on his way to accept the throne of Poland – such were the complex webs woven in the sixteenth century! Because these men were now unemployed, the opportunity to fight against Spain in The Netherlands was very welcome for them.

The Spanish response to the threat was immediate, and their rapid advance persuaded Count Louis to engage them in battle at Mookerheyde. Time was not on Louis's side, however, because nearly all his army consisted of newly acquired mercenary troops, and mercenaries expected results. Whereas it was the habit of the Spanish army to mutiny after a victory was gained, the prospect of a German mercenary army mutinying before a battle was even fought plunged Louis into considerable despair.[13]

Scouts reported that Sancho de Avila, the Spanish commander, had constructed a bridge of boats over the River Maas, and was now preparing to give battle. Avila had chosen his position well. He knew that Louis was superior in cavalry and therefore Avila arranged his own army in a confined space between the river and some low hills, where that arm could not be exercised to its best advantage. After some skirmishing, reinforcements arrived on the Spanish side, and with them came the news that more men still were on their way. Caution would have seemed advisable, but the Spanish commander knew that Louis's primary objective was to make contact with his brother, William, and that his mobile army would be very likely to give the Spanish the slip if an attack was not pressed home immediately. The Spanish therefore redoubled their efforts, to which Louis responded with a vigorous cavalry charge. While the infantry of both sides were engaged in the centre, Louis sent his *reiters* against the cavalry on the enemy left. The *reiters* attacked a force of mounted arquebusiers using the *caracole* system. At first all went well because they broke Avila's arquebusier cavalry. But behind them was a second line of men-at-arms with lances. By now a large number of *reiters* had already moved to the rear to reload their empty pistols, and others were showing their flanks as they proceeded on their way back. The disordered formation, always the weakest part of a *caracole*, invited a charge, so in went the Spanish knights with their lances lowered to gain a stunning victory of lance against pistol.

Yet within days of the Battle of Mookerheyde nearly all the advantages the Spanish had gained were dissipated, as their victorious army mutinied. Apparently, the men had not been paid for three years, and until the arrears were settled the Siege of Leiden would not be rejoined. Gold had triumphed over gunpowder.

The Great Siege of Leiden

As soon as his army was both paid and placated, de Requescens resumed the Siege of Leiden in May at the head of eight thousand Walloon and German troops. Siege lines were constructed around the city in a ring of sixty-two redoubts. The citizens rose to the occasion, although they had previously infuriated William of Orange by their astounding complacency and lack of urgency over the restoration of their fortifications while the Spanish were otherwise occupied at Mookerheyde. The return of the Spanish besiegers seemed to wake the people of Leiden from their torpor, and by the end of June the citizens were placed on a strict ration of food, with a handsome reward on offer to any man who brought within the gates the head of an enemy soldier.

William of Orange was not inside the city but in a fortress called Polderwaert. It lay between Delft and Rotterdam, a position that gave him the opportunity to contribute to the defence of Leiden in a similar fashion to the relief of Alkmaar. In the immediate area were the dykes of the Maas and the Ijssel. William's plan was that these dykes should be pierced and that the great sluices at Rotterdam, Schiedam and Delftshaven should be opened. This drastic plan envisaged a destruction of land on a scale every bit as great as the Alkmaar scheme, but it met with resigned yet patriotic support. 'Better a drowned land than a lost land' was the cry.

The flooding of the Leiden hinterland also promised military benefits that had not pertained at Alkmaar, because it was expected that the inundation would be extensive enough to allow necessary supplies of food to be brought to Leiden by boat, across the former fields. Meanwhile, Valdez, the Spanish commander on the scene, tried to tempt the citizens with offers of a pardon. His master, de Requescens, was no Duke of Alba, but that monster's excesses had ensured that any such suggestion would fall on deaf ears.

The besieging Spanish army soon realised that the waters around Leiden had risen by about ten inches since the Siege had begun. Through the use of the weapon of flood, the attackers had become the attacked. For the citizens of Leiden, however, the view that met the eyes of anyone who ascended the great tower and gazed out beyond the walls was not very reassuring. The land was being slowly flooded, that was clear, but did that in any way promise to bring their relief? Might it even mean that their rescue from starvation, if not from the swords of the Spaniards, became even less likely than it had been when the land was dry?

The operation to transport supplies into Leiden across the ruined fields was in the hands of the Sea Beggars. The distance from Leiden to the broken outer dyke was about fifteen miles, but between it and the city were other dykes built to prevent just such an inundation occurring by accident rather than design. These barriers were doing their job well, and in spite of the massive floods already released the waters were still a good eighteen inches from the top of the first dyke. For the fleet to proceed further these inner dykes had to be cut, and they were as heavily defended by the Spanish as were the walls of Leiden itself.

A fight thus began for the first dyke, and no sooner was it taken by the Dutch than they demolished their prize. In rushed the water and on sailed the fleet, only to be confronted by another dyke three-quarters of a mile further on. This, too, was captured. Beyond it lay a lake, which the relieving fleet had hoped would provide an unobstructed passage. Unfortunately for them, the wind had dispersed the waters and made the lake too shallow – the only channel left through this area followed a canal. The canal was deep enough, but it led to a bridge that the Spanish had prudently fortified. In spite of directing cannon fire against it, the Dutch fleet came to a halt. In one week, the fleet had proceeded only two miles towards Leiden, which was now feeling the pangs of starvation more acutely that even Haarlem had suffered. The waterborne army lay motionless and helpless, but once again the weather came to its aid. On the eighteenth of the month the wind shifted to the north-west and blew a gale. When the waters rose again the commander of the fleet was informed that he could now bypass the canal and the bridge in a wide detour. This took them towards a small dyke defended by a Spanish army detachment, who were terrified in equal part by the inexorable disappearance of dry land on which to operate as soldiers, and the approach of a naval force that threatened to turn them rapidly into sailors.

It was not long before the first ships reached the fortifications on the outside of Leiden that the Spanish had appropriated. These were set alight, and the flames gave hope to Leiden's starving citizens. Yet once again the weapon of wind played a role, and when it changed direction again the fleet was immobilised anew within sight of the last dyke. Inside the city its inhabitants were falling dead in the streets, and such was the discontent in some quarters that a dead body was placed on the doorstep of one of the leading burghers as a request for him to call for a surrender. In a dramatic speech, the commander of Leiden offered his own body as food for the starving citizens (*see* plate 28). Nevertheless, carrier pigeons brought the news into Leiden that just over the horizon lay their means of salvation.

The Relief of Leiden

All that was needed was a blessing from the Dutchman's great allies of wind and flood, and soon it came. Within the space of twenty-four hours a north-westerly gale caused the water level to rise by two feet, and the relieving vessels were able to engage with those outposts in the Spanish siege lines that had escaped inundation (*see* plate 29). Here the final battle for Leiden took place. The Spanish fled, leaving their pots of beef stew behind, a detail still commemorated every year on the anniversary of the raising of the siege. The canals and quays of Leiden were soon lined with the famished spectres that were its citizens as the supply boats finally made their triumphal entry. Some people choked to death as they rushed in a frenzy to feed themselves. But Leiden had been relieved, and a powerful message had been sent to the King of Spain. As William of Orange noted:

> If the poor inhabitants here, forsaken by everyone, persevere despite everything, as they have done until now ... it will cost the Spaniards half of Spain in goods as well as in men before they have finished with us.

This second dramatic demonstration of how the power of flood might be enlisted as a weapon in warfare in the Low Countries was a lesson that was not lost on the Spanish, who began to draw their own conclusions. Inundation could be made to work for Spain as well, and during the winter of 1574–5 a debate was held over whether the solution to the problem posed by the Dutch might be to destroy the dykes and flood the whole country. This drastic response was in fact rejected, partly because the destruction it would cause might never be reversed, and partly because places loyal to the king would suffer as well. It would also give the Spaniards a reputation for cruelty on an immense scale. But having turned down this course of action, the only alternative was to continue with the slow and ugly business that had characterised the past few years. In 1577, when still no end was in sight, a certain Spanish minister gloomily predicted that the reduction of The Netherlands would take fifty years of fighting. History was to prove him wrong on two counts: the Spanish lost, and it took eighty years for them to do so.

Chapter 12
Innovators and Enemies

The great city of Antwerp lay on the River Scheldt, between the provinces of Brabant and Flanders. Two thousand ships of the largest capacities could easily find room in its ample harbours, protected by the mighty river that flowed north-west to divide itself into innumerable estuaries around the isles of Zeeland – the lair of the Sea Beggars who had been the first to defy Spanish rule.

For the first few years of the Dutch Revolt it had been unquestionably true that the burghers of Antwerp were having a good war. Commercial traffic was largely uninterrupted, and was even somewhat enhanced by the increased demand for goods and services that always attends a major conflict. Yet certain developments were beginning to cause anxiety among Antwerp's merchants, who had always known that their city would be a rich prize for the Dutch rebels. This fact was also crystal clear to the Duke of Alba. Employing the cold and calculating mind that was his hallmark, Alba had worked out that if the earlier pattern of the Dutch Revolt was replicated in Antwerp then it was likely that an insurrection would develop within the city itself, rather than through some attack from outside. Precautions had to be taken.

The resulting fortification plan that Alba drew up for Antwerp provided a subtle political variation on the accepted role of the angle bastion. Antwerp's modern citadel was less to provide a defence against an enemy at the gates and rather more to encourage potential rebels within. Its centrepiece was a magnificent set of bastions designed by Paciotto, the Italian military architect whose star-shaped citadel at Turin had already led to his recognition as being at the cutting edge of military architecture. The citizens of Antwerp, therefore, witnessed the erection of an edifice ostensibly for their protection, but which also allowed a Spanish garrison to control the city from a position of safety. To add insult to injury, Alba also commissioned a statue that depicted him in a heroic pose crushing Dutch rebels.[1]

At first, the burghers accepted the existence of the citadel with a grudging resignation, although the replacement of the Duke of Alba by de Requescens in

1573 was widely welcomed, particularly when de Requescens removed the statue of his predecessor and placed it discretely out of public view. What now caused most concern was not the citadel's impregnable bricks and mortar, but the garrison within it. As was indicated in the previous chapter, the Spanish army of The Netherlands was not a loveable creature. It was an alien being made worse by mercenaries and regularly maddened by the Spanish government's frequent inability to pay its wages. Campaigns had already been lost through the weapon of gold withheld, and the army mutinies that often followed such situations were terrifying displays of anarchy.

So, when a mutiny occurred within the Antwerp citadel in 1576, the citizens became very worried indeed. The Antwerp mutineers were in constant communication with other rebel garrisons in towns and fortresses nearby, and only awaited the opportunity to make a devastating attack on the city outside their protecting bastions. The citizens took what precautions they could, and, following the arrival of German and Walloon troops sent to protect them, began a frantic programme of building earthworks and palisades against the citadel. It was to no avail. Some approaches were so weakly defended (one major road had only an upturned wagon dragged across it as a rampart) that when the incursion began the Spanish mutineers carried all before them. Resolving to 'dine in Paradise or sup in Antwerp', the garrison and a group of newly arrived colleagues erupted on to the 'honey pot' below. The result was one of war's most notorious massacres, which has gone down in history as the 'Spanish Fury'. No other incident in the Eighty Years War in The Netherlands was to provoke such revulsion as the Sack of Antwerp. Over the course of three days, as many as eight thousand people were murdered, while the city itself was thoroughly looted and extensively burned.[2]

Because the Spanish Fury was the result of the actions of an unofficial mob of soldiers, the citizens were left to recover from the shock when the pillagers withdrew. This they did after much painful rebuilding and readjustment. In March 1577 they discovered that the newly appointed governor of the Spanish Netherlands, Don John of Austria (of Lepanto fame), had chosen not to garrison the Antwerp citadel. It had in fact been abandoned, so the citizens interrupted the rebuilding of their lives for a spontaneous act of demolition. Old and young, noblemen and commoners alike, took pick and shovel and laid low the walls that had symbolised their oppression and sheltered their tormentors. In the course of the operation, the statue of the Duke of Alba was discovered in a forgotten crypt. It was dragged into the daylight as if it were the captive body of Alba himself, and set upon by dozens of sledgehammers until the bronze effigy was beaten into a shapeless mass.[3]

The demolition of the Antwerp citadel by the people of Antwerp in 1577

The Battle of Gembloux

Later that same year Don John of Austria summoned to the Spanish Netherlands as his aide his nephew Prince Alexander Farnese, who later became the Duke of Parma. He too was a veteran of Lepanto, and was both able and resourceful. He excelled in diplomatic affairs as much as he did in military ones, and as the heir to an Italian dukedom and a nephew of the King of Spain he had all the necessary connections. Yet it was as a mounted knight, lance in hand, that Parma was to make his first impact on the Dutch Wars.

Alexander Farnese, Duke of Parma, who successfully captured Antwerp after a long siege

Early in 1578, the army of Don John prepared to make a move against the Dutch rebels. The rival armies met close to Namur. The original intention of the rebels was to attack the Spanish, but when it was learned that Don John was advancing against them the rebels' cautious commander, Sieur de Goignes, resolved to fall back to a better position at Gembloux, about nine miles from Namur.[4]

The army moved off in three divisions. In the van was the infantry, protected by light horse. The centre company included some Scottish and English contingents, while the heavy cavalry brought up the rear. Don John immediately ordered a pursuit. In front was nearly the whole of the Spanish cavalry, with two squares of infantry behind them. Over Don John's head streamed a banner embroidered with a crucifix and bearing a motto in Latin that read, 'In this sign I conquered the Turks, and by the same I shall conquer the heretics'.

Small detachments of mounted men were sent forth as scouts to flush out any ambushes that may have been laid against them, and the intentions of the Dutch army were confirmed by intelligence gained from prisoners taken. Soon the rear ranks of the retreating rebels came into view. Don John selected six hundred horsemen and a thousand foot-soldiers, divided them into two and sent them forward to do as much damage as possible without risking a full engagement. The orders were at first strictly obeyed, but at least one spirited cavalry officer had to be recalled from too risky an advance.

In the midst of the skirmishing, Parma rode up to reconnoitre and observed that the retiring army was proceeding along the borders of a deep valley filled with mud and water. So boggy was the surface that it was proving as much of a hindrance to the marching men as if it had been a broad river. Parma's keen military eye noticed how the points of the pikes were swaying about as the cursing infantrymen tried to get a foothold in their passage through the mire. Mounting a fresh and powerful horse he signalled his intention of leading a charge against these disorganised enemies. 'Tell Don John of Austria', he shouted, 'that Alexander of Parma has plunged into the abyss, to perish there or come forth victorious!'

Parma led the way through the swamp, and, with his lance couched in its rest, waited for his men to follow. After a short break, he drew up his force in a compact column and sent it against the unsuspecting rear ranks of the foe. The rebel cavalry fled, leaving the centre of the army exposed. Parma charged afresh into the confused mass of foot-soldiers, who were so overwhelmed that few of them offered a blow in return. Hardly a man in the Spanish army was wounded. In fact, none of the Spanish infantry seems to have been involved, while in the course of an hour and a half almost the entire enemy force, some ten thousand in all, were cut down. Thirty-four standards, many cannon and six hundred prisoners were taken. Many of the latter were then hurled to their deaths from the bridge at Namur.

On 29 September of that same year, Don John was once more back in a fortified camp, but this time dying from a plague that had swept through his lines. On his death bed he named Alexander Farnese, Duke of Parma, as his successor to the governorship of the Spanish Netherlands. It proved to be a wise choice.

Parma knew that in the south of The Netherlands the mainly Catholic areas had effectively seceded from the common cause. In the north it was different. The Protestant provinces had united under the terms of the Union of Utrecht, and were committed to fight for total victory. Parma therefore initiated a policy of reconciliation with the southern Catholic provinces, while delivering a heavy blow against William the Silent by taking the great stronghold of Maastricht in 1579.[5]

The Siege of Antwerp

Over the next few years the Duke of Parma consolidated the line between the loyal south and the rebellious north, and set about reducing the northern strongholds by means of a long succession of sieges, a process that culminated in the thirteen-month-long Siege of Antwerp – one of the most fascinating operations of the Eighty Years War.[6] Parma's plans involved cutting the city off from the north by building a bridge across the Scheldt. To many this was the strategy of a lunatic. That a river half a mile wide could be bridged while there were so many rebels around to prevent its construction was one reason for the scepticism. The other reason was that some years previously, when Antwerp was still in Spanish hands, William the Silent had attempted to build a bridge, only to see his creation swept away with the coming of winter and the pounding of ice floes. Nevertheless, William remained one of the few people to take Parma's threat seriously, and he proposed a drastic course of action to frustrate Parma's plans.

William's plan involved the almost total inundation of the area. Downstream from Antwerp, the Scheldt was confined within its banks by a complex system of dykes, the most important of which extended along its edges towards the sea in parallel lines. On the right bank this barrier became the mighty Blauwgaren dyke, which was met at right angles by the equally formidable Kowenstyn dyke. Not far from where they joined, the Dutch had a strong fortress called Lillo. If the Blauwgaren dyke was pierced, it would take the Kowenstyn dyke with it and would cause such an extensive flood that Antwerp would become a city with a harbour on the sea. It would then be almost impossible to starve out.

Had William the Silent's orders been carried out immediately, then Antwerp might indeed have been safe, but a fateful and time-wasting debate took place, and just a few weeks later William was assassinated. The idea of a massive flood was certainly not well received. In an echo of Alkmaar, it was pointed out that twelve thousand head of cattle grazed upon the fields protected by the two dykes. If Parma was intent upon starving Antwerp's citizens, then surely there was no better way of helping him than by the Dutch destroying such a huge food supply.

Parma's bridge across the Scheldt at Antwerp

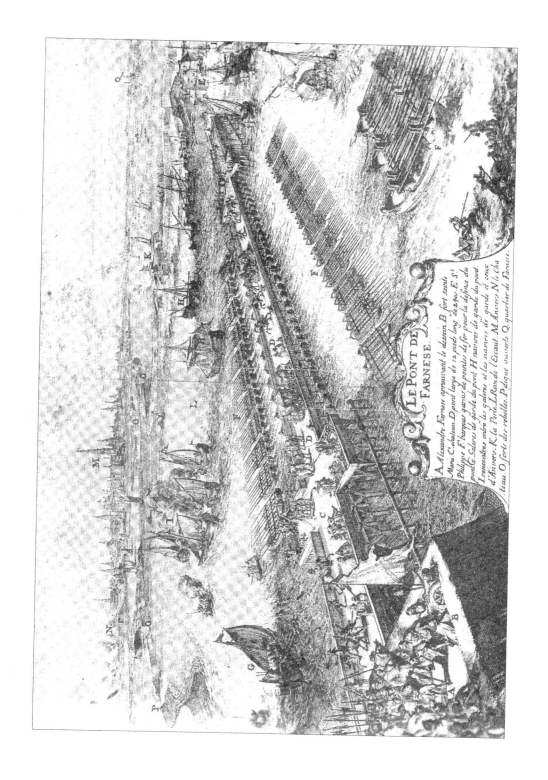

LE PONT DE FARNESE.

A Alexandre Farnese approuvant le dessein. B fort sainte Marie C chasteau. D pont large de 12 pieds long de 2400. E S.t Philippe F barque garni de pointes de fer pour la defense du pont G Galeres de garde du pont H navires de garde du pont. I monstres entre les galies et les navires de garde et ceux d'Anvers. K la Porte. L Ron de l'Escaut. M Anvers. N le chateau O forts des rebelles P digue ouverte Q quartier de Farnese.

The tiny village of Kallo, which lay about nine miles from Antwerp, became the construction site for Parma's bridge, but the scheme was such a huge undertaking that by the autumn of 1584 little seemed to have been achieved. Antwerp continued to be supplied by flotillas of craft, which exchanged fire with Parma's forts as they boldly made their way upstream. The Antwerp authorities then made an astounding blunder. It transpired that grain bought in Holland could be sold for four times its original price in beleaguered Antwerp, a mark-up that was attractive enough to make Spanish cannon fire an acceptable hazard. But the city fathers then set a fixed price for supplies brought in, and simultaneously regulated the accumulation of grain in private warehouses. Seeing their profit wiped out, the ships' captains stopped the traffic stone dead. Even Parma could not have created such an effective blockade!

At the same time, the inundation urged by William the Silent had actually begun, albeit in a much-reduced fashion. Yet, ironically, the opening of the sluices on the Flanders side actually made Parma's communications that much easier, because the flooded countryside now enabled him to give Antwerp a wide berth. By the time it was finally decreed that the dykes of Blauwagaren and Kowenstyn should be cut there were strong Spanish garrisons in place to prevent this happening. The Kowenstyn in particular now resembled a long, bastioned city wall bristling with cannon and pikes.

Meanwhile, the bridge grew slowly. On the Flemish side a fort called Santa Maria was erected, while on the Brabant side opposite developed one named in honour of King Philip II of Spain. From each of these two points a framework of heavy timbers spread slowly towards the middle of the river. The roadway was twelve feet wide, defended by solid blockhouses. Numerous skirmishers attacked the workmen in order to prevent the two halves meeting, but skirmishes is all that these attacks were. In spite of entreaties from Antwerp the vacuum of power since the death of William the Silent prevented any concerted attack from occurring.

Parma was also suffering from a lack of money. His army had not been paid for two years, and he was not yet in a position to promise early payment from loot. A botched attempt by the rebels to capture s'Hertogenbosch, Parma's main supply centre for the siege, served only to increase the commander's determination to complete his bridge, against which the wintry weather was now providing the only real challenge. The ocean tides drove blocks of ice against the piers, which stood firm, but in the centre portion of the construction the current was too strong to allow pile-driving, so here the bridge had to be carried on the top of boats. There were thirty-two of them altogether, anchored and bound firmly to each other and armed with cannon.

Parma's bridge was completed on 25 February 1585. It was twice as long as Julius Caesar's celebrated Rhine bridge, and had been built under the most adverse weather conditions. As an added precaution, on each side of the bridge there was anchored a long heavy raft floating upon empty barrels, the constituent timbers lashed together and supported by ships' masts, and protected with iron spikes that made the construction look like the front rank of a pike square. An entire army could both sit on the bridge and walk across it, and, to impress the citizens of Antwerp, Parma's soldiers proceeded to do both.

So that they should be under no illusions as to the strength and size of the edifice, a captured Dutch spy, who expected to be hanged, was instead given a guided tour of the bridge and sent safely back to relate in wide-eyed wonder what he had seen. 'Tell them further', said Parma to the astonished secret agent, 'that the siege will never be abandoned, and that this bridge will be my sepulchre or my pathway into Antwerp.'

The Diabolical Machine

The besieged citizens of Antwerp, however, still possessed one possible winning card. In their city lived a sympathetic Italian engineer by the name of Gianibelli, and in a similar display of enthusiasm to that with which Parma had built his bridge, so did this Gianibelli determine to destroy it using exploding ships. His proposal to the city authorities involved the construction of a fleet, but by the time his project was approved the parsimonious city fathers had reduced the fleet to two ships, which disgusted Gianibelli, even though each of the vessels, to be optimistically named *Hope* and *Fortune*, was enormous. The two ships were nothing less than artificial volcanoes. In the hold of each was a chamber of marble, along their entire length, built upon a brick foundation. This chamber was filled with gunpowder under a stone roof, on top of which was a 'cone' – also of marble – packed with millstones, cannonballs, lumps of stone, chain-shot, iron hooks, ploughshares and anything else that could be requisitioned in Antwerp to cause injury when blown up. On top of all of this were piles of wood that gave the vessels the appearance of conventional fireships. The one difference between the two ships lay in the means of ignition of the volcanoes within. On the *Fortune* this was to be done by means of a slow match. On the *Hope* the business would be done by clockwork and flint, rather like an enormous wheel-lock pistol. The progress of these infernal floating mines was to be preceded on the ebb tide by thirty-two smaller vessels laden with combustible materials, which would keep the defenders of the bridge busy until the two great ships reached Parma's masterpiece and utterly destroyed it.

The date for the attack was to be dusk on 5 April 1585, and the enterprise was placed into the hands of Admiral Jacob Jacobzoon. He began badly, sending all the thirty-two vanguard ships down the Scheldt almost all at once rather than in the steady progression previously agreed upon. On each bank, and from every dyke and fortress, the Spanish troops gathered in their thousands to gaze at the burning flotilla that was turning the night back into day with its ruddy glow. Some of the boats hit the forward barges of the bridge and stuck on the spikes, where they burned themselves out ineffectively. Others struck the banks or ran aground. Some simply sank into the river as their own fires consumed them.

To the guardians of the bridge the attack seemed to be having no effect, but behind these minor vessels there now loomed the two great ones. They meandered somewhat aimlessly with the tide and the current, because their pilots had long since abandoned them. There was a moment of concern for the Spanish when the *Fortune* swung towards the side of the river, completely missing the forward protective raft. It eventually ground itself while, unknown to the Spanish defenders, the slow match burned through. There was a small explosion, and some minor damage, but so slight was the effect that Parma sent a boarding party to examine the interior of the ship.

They did not stay long, because the *Hope* had now followed its sister downstream. Its precision in finding its target could not have been better if it had been guided until the very last moment, because it managed to hit the bridge next to the blockhouse where the middle pontoons began. However, as Parma had confidently expected, the bridge had been so strongly built that the impact alone caused it no damage. Expecting it to be another fireship, Spanish boarders leapt on to the deck, and with excited whoops of laughter promptly extinguished the decoy fire. With some sixth sense, an ensign rushed up to his commander and begged him to leave the scene. So earnest were the man's pleas that Parma reluctantly withdrew to the Fort of Santa Maria. This saved his life, for at that very moment the *Hope* exploded.

Not only did the ship vanish, so did much of the bridge, the banks, the dykes, the fortresses, and for a brief moment even the waters of the Scheldt, as possibly the largest man-made explosion in history up to that date lit up the night sky. The facts and statistics of the act took months to establish, and still have the power to cause amazement. The entire centre section of the bridge disintegrated. More than a thousand Spanish soldiers died instantly, and their bodies were never found. Houses nearby collapsed as if hit by an earthquake, and the pressure wave blew people off their feet. From the sky there began to fall the cannonballs and stones that had been crammed into the ship, accompanied by the mortal remains of its immediate victims. Slabs of granite were later found buried deep in the ground having travelled six miles from the scene of the explosion.

The personal tales were also quite remarkable. One Marquis Richebourg, who had been in command on the bridge, simply disappeared. His body was located several days later, its progress through the air having been arrested by one of the chains Parma had strung across the river. Seigneur de Billy's body was not located until months afterwards when his golden locket and an unpleasant stain on one of the surviving bridge supports provided identification. The fortunate Duke of Parma was merely knocked unconscious by a flying stake. One captain was blown out of one boat and landed safely in another. A certain Captain Tucci was blown vertically into the air in his full armour and dumped in the river, where he still retained the presence of mind to remove his cuirass and swim to safety. Another young officer was blown completely across the river and landed safely after a flight of half a mile.

The original plan was that immediately after the expected explosion Admiral Jacobzoon should launch a signal rocket that would send boatloads of armed Dutchmen pouring on to the scene. Instead, he was totally stupefied by the explosion and gave no order. No rocket was fired and no one advanced. During the hiatus Parma regained consciousness, and by displaying leadership skills of unbelievable quality he managed to marshal his men to begin to repair the damage. Even though the Dutch advance was expected at any moment, it never came. By daybreak, even Parma began to believe the unbelievable – that the Dutch rebels, having set off the largest explosion since the introduction of gunpowder to Europe and blown a hole in his bridge, were now going to let him mend it. Yet this is precisely what happened.

The Kowenstyn Dyke

With the initiative lost it took the defenders of Antwerp a full month to mount another attack on Parma's besieging army. The new attack was not against his damaged bridge but on the mighty Kowenstyn dyke. As the target was an earthen dam explosives would not have been effective, so the goal of breaking the great barrier would be made by men capturing the dyke with pike and musket and then cutting it with pick and shovel. It was a low-tech solution, and it was likely to be a very bloody one.

Following a successful landing a fierce 'push of pike' began on top of the Kowenstyn dyke. The rebels could well have been shoved back into the water had it not been for the arrival of the other half of their army downstream from Antwerp. For once in this campaign a co-ordinated effort had actually worked, and three

The battle for the Kowenstyn dyke

thousand men now occupied this small section of the dyke. Among them was an eighteen-year-old youth called Maurice of Nassau, the son and heir of William the Silent, who was experiencing his first real taste of combat in what was to become a renowned military career. While two walls of soldiers shot, cut and speared their enemies, the sappers began two very different but complementary operations: to reinforce the dyke with trenches and mounds, and also to cut a hole through it. At last a loud cheer went up as the salt water rushed in a torrent through the newly created gap. A few moments later a Zeeland barge sailed through.

It is to the great credit of the Spanish commanders on the scene that they did not immediately panic; they stayed calm, even though their leader was some distance away. They were also sensible enough to realise that a breach sufficient to allow a Zeeland barge through was by no means sufficient to permit the passage of an entire fleet, and if the dyke could somehow be recaptured then the rupture might even be repaired. Five attacks followed along the dyke in a manner that demonstrated beyond all doubt why the Spanish were regarded as the finest infantry in Europe. The last assault was successful, and it was not long before intelligence arrived in Antwerp that the wild celebrations currently taking place were somewhat premature.

The failure plunged Antwerp into despair and forced its rulers back to the negotiating table. They sought three reassurances from Parma: that religious freedom would be granted, that troops would not be stationed in the city, and that the hated citadel would not be rebuilt. Knowing that King Philip II would accept none of these 'exorbitant ideas', as Parma termed them, he reminded the citizens of Antwerp of the stranglehold he still had on their city. But he had other cards to play, and drew their attentions to the role of Antwerp as the 'great opulent and commercial city' that it had been in the past and could be again. What cause, what real cause, did rich Antwerp have with the heretical Sea Beggars of Holland and Zeeland? Surely the loyal south was more to their liking?

Parma's own fears lay with the winter that was fast approaching. It turned out to be so severe that Parma's bridge would have been unlikely to survive, but by the time winter came a settlement had already been reached. A minor concession regarding the troops to be stationed in Antwerp proved sufficient for all parties to be satisfied, and Antwerp capitulated with honour on 17 August 1585 without a shot having been fired at the city itself. There was no massacre, no sack, no pillage and Parma's soldiers were paid not by loot but in hard cash. The noble Duke of Parma had achieved his objectives, and, unknown to him at the time, he had actually achieved something quite remarkable. By detaching the fate of Antwerp and the lands to the south from the United Provinces of The Netherlands he had effectively created a recognisable and workable border. In 1648, as part of the Treaty of Westphalia, this border was to be given both recognition and reality, confirming that Alexander Farnese, Duke of Parma, had invented Belgium.

The Dutch Infantry Reformers

Political events, rather than strictly military ones, prevented Parma from consolidating his gains in the years that followed the Siege of Antwerp. In 1590 he was required to move his Army of Flanders into France to support the Catholic cause.[7] The Dutch recognised the opportunity this presented, but were unable to capitalise upon it to any great extent in that same year – their only real success being the capture of Breda in March, the first major town to be taken by the Dutch rebels since 1580.[8]

The success at Breda inspired them on to great things in 1591. The Dutch were now under the overall command of Maurice of Nassau, the son of William the Silent, who was determined to make gains at Parma's expense before the latter returned from his duties in France. Maurice adopted Parma's own tactics by trying to create a zone of control, with defensible borders and space for manoeuvre. To achieve this he targeted the towns in the north-east that Parma had captured during the 1580s. Maurice led an army ten thousand strong with considerable artillery support, and captured Zutphen in May 1591 and Deventer in June. These were operations that exposed the weakness in the theory of the invincible angle bastion that was discussed in an earlier chapter. Without a field army to support them, the garrisons of the finest defence works found themselves hopelessly isolated.

When he returned, the Duke of Parma found that he was powerless to stop the new Dutch advance. He had left six thousand of his best men in France. A further two thousand men had mutinied over arrears in pay, and when he failed to relieve Nijmegen he withdrew towards the south. When he was again summoned to France, Maurice redoubled his efforts, so that when Parma returned to the Low Countries for the last time in 1592 it was to find even more fortresses back in Dutch hands. In November 1592, worn out by his exertions, the great Spanish commander died at Arras.[9]

During the following years, by means of an intermittent war of sieges, the Dutch army under Maurice recovered the whole of the north-east of The Netherlands, so that by 1597 the heartland of the Dutch Republic was secure.[10] It is not only as a master of siegecraft that Maurice of Nassau is known to history but also he and his cousin William Louis are regarded as major innovators in infantry tactics through their introduction of volley firing.[11] Unlike many military 'discoveries', this

one can be dated quite precisely to 8 December 1594, the day on which William
Louis of Nassau penned a letter to his cousin. William Louis had been studying
Aelian's description of the drill practised by the Roman legions, and he writes to
Maurice to express his excitement at the idea that was forming in his mind. The
Romans, apparently, kept up a constant fire from their javelins and slingshots by
operating a rotating volley system. The front rank discharged their missiles, then
moved to the rear to allow the second rank to do the same. With the assistance
of a diagram William Louis suggests that the Dutch could do the same with six
ranks of musketeers.[12]

The enthusiastic Count of Nassau, of course, did not claim that his idea was
totally original. Quite apart from the Roman inspiration, the 'European Countermarch' had more than an echo of the cavalryman's 'dainty' *caracole*. Unlike the *caracole*, however, this system of volley firing by infantry appeared to work, although
ten ranks, not six, were needed at first to maintain a constant fire. But that was not
all that was needed. From an external viewpoint the key to success was drill, and
from an internal viewpoint it was discipline, and it was not long before Maurice,
William and Maurice's brother John were drumming both into the foot-soldiers of
the army of the Dutch Republic.[13]

The originality of the European Countermarch system, therefore, lay less in
the idea itself than in the enthusiastic and systematic way that the Dutch trio put
it into operation. Convinced that this was the way ahead, they tackled every aspect
of their army's organisation to enable it to deliver the sustained volley firing that
was the goal. The army was divided into smaller formations, but the men in these
smaller formations were drawn up in ranks that were as long as possible. This was
more efficient than the *tercio* in terms of delivering fire, but its lack of flexibility
rendered the men more vulnerable to attack.[14] The system of drilling that became
the norm therefore had two purposes. Not only did it enable the individual soldier
to fire his weapon almost without thinking but it also allowed a section to turn
about quickly and efficiently to receive an attack in flank. So these Dutch soldiers
were drilled incessantly, both in the manner of keeping their places and in the
complex business of loading and firing a musket. To assist with the latter two important innovations occurred. First, Maurice was able to secure enough money to
equip the entire army with weapons of the same size and the same calibre. Second,
John studied the process whereby a musket was brought into action. The process
was broken down into twenty-five stages, numbered and illustrated with drawings
in a drill book. By 1606 the sequence for musket drill had been further subdivided
to yield forty-two movements.[15] Maurice also included drill sequences whereby a
unit broke ranks and then reformed at speed to the beat of drums. He reported in

1612 that, because every man knew his position, two thousand men could reform their ranks in twenty-two minutes, whereas it usually took one hour to reform a thousand men. It was a system that Maurice was not willing to modify any further. Every man knew his place.[16]

Over the following decade the fame of the Dutch system spread throughout Europe. John of Nassau's drill manual was translated into other languages, and in 1616 he opened a military academy.[17] It succeeded on the drill ground. It succeeded in the drill manuals, but did it succeed on the battlefield? This is a difficult question to answer, because around the turn of the century the Dutch army was rarely placed in a position where its theories could be tested. Only twice was there a pitched battle where musketeers and pikemen could be drilled and commanded. These were the battles of Tournhout in 1597 and Nieuwpoort in 1600. At the former, which was a victory of cavalry over a mixed force, none of the Dutch infantry was involved save three hundred arquebusiers in the vanguard.[18] The latter was a Dutch victory, but a costly one, that only took place in direct opposition to Maurice's best judgement. Nevertheless, even though they lacked the acid test of a glorious victory, the Dutch cousins' theories won wide acceptance. By the beginning of the seventeenth century their ideas were being widely copied. The Dutch system was accepted, unquestioned and as yet unchallenged.

Chapter 13
Cavalry and Curiosities

While the Dutch Wars were still continuing, other military campaigns were taking place in northern Europe. They are less well known than the campaigns of the Low Countries and the Mediterranean, and have often been seen as taking place in an ignorant military backwater. But this was not the case. Military change took place here, just as it did elsewhere, in response to the specific geographical, social and economic circumstances of the particular area – differences were fully appreciated by those who fought there. In 1581 Jan Piotrowski, the Polish royal secretary on campaign against Pskov, noted in his diary the complaints made to him by a foreign mercenary company, and summed up the situation in the words, 'We are not fighting in France or The Netherlands'.[1]

Piotrowski was fighting in the service of King Stefan Bathory, whose contribution to military development will be examined in this chapter. He is celebrated in Poland for being its great warrior leader of the sixteenth century, yet in spite of ruling the huge area of the Commonwealth of Poland and Lithuania, a political union that had existed since the fourteenth century, Bathory was neither Polish nor Lithuanian. This was a situation that arose from Poland's practice of electing its monarchs. It was a system that had its weaknesses and threw up certain failures, but on occasions the end result could be to produce a great success. The election in 1576 of Stefan Bathory, a prince of Transylvania, was one of those successes.[2]

Bathory was a born soldier with many years of military and political service to his credit. He had studied at the University of Padua, had served at the imperial court in Vienna and had been wounded on campaign against the Ottomans. Out of all his talents, however, his military experience was the one that loomed largest in the minds of the Polish electoral council in 1576. Only a year earlier the biggest Tartar raid in Polish history had occurred, and Ivan the Terrible of Muscovy, who, somewhat bizarrely, had offered himself as a candidate for the Polish throne, was currently ravaging Poland's eastern provinces. The country needed a warrior.

Bathory entered Cracow to be crowned on 1 May 1576 and soon proved to be the new broom that would sweep clean. He began with domestic problems.

Stefan Bathory, the Transylvanian prince who became King of Poland

A revolt in Danzig was put down by force, after which he turned his attentions to army reform. A corps of infantry armed with muskets was created, while the Polish mounted arm began its transition into the famous 'winged hussars' who were to have such an impact on eastern battlefields over the following century. The Polish hussars were a creative response to the changing needs of warfare in Eastern Europe. Each man was mounted on a fairly small, nimble charger and was armed with a long lance. These lances were designed to be decisive on first contact and often shattered on impact, after which the hussar would draw his curved sabre. The hussars also carried bows, which enabled them to deliver far more missiles than the contemporary pistol-wielding heavy *reiters*.[3] It was all a question of timing.

The range and speed of fire of the arquebuses and wheel-lock pistols in use at the time allowed only one or two salvoes before cavalry could close in on them. The Polish winged hussars always charged in waves. Between three and five ranks would charge in succession, in the belief that even if the initial volley stopped the first wave it was unlikely to stop the second. To minimise casualties the Poles rode in extended formation until the enemy had fired their volley. They then closed their order for the maximum impact. This was 'the essential of cavalry tactics – the utilisation of the impact of man and horse to disrupt the enemy formation . . . wholly lost – except in Poland'.[4]

Ivan the Terrible

When he was elected to the throne Bathory had promised action 'for the defence of Christendom'.[5] Had these words fallen from the lips of any other European monarch the reasonable conclusion to be drawn would have been the promise of leading his winged hussars in a crusade against the Ottomans. But Constantinople was not at present on the target list for Bathory, who admired Ottoman culture and had long accepted Ottoman suzerainty over his native Transylvania. Bathory's concern was instead with Poland's eastern neighbour, the Duchy of Moscow, under its ruler Ivan IV, known to history as Ivan the Terrible – the first Muscovite ruler to take the grand title of tsar.

For almost two centuries the primary foreign policy objective of Ivan and his predecessors had been to gain free access to the Baltic Sea. Most of the Baltic coastline had been in the hands of the Livonian (i.e. Latvian–Estonian) branch of the Teutonic Knights since the thirteenth century. But that organisation's power had been in decline for many years, and Moscow was but one of several rivals who tried to take advantage of the situation. Ivan the Terrible's intervention in 1558 was particularly decisive, because a Muscovite invasion of Livonia in that year led to the Livonian Order making its last stand. In 1560, in a dark Latvian forest at a place called Ermes, the last of the Teutonic Knights were crushed by Ivan the Terrible's army. Half the Order's force was killed or captured, and its leaders were dragged to Moscow to be executed. It was an ignominious end to a long history.[6]

Long before 1560, however, the decline of the Teutonic Knights had created a dangerous political vacuum in a region that was proving to be of increasing interest throughout northern Europe. Trade through the Baltic area had surged during the fifteenth century and promised lucrative rewards to whoever controlled its ports and cities. Most of the major trade centres belonged to the old Hanseatic League centred on Lübeck, but their prosperity now depended on the attitudes of local rulers and the ambitions of the great powers of Sweden, Denmark, Poland–Lithuania and Muscovy. The Poles had captured Danzig (Gdansk) in 1466, and the collapse of the Livonian Order made places like Riga, Reval (modern Tallinn) and the great fortress of Narva look highly vulnerable. These places were likely targets for the duchy of Muscovy, which had grown rapidly at the expense of other, smaller, Russian principalities. In 1478 Ivan II captured Novgorod, and in 1492 he founded Ivangorod on the Gulf of Finland, just across the river from Narva. The capitulation to Muscovy of the Prince of Pskov in 1510 cemented the Muscovite presence in an area for which it was to fight Poland–Lithuania for decades to come.

Ivan the Terrible launched his major advance against Livonia in 1558, but the collapse of the Livonian Order at the Battle of Ermes turned out to be his only real success. Livonia's greatest prizes – the key port cities of Riga and Reval – held out against him from behind modern fortifications. Reval had acquired several round artillery towers to augment its medieval walls, including the six-storey cannon tower nicknamed Kiek in de Kok ('peek into the kitchen') after its lofty eminence, and a huge squat roundel known as Fat Margaret, which covered the harbour gate. By 1560 the fortress of Narva possessed three angle bastions, a modern touch that nevertheless failed to prevent it falling to the Muscovites.[7]

After repelling Ivan's attack, Reval and Riga decided to augment their physical defences by placing themselves under the protection of friendly foreign overlordship: Sweden for Reval in 1561, and Poland–Lithuania for Riga in 1562. To Ivan the Terrible these were provocative moves, so he returned to Livonia in 1570, when Reval held out successfully for eight months against his army. But in 1572 he captured nearby Weissenstein (Paide), and in 1577 the army tried again to capture Reval as a prelude to a summer assault to be led by the tsar in person. Ivan's advance through Latvia was successful until he reached Wenden (Cesis). The town soon fell, but the castle that had once been the capital of the Livonian Order held out against him. While Ivan the Terrible was inspecting the defences a cannonball narrowly missed him, a provocation that led to a promise to slaughter the inhabitants when the castle fell. The garrison of three hundred men, women and children did not wait to discover whether he was serious. They locked themselves in a tower and blew themselves up with four tons of gunpowder.

After this triumph only Riga, Reval and the isolated island of Oesel (Saaremaa) held out, but Ivan the Terrible was unable to consolidate the gains he had made. With the help of Sweden, still clinging doggedly to its toehold of Reval, Stefan Bathory of Poland–Lithuania led the fight back. Wenden was recaptured before the year was out and was then successfully defended against a Muscovite counter-attack in February 1578. Meanwhile the Swedes moved against the Muscovite gains in western Estonia, retaking Leal (Lihula) and Hapsal (Haapsalu).

By September 1578 Ivan the Terrible was so battered that he was ready to dis-cuss peace terms, but Bathory was not interested – his aim was to expel Muscovy completely from Livonia. Bathory, however, reckoned that a direct strike at Ivan's possessions in Livonia would be unlikely to guarantee a quick victory. Instead he proposed a bold strategy of taking the fight directly to the enemy, and three strikes against Muscovy followed in quick succession. In 1579 the Polish king recaptured Polotsk. The following year Bathory's Crown Chancellor Jan Zamoyski cut his way through trackless forests for three weeks before destroying the fortress of Velikie Luki. Hungarian engineers then built a firm road back to Polotsk. A wedge had now been driven between Moscow and Livonia.[8]

In 1581 the campaign moved northwards again in the general direction of Pskov, but by now Bathory was under different pressure. His parliament had voted two years worth of funds towards the war on condition that the matter was brought quickly to a close. Seeking a quick solution for his money Bathory recruited an ex-pert force of foreign mercenaries. The army that Bathory was eventually to deploy at Pskov included 838 *reiters*, the majority of whom were German; there were also several Scottish regiments and a number of Italian, French and Spanish captains. It is no wonder that Ivan the Terrible complained that he was being attacked by the whole of Italy![9] With this international brigade under his command Bathory advanced against his first major objective, and laid siege to great city of Pskov.

The Siege of Pskov

The Siege of Pskov in 1581 provides an important illustration of how the dissimi-lar conditions of warfare in north-eastern Europe required an approach that was different from the tactics adopted in western sieges. Both in terms of fortifica-tions and the use of cavalry, Piotrowski's comment that 'We are not fighting in France or The Netherlands' was very apposite. In the sixteenth century Pskov was the third Russian city of importance after Moscow and Novgorod. The Kremlin, the inner citadel where the Cathedral of the Holy Trinity stood, was located on a narrow promontory created by the confluence of the Velikaya and the Pskova rivers like a miniature version of Constantinople or Belgrade. Surrounding the Kremlin was a remarkable system of medieval limestone walls that had been strengthened during the previous half century by the addition of round artillery towers (*see* plate 30). The Pokrovskaya Tower ('Tower of the Intercession of the Virgin'), which lay at the south-western corner beside the Velikaya river was the strongest of all with walls that were twenty feet thick. Its alternative name, 'Tower of the Virgin's Veil', referred to the tradition of the Virgin Mary as the protector of the city by covering it with her veil, a pious belief that originated in Constantinople.[10]

Unlike Belgrade and Constantinople, however, the land walls of Pskov did not merely cut off the peninsula but extended over the small Pskova river in an outer ring. The freezing of both rivers in winter was no doubt one consideration in this design. Water gates with opening lattices were built at the two points where the walls actually crossed the river. The Gremyachaya Tower, on which the northern water gate was anchored, dated from 1525 and provided a formidable stronghold at the Kremlin's northern point. The total extent of the outer walls was more than five miles, and there were thirty-nine towers in all. Even Pskov's numerous churches played their part in the city's defence. The city was divided into six sections, each based on an individual church. The men of each section had defensive responsibilities for a designated sector of the walls, while gunpowder was stored in the church crypt. Just before the siege began a fortunate apparition of the Virgin Mary was granted to one of Pskov's gunsmiths, instructing him where to place the artillery to its best effect and assuring him that the city would not fall.[11]

Although Bathory's main thrust was directed against Pskov, massive Polish attacks were expected – and actually occurred – along the entire Russian–Lithuanian border. Swedish attacks against Novgorod were also a possibility, so Ivan the Terrible decided to keep the majority of Russian troops in reserve, leaving Pskov under the command of the able Prince Ivan Petrovitch Shuisky. He led a garrison of seven thousand *strel'tsy* (musketeers) together with two thousand cavalry for mounting sorties supplemented by ten thousand men of the city.[12]

Bathory's approach to Pskov lay through a trackless, forested wasteland where the rain poured down, so that Piotrowski noted that they were 'in this dark wilderness, as if plunged into the deepest circle of Hell'.[13] The comparatively few guns he possessed were floated down river or more often dragged laboriously through the mud. By August siege lines were in place, and the attack was ready to begin.

A lively source for the events of the Pskov campaign is *The Story of Stefan Bathory's Campaign against Pskov*, which was produced in the style of an epic by an anonymous and very patriotic Russian author writing within a few years of the events he describes.[14] He begins with the words:

> Dreadful and cruel times have come . . . Similar to insatiable hell, which opens its jaws to swallow its victim, so also did the Polish–Lithuanian king prepare to take the city of Pskov in the pincers of his regiments.[15]

Bathory's cannon were concentrated on making a breach on the southern, landward side of the city, where the first major assault against Pskov was launched on 8 September. The bells of the church of St Basil the Great sounded from the hillock in the middle of the city to warn the citizens to be ready, while the Russian artillery opened fire on the advancing troops. The chronicle continues:

> At six o'clock of this same day they heard a noise comparable to that of approaching gigantic waves or of powerful thunder. And the entire enemy army howled and ran to the breaches in the fortress wall, covering themselves with their shields, muskets, lances and other weapons, and thus appearing to be under a roof . . . But our Christian warriors remained as firm as the stars in the sky, and did not permit the enemy to scale the walls.[16]

The chronicler goes on to relate how the Polish artillery succeeded in creating a breach wide enough even for cavalry to go through. Its location is remembered in Pskov to this day as 'Bathory's Breach', a battered stretch of rubble that lies between the Tower of the Intercession of the Virgin and the site of another tower called Svinuzskaya Tower (Tower of the Hog), which was destroyed in the fighting. This is where a modern memorial to the siege has been erected. The Russians began building temporary fortifications inside, and although Polish fire hindered their efforts a second line of defence was created from timber and earth:[17]

> And two thousand selected storm troops and personal guards of the king began the assault on the Hog Tower, which was already destroyed on their side, and they began shooting through the windows of the walls at the Christian people, and at the Russian militia. Their bullets fell like drops of rain from a storm cloud, and flooded the Russian warriors. These bullets were killing the Christian people as if they were the stings of serpents. Other enemy troops stormed through the break in the Virgin's Veil Tower, and cleared the tower of Russian warriors, preparing the way for the final taking of the city.[18]

The Relief of Pskov

But the city did not fall. As the news came in of the Polish seizure of the Virgin's and Hog towers the Orthodox priests and monks offered prayers in front of the Cathedral's holiest icons for deliverance from the Roman Catholic Bathory with his 'lawless Latin heresies'. As if in response to their prayers a shot from the great Russian cannon named 'Leopard' scored a direct hit on the Tower of the Hog. The chronicler also tells us that a large quantity of gunpowder was exploded under the occupied tower. This may well have been a mine introduced by Russian defenders who were familiar with the cellars beneath it. It had a dramatic effect:

> And the overproud knights, courtiers and nobles of the king, who had begged their king for permission to take the city of Pskov ... were blasted into the air according to God's design ... And the best of the royal nobles, who had boasted that they would bring the imprisoned Russian command- ers to the king, remained under the ruins of the Hog Tower, prisoners of death until the Last Judgement.[19]

It was time for a counterattack, preceded by a procession of clergy bearing the most sacred icons of the city against the enemy. A surge of inspiration ran through Pskov. Women joined their menfolk on the walls to appropriate the guns aban- doned by the Poles. Others helped carry water and rocks to the defenders who were still fighting. The decisive moment came with the recapture of the Tower of the Intercession of the Virgin, as 'with the Grace of Christ, the stone wall of Pskov was cleansed of the evil Lithuanian feet' (see plate 31).[20]

This attack of early September turned out to be the only major assault that took place against Pskov during what was to be an eight-month-long siege. The Polish king was short of both cannon and powder – he had only been able to bring twenty heavy cannon against Pskov – and the experience of the past few days had shown that when breaches were created the defenders rapidly met the storming parties with internal defences and barriers of timber and earth. Russian morale was also very high. Under these circumstances, a siege to starve out the garrison was the only realistic alternative. We noted earlier that, even if a fortress ultimately surrendered, its long resistance (sustained by the hope of relief) could do dreadful damage to a besieger. Bathory clearly appreciated these points when he began the Siege of Pskov, but his conduct of the operation differed greatly from western Eu- rope. It depended to a very large extent on his use of cavalry. In the west, cavalry were regarded as a useless encumbrance in a siege situation. In the Baltic lands and the plains of western Russia they were an asset.

Their first use was as a means of distracting and disorganising relief operations. Before the siege began about five thousand six hundred men had covered the eastern flank of Bathory's march on Pskov and kept Muscovite forces well away from the centre of operations. Another vital function was to secure the supplies upon which the besieging army depended. The supplies that the Polish army brought with it would not last for ever. By late August there were already shortages of bread and beer, and by the end of September there was not much left of hay and oats with which to feed the horses.

Because Ivan the Terrible had devastated the border regions, in which there were precious few villages anyway, Stefan Bathory's army had to forage far afield. Parties of a hundred and twenty horsemen were assigned for foraging expeditions that could take up to six days and faced the perils of winter such as a sudden thaw that overtook one foraging party crossing the frozen Lake Peipus. An astonished Ottoman envoy who observed the Siege of Pskov commented that the sultan would never be able to persuade his troops into the field at such low temperatures. By January 1582 these trips had been extended to one month and took in the Baltic coastline, so enormous was the distance to be travelled. An infantry army would have starved.[21]

Bathory's hussars also provided vital assistance in the siege lines. Nine hundred cavalry were permanently on duty at Pskov, keeping a watch on the fortress and acting immediately to counter any sortie. They were also both willing and able to dismount and take their places in the trenches along with the infantry. When much of the German mercenary infantry left Pskov in December 1581, Jan Zamoyski ordered seven cavalrymen out of every company of a hundred and fifty, and five out of every company of a hundred, to serve on foot. Squads of highly mobile mounted troops therefore replaced the elaborate lines of circumvallation that were becoming the norm elsewhere, and on his return to Cracow Bathory specifically praised the cavalry for their willingness to undertake such humble tasks.[22]

The use of cavalry in such a fashion also reflected a different attitude towards fortresses from Western Europe. Few communities could afford to erect elaborate stone castles and walls. Pskov and the former castles of the Livonian Order were notable exceptions to a pattern of smaller and predominantly wooden fortifications that were unlikely to face a long siege and whose military effectiveness was doubtful. In fact, when, in 1567, it had been suggested that a fortress line should be built along the Muscovite frontier, the great *hetman* Jan Chodkiewicz (1560–1621) scornfully remarked that the Polish army should not sit dispersed on hilltops but should be with the king, ready to destroy the Muscovite army in one blow. The smaller Muscovite garrisons could then be safely ignored, because, 'if the Lord

grants us victory over this enemy, then all these chicken coops will have to surrender anyway'.[23]

Pskov, of course, was no chicken coop, and in spite of all Bathory's skills and
patience it held out against him, and when the factor of time came into operation
it was the Polish side that cracked first. A companion of Bathory recorded the
king's admiration for the Russian defenders:

> When they are defending towns the Russians give no thought to their lives.
> They steadfastly man the walls and defend the ditch, fighting night and day
> regardless of whether they have been torn by shot or steel or hurled into
> the air by mines, or whether their rations have run out and they are dying
> of hunger. They will not surrender, for their one concern is the welfare of
> the realm.[24]

Impressed maybe, but exhausted and defeated, Bathory abandoned the Siege of
Pskov in 1582. Both sides claimed it as a great victory, for which the Poles probably
had the greater justification, because the Peace of Yam Zapolski, which brought
the fighting to an end, was signed on 15 January 1582 while the siege was still continuing, and gave Poland–Lithuania the whole of Livonia. The Poles returned to
Moscow the gains made immediately prior to the siege apart from Polotsk, which
they retained.

Resting on his laurels, Bathory began dreaming greater dreams of conquest.
The year 1583 was to see him wooing Ivan the Terrible for a joint crusade against
the Crimea. By 1584 he was thinking of Constantinople, and when Ivan the Terrible died in that year Bathory had an image in his mind of a great union of Poland,
Lithuania, Livonia, Hungary and Moscow marching against the Ottomans. But his
subjects, particularly those who voted for or against his taxes, were not impressed.
Shunned by his adopted countrymen, Bathory sulked and drew up a will from
which his native Transylvania would be the major beneficiary. He died suddenly in
1586. Poison was suspected.[25]

For the Muscovites, however, Bathory's campaign against Pskov was to have
an outcome no one could have foreseen. In the winter of 1581 the Tsarevitch Ivan,
Ivan the Terrible's son and heir, had begged his father to be allowed to lead the
relief of Pskov in person. The tsar flew into one of his periodic rages and struck his
son with his staff with such force that the youth died a few days later.[26] The eventual death of Ivan the Terrible in 1584 led to a weaker son inheriting, thus plunging
Russia into its dreadful 'Time of Troubles', when Polish armies would once again
threaten its borders.

Chapter 14
The Shock of the New

Thanks to Stefan Bathory, by the beginning of the seventeenth century, Poland had a mounted arm that was loyal, flexible and visually impressive. A senior official under King Jan Sobieski, who led them to victory at the Siege of Vienna in 1683, was to describe them as 'the most beautiful cavalry in Europe'. Armed with lances and sabres, and gorgeously costumed, they presented an aspect of awesome splendour. But of all the features in their costume and equipment it was the presence of the wings of feathers that most stood out. There is still some dispute over their significance. Theories have been put forward to explain them as a defence against sword cuts or lassoes or even an attempt to make the riders look like a horde of avenging Christian angels! They certainly functioned as a device to scare an enemy, if not by the whistling sound they are alleged to have made then at least by the visual impact they created.

The Siege of Pskov had seen the prototype hussars serve in siege lines, and it was to be twenty years before they faced a real challenge on the battlefield to their role as cavalry. Yet this was the new age of the Dutch system of the European Countermarch and the pistol-wielding *reiters*. How would hussars cope against them? All was to be revealed in 1605 and 1610, when Poland's apparently medieval anachronisms came up against armies that, according to the theory that lay behind their modern methods, should have driven them from every battlefield.

The Challenge from Sweden
As the seventeenth century began, the Swedes replaced the Muscovites in the struggle for Livonia. In preparation for his campaign, Charles IX of Sweden had sought the service of John of Nassau to train his troops in the Dutch methods of heavy infantry armed with pikes and muskets and perfectly drilled – the supposedly perfect antidote to cavalry charges. But Sweden was not Holland. It had taken the Nassau cousins several years to train and discipline their men to fight to the European Countermarch system. There was no time to improve the Swedish

discipline and training, although John did his best. In the few months that he was there he taught them drill, but they lacked equipment; nor was there a trained pike unit to protect the musketeers as they went about their meticulous sequence of movements. When he eventually left Sweden in 1602 John left behind a half-trained army that could create chaos on a battlefield for its own commander.[1]

Needing a pike hedge, Charles IX acquired eight thousand of the weapons, and at Kokenhusen (modern Koknese in Latvia) the Swedish foot-soldiers based their defence against the Poles on a *wagenburg* strengthened with a hedge of sharpened stakes. But once the Swedish cavalry was routed in the first phase of the battle the infantrymen were left completely exposed. Cossacks pursued the fleeing Swedish horsemen while the Poles combined firepower and manoeuvrability to mop up the foot-soldiers. The following year the Polish *hetman* Stanislaw Zolkiewski (1547–1621) confronted a Swedish force outside Reval (Tallinn). Finding his way blocked by infantry armed in part with pikes and occupying good ground, he kept the enemy occupied by repeated charges while his Cossack cavalry made a wide detour to take the preoccupied Swedes in the rear.[2]

The Swedes were soon to provide the Poles with one of their most celebrated cavalry victories. It happened at Kircholm, a few miles from the city of Riga on the banks of the Dvina (Daugava) river. The Swedes outnumbered the Poles, yet suffered a catastrophic defeat. Charles IX left three thousand men besieging Riga and chased *hetman* Jan Chodkiewicz along the river. Sensing an easy victory, on the morning of 27 September 1605 Charles drew up his army in battle array on the crest of a ridge in a narrow corridor between the Dvina and a heavily wooded hill. He prepared well, leaving gaps between his infantry formations that the Swedish cavalry could utilise. The infantry were arranged in squares of pike and shot.

Chodkiewicz sought to lure the Swedes out of position. He sent his light cavalry to skirmish between the two armies and ordered his force to close ranks to make it look even smaller than it actually was. After fours hours of waiting Chodkiewicz pretended to withdraw, and the trick worked. The Swedes had marched overnight in pouring rain to confront the enemy. It was now very hot, and they were certainly not going to let them get away. As they advanced Chodkiewicz timed his attack perfectly. His hussars smashed into one of the Swedish infantry squares in the centre. They suffered casualties before withdrawing, but the attack was not designed to break the enemy. That was planned to happen on the flanks. On the left wing, supported by steady infantry fire twelve hundred hussars and Cossacks charge home against the Swedes, who were shattered after the briefest resistance. As they fled they disorganised the infantry of the third line. On the right, although the numbers were smaller, the charge had a similar effect.

Both commanders committed their reserves, and within half an hour the Swedish cavalry was in retreat on both flanks. The light cavalry was left to pursue while the heavier hussars concentrated on the infantry in the centre. The result was a massacre of the Swedes. Kircholm was one of the bloodiest encounters in history relative to the numbers engaged. The road to Riga was littered with the bodies of the Swedish cavalrymen.[3]

The Time of Troubles

It was not long before the Polish hussars had the chance to tackle once again the armies of Muscovy, where Boris Godunov had ruled as tsar since 1597. To his opponents Godunov had usurped the throne, but the powerful *boyars* (nobles) were faced with a stark choice: either accept Godunov as tsar or find an alternative candidate. Then in 1603, to everyone's astonishment, just such a candidate appeared out of the blue. He was a monk currently living in exile in Poland, who told everyone that he was Prince Dimitri, the youngest son of Ivan the Terrible. If the mysterious monk was actually a pretender it was a strange choice of false identity, because everyone believed that this particular child had died in 1591. Dimitri had epilepsy, and one afternoon had been playing in the courtyard of the palace with four young companions. Their game involved throwing a sharp knife about, and while Dimitri had the knife in his hands he suffered a violent epileptic seizure and cut himself so badly that he bled to death. Twelve years later, this strange monk appeared out of nowhere, with the explanation that the tragic accident with the knife had actually been a botched assassination attempt by agents of Godunov; and that another boy had died in his stead.

The true origins of the supposed Dimitri will never be known, but his actual identity was a less important factor than the use to which he was put. There was much to be gained for Poland from supporting the 'First False Dimitri' as he became known to history, but to convert that support into military intervention was a very controversial step. For a start, Poland had a twenty-year armistice with Muscovy, and to break it on behalf of a man whose rights to the throne and his chances of actually reaching it were, to say the least, slim would be a very risky business. King Sigismund III of Poland therefore held back from officially supporting Dimitri, but he allowed the pretender to recruit a private army.

In October 1604 False Dimitri crossed the border into Russia with an army of Polish and Cossack mercenaries, having already sent proclamations to Muscovy inviting its lords to pledge their allegiance to him. Some of the support he eventually received was undoubtedly based on the belief that he was the rightful tsar. Others followed him simply because he was opposed to Godunov, who obligingly died on

13 April 1605. Had Godunov been assassinated? No one was sure, but his opponents followed up the fortuitous death by murdering Godunov's heir. This allowed a triumphal entry into Moscow for False Dimitri, who was solemnly crowned tsar on 21 July. The following May his Polish bride arrived in Moscow to be crowned as tsarina. It was then that things began to go badly wrong.

The Second Death of Dimitri

The celebrations for the tsarina's coronation made Moscow look like a Polish city. The Polish magnates brought large retinues with them, but behaved with unwise arrogance that alienated them from the local population. The *boyars*, headed by Vasili Shuisky, felt that the moment to strike had arrived. During the night of 17 May the conspirators occupied all the Kremlin gates, allowing no one to go either out or in. When the bells of Moscow rang at 4 a.m. Shuisky was waiting in Red Square, mounted and armed, and it took little encouragement to persuade the populace to raid the lodgings where the Poles were staying. Amid the confusion the *boyars* penetrated the royal palace in the Kremlin to seize False Dimitri. A foreign visitor wrote:

> He was presently pursued by his enemies, so that he leaped down out of a window, falling a marvellous height upon the pavement; for his lodging was in the top of the castle, so as it was a great wonder that he broke not his arms and legs or that he was not crushed all in pieces.

Dimitri was unable to move and was speedily done to death, after which his naked body was tossed contemptuously into Red Square for all to see and abuse. Finally his mangled corpse was treated with the ultimate indignity when it was fired out of a cannon. In the early morning of 19 May 1606 Shuisky was proclaimed Tsar of Russia. The Polish interference in Russian politics had therefore been disastrous for all concerned, but a further tragic intervention was soon to come.

For a while the Poles stood back as Russia dissolved into civil war. Shuisky was not universally popular, and soon a further threat appeared in the west in the shape of yet another pretender. The new candidate, who again had Polish support, also claimed to be Prince Dimitri, who had now risen from the dead twice! Just as before, the actual identity of the second False Dimitri mattered less than his vital function as a figurehead, and by the spring of 1608 the new pretender was ready to march on Moscow with Polish support. He made his headquarters at Tushino, about eight miles west of Moscow. At this point the sorry tale descends into farce, because the ex-tsarina was still alive and False Dimitri II's supporters needed her to recognise the impostor as her husband. At first she refused to have anything to do with the crazy plot, but her father's wishes prevailed, and to create legitimacy she was forcibly and secretly married to False Dimitri II.

False Dimitri II's military strategy against Shuisky was to encircle Moscow and cut off its supplies. This turned out to be a licence for indiscriminate raiding and destruction, even when the towns they attacked stated their support for him. One famous operation began in September 1608 against the Monastery of the Trinity and St Sergei, in a siege that inspired a memorial tablet stating that the monastery had survived three plagues in its history: 'Typhus, Tartars and Poles'. False Dimitri II expected it to be an easy operation, but the monastery's strong walls, defended by the monks and an army of local gentry, militia and peasants, held out for three months and prevented the circle round Moscow from being closed completely.

Shuisky was nevertheless in a desperate state, so he signed a pact with the one country that could really help him, but which would be certain to provoke official Polish intervention for the first time. On 28 February 1609 the tsar allied himself with King Charles IX of Sweden, who had been watching the developments in Russia for some time. He received important pledges from Shuisky concerning disputed territories before his expeditionary force arrived at Novgorod in April 1609. It was a motley crew of fifteen thousand men, the majority of whom were mercenaries from Germany, Holland, England, Scotland, France and Spain. Jacob de la Gardie, who had previously fought against Ivan the Terrible, commanded them. The Swedes were joined by three thousand Russians.

In response, King Sigismund III of Poland invaded Russia in September 1609. Smolensk became the first target in the Polish advance, which was led by one of Poland's finest soldiers – the *hetman* Stanislaw Zolkiewski (1547–1620). We are fortunate that Zolkiewski left a detailed personal account of the expedition. It was written to justify the course of action he was forced to take by his king, who commanded the army in person and overruled Zolkiewski every time there was a point of difference.[4]

The first disagreement concerned Smolensk. It had a long wall with high, thick yet very cramped brick towers unsuitable for heavy artillery, but was still formidable. Zolkiewski was for bypassing Smolensk and heading straight for Moscow, but the king gave first priority to the fortress and ordered a siege. Its defenders, safe behind their mighty walls, refused to discuss terms, so a Polish council of war was held, and '. . . one old colonel, a Scot, who, asked his opinion, said at length that it was a zoo, not a castle, so it would easily be taken.' Zolkiewski did not agree, and urged the king not to go ahead with an assault, but 'His Majesty, persuaded by some that stratagems might have good effect, insisted on trying them'.

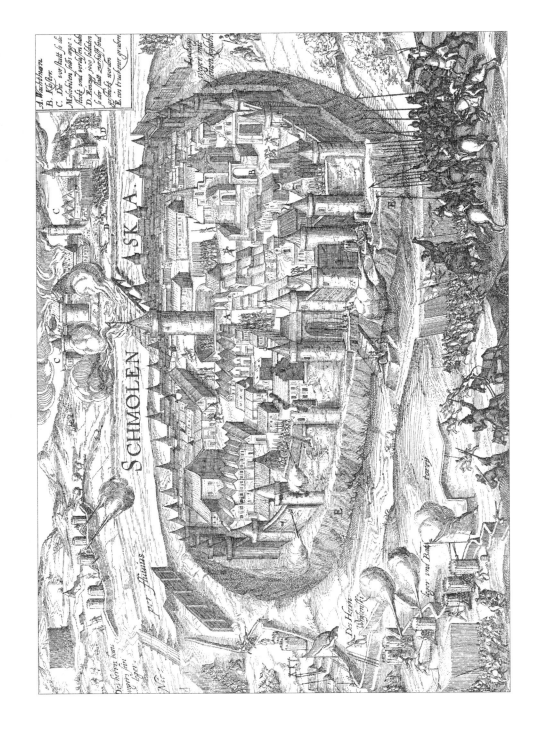

SCHMOLEN SKA

The first stratagem concerned petards, those bizarre explosive devices that blew in gates very effectively, but actually had to be placed by hand against a target to work properly. The approach to the gates of Smolensk was by means of a narrow path only wide enough for one man on a horse, and:

> Pan Nowodworski had to go along this path with his petards, bending below the lower guns in the wall. He planted a petard by the first and another by the second gate and blew them both up. But as in such an operation the noise is great, with heavy firing both from cannon and various guns, we did not see if the petards had any effect, since the gate could not be seen because of the structure which concealed it. Consequently those who were in front, not knowing what was happening there, did not enter the narrow path.[5]

A trumpet signal that should have announced the success of the petards also failed as the trumpeters 'got lost somewhere in the tumult'. A fine initiative was therefore wasted, and when artillery fire and tunnelling also failed to produce any effect Zolkiewski again urged the king to mask Smolensk and advance on Moscow.

King Sigismund also refused to send for gunfounders to recast the damaged guns or to hire more troops (for which he pleaded poverty) but did arrange for heavier guns to be brought up from Riga.[6] But all this took precious time, and in fact the Siege of Smolensk went on to last two years. It was a major strategic blunder, because throughout this time the Swedish army was active in the north. They first defeated False Dimitri II's troops in a two-day-long battle, but their commander did not have enough resources to pay the mercenaries. Many marched home, pillaging on the way. Somehow de la Gardie rallied them, and the newly recombined army headed against False Dimitri II's siege lines at the Trinity and St Sergei Monastery. The monastery was relieved on 12 January 1610, and the allied army entered Moscow in triumph three months later.

Much alarmed, False Dimitri II fled to Kaluga, where he found that his Polish allies were willing to betray him for their own ends. In a treaty signed outside Smolensk any personal desires of False Dimitri II were overruled, and instead it was proposed that King Sigismund's own son Prince Wladyslaw should become Tsar of Russia.

This new development reached the ears of Tsar Vasili Shuisky, who proclaimed a holy war against the 'Catholic crusader' from Poland. He ordered a march to relieve Smolensk, and forty-six thousand men headed for King Sigismund's siege lines. The result, however, was one of the greatest victories in Polish history.

The Siege of Smolensk by the Poles between 1609 and 1611

The Battle of Klushino

When Zolkiewski headed towards Moscow to confront his enemies the first obstacle he met was the town of Tsarovo Zamyestye, located beside a stream that had been dammed to form a small lake with a very wide causeway across it. Its fortifications, however, were still in course of construction, so the Poles determined to attack it before the defensive works were completed. A preliminary scouting party under Zolkiewski himself took fire from off the causeway. The Russians had concealed several hundred musketeers in the ditches and among the reeds by the causeway, but Zolkiewski was not fooled, and eventually the ambushers grew impatient and revealed themselves. So Zolkiewski ordered some Cossacks to dismount and sneak forward:

> As soon as these drew level, others jumped on them openly on the causeway, while those who were below it forced their way on to it, shooting and fighting hand-to-hand. The Muscovites immediately took to flight through the rushes, with our men chasing them.[7]

The capture of the causeway allowed the safe passage across of the Polish army. The Fort of Tsarovo Zamyestye still remained untaken, but the Poles erected small forts to bottle it up (the tactic Zolkiewski had urged on King Sigismund at Smolensk) and prepared to meet the advancing Russian army. Information obtained from captured prisoners provided evidence that the Russians were planning to spend the next night at Klushino.

Zolkiewski had already decided to meet the Russian army on the road, but he did not divulge his decision even to a council of war for fear of being betrayed, and when the army marched it was without trumpet or drum. It took the whole night to move the army four miles through the woods. Fortunately for them, the Russians were not on their guard, and most of their camp was asleep. Zolkiewski could possibly have taken the whole army by surprise, but there were complications:

> If the whole of our army had been available, we should have got them up unclothed, but it was not possible to get them out of the wood quickly. The *hetman* had taken two falconets with him, which blocked the way so that the army could not move ahead of them. There was another obstacle which prevented us from striking at them at once. Athwart the whole field leading to the enemy camp hedges had been planted and between these hedges were two hamlets. It was thus necessary to await the arrival of the army in order to break down these hedges.[8]

The two hamlets were set on fire, and this roused the Muscovites from slumber. As the Poles dressed their ranks drums and trumpets sounded, and the army made contact with the men that the Russians had stationed behind the hedge.

> At this point the falconets arrived with some infantry and met a great need. For the gunners discharged the falconets at the German infantrymen who stood by the hedge, and our infantry, not numerous but tried and experienced in many battles, rushed at them and at once several of the Germans fell.[9]

When the infantry had been driven back from the hedge, it was the turn of the Polish winged hussars to go into action. An eyewitness of the Battle of Klushino, Samuel Maskiewicz, counted eight or even ten separate charges against the enemy. The effect was tremendous and the Muscovites withdrew towards their camp, with the Poles following with their sabres.[10]

The vital phase of the battle that followed was a tremendous demonstration of the effectiveness of Polish cavalry tactics, but, very surprisingly, Zolkiewski himself does not describe it in detail (*see* plate 32). He notes merely that:

> Our men, coming against the Muscovite troops, had the easier task, for the latter did not hold out but began fleeing with our people in pursuit.[11]

Instead we are dependent upon Samuel Maskiewicz for a vivid account of what happened next. The hussars were frustrated at first by the presence of the hedge (which Maskiewicz calls a palisade). Whatever the exact nature of the obstacle, it had only partially been destroyed, and the gaps were scarcely large enough to allow ten horses to pass through in close order. This prevented them from attacking in their usual formation. Steady fire from the Russian musketeers also took its toll. The Muscovite cavalry, however, were beginning to give way, so Shuisky asked de la Gardie to support it with his cavalry. De la Gardie's response was to order his *reiters* to perform a *caracole*, and the Polish hussars seized their opportunity:

> They handed us the victory, for as they came to us we were in some disorder, and immediately, having fired their carbines, they wheeled away to the rear in the normal fashion to reload, and the next rank advanced firing. We did not wait, but at the moment all had emptied their pieces, and seeing that they were starting to withdraw, we charged them with only our sabres in our hands; they, having failed to reload, while the next rank had not yet fired, took to their heels.. We crashed into the whole Muscovite force,

still drawn up in battle order at the entrance to their camp, plunging them into disorder.[12]

In other words, the Poles attacked the Russian cavalry with their sabres as they were just completing a *caracole*.[13] The victory was completed when their Swedish mercenaries, who also outnumbered the Polish army, changed sides.[14]

When news of the Polish victory at Klushino reached False Dimitri II, he raced to Moscow to claim his throne before the Poles got there. The defeated Tsar Vasili Shuisky was arrested and forced to become a monk, but the *boyars* would not allow False Dimitri II to be crowned. Believing that he held the balance of power, the victorious Zolkiewski began negotiations, but the *boyars* sensed that they could make more demands than hitherto. Zolkiewski was forced to agree that Prince Wladyslaw should convert to the Orthodox faith before heading for Moscow to be crowned, where he would marry an Orthodox bride. It was an amazing concession to make, but there was a stumbling block even more difficult to surmount than the conversion of the Crown Prince of Poland. His father, King Sigismund III, had decided to become tsar himself!

Zolkiewski was astounded that his victory had been placed in jeopardy by such bizarre rivalry, and it was because of this final and irreconcilable difference of opinion between the king and his loyal *hetman* that Zolkiewski eventually wrote the memoir that has provided us with so many vivid military accounts. But from the Russian point of view the matter was simple. Their capital was now occupied not by a Russian pretender to the throne but by the troops of a foreign invader, and when it was discovered that False Dimitri II had been murdered the opposition to Poland grew rapidly into a national crusade. In January 1611 a revolt began in Riazan. Nishni-Novgorod and Kazan soon followed suit, and by March the advance forces of what was effectively a Russian national army were nearing Moscow. On 13 March a brawl broke out in Moscow between Russians and Poles.

Tension was running high, so to prepare against any attack from outside the Polish commanders ordered some Moscow carters to haul the Polish cannon up on to the walls of the Kremlin. The carters refused and a riot started. The mercenaries in Polish service then took the opportunity to attack the Muscovites and a major incident developed. Elsewhere in the city the Russians had time to collect arms and build some makeshift barricades. The Poles responded by setting fire to Moscow. It caused a terrible conflagration, as Zolkiewski notes:

Our men then resolved among themselves to set fire to the wooden city and the one inside the White Wall, to shut themselves in the Kremlin and

Kitai-gorod and to attack the *strel'tsy* and anybody else they met. On the Wednesday before Easter they did so. Having been drawn up and marched out by regiments, they set fire at once to the wooden town.

Looting by the Polish army was widespread, and in a marvellous hyperbole we are told that the Poles captured so much treasure that they fired pearls out of their muskets rather than lead bullets. 'So,' Zolkiewski was to write, 'Moscow burned with much bloodshed and incalculable loss, for it was a large and rich city of great circumference'.

The immediate outcome, however, was that the Poles found themselves under siege in the Moscow Kremlin for the next nineteen months. Three times Polish military expeditions reached Moscow to reinforce the garrison and bring food, but conditions rapidly deteriorated. Meanwhile, far off to the west, King Sigismund's futile Siege of Smolensk was still going on. When Zolkiewski had left to fight the Battle of Klushino the Smolensk operation had been handed over to the Palatine of Braclaw, who was delighted to be given the opportunity to earn himself some glory by capturing what he contemptuously referred to as a 'hen house'. But it was by no means as easy as he expected, and in his memoirs Zolkiewski is scornful of his successor's efforts:

> He did not take into consideration that immediately beyond the wall, at a distance of a dozen or so yards, there was an old wall, which in our ancestor's time had been the castle's defence, stronger than the stone wall erected in the time of Tsar Theodore. Even if the stone wall had been destroyed, as would not have been difficult with good guns, nevertheless that other wall, being so high, barred access to the castle, as the event proved.

When the men were ready to follow up a breach Braclaw's guns blasted a hole in the stone wall, but flanking fire gave them no chance of passing through. So Smolensk stood, but as the months passed the defenders began to fall ill from plague. The time finally came when the defenders were so decimated by hunger and disease that an all-out assault could be risked. Information received from within the city suggested that a sewer outlet by the walls might be a good pace to blow a breach, and so it proved.

On the night of 3 June 1611, after a heavy bombardment and the blowing of a charge next to the sewer, the Poles succeeded in taking the city by storm. Most of the defenders died fighting, and the survivors sought refuge in the cathedral. Not wishing to surrender they set fire to the powder store in the crypt and perished in the explosion. 'Almost the whole castle was burned out,' writes Zolkiewski, who noted many unused cannonballs still in store, together with much food, including rye, oats, geese, hens and even peacocks. Sixteen days later two children were dug out alive from a destroyed building.

The Retreat from Moscow
The fall of Smolensk may have brought some cheer to the Polish defenders of Moscow, but pressure on the capital steadily increased. After a further year of occupation the soldiers were reduced to eating the leather from their saddles and parchment from books, and may even have descended to cannibalism. When the Russians finally stormed the walls on 22 October 1612 the Kremlin garrison surrendered. Despite the terms of capitulation, some Polish soldiers were murdered and the rest imprisoned, and King Sigismund began his retreat from Moscow. On 25 October the gates of the Kremlin opened to allow in the victorious Russian army (see plate 33), and in January 1613 a new tsar was crowned. His name was Michael Romanov, whose family name was to become famous for centuries to come.[15]

Although cruel in its effects on the population, the 'Time of Troubles' is cherished in Russian memory for its example of how a cruel invader was driven out. But in spite of its colourful winged hussars, Poland never really possessed the military resources to contemplate subduing Russia, and her adventure was an act of minor romantic opportunism amidst a serious civil war. As his memoirs show, the *hetman* Zolkiewski opposed the futile campaign from the start, and it was only his loyalty and sense of duty to his king that drove his service along. King Sigismund of Poland may have experienced a retreat from Moscow, but 1612 was not 1812, and he was no Napoleon.

Chapter 15
Mercenaries and Marvels

While The Netherlands and Livonia experienced long periods of war, the border between the Ottomans and the Austrian Habsburgs remained quiet until 1593. When hostilities recommenced it was the front-line state of Hungary that saw most of the fighting once again. From the European side the fight rapidly assumed the character of a crusade, in spite of all the contempt that the Reformation had heaped upon that long-discredited concept. This Christian optimism was sustained by the persistent belief that once serious warlike moves were made against the Ottomans the peoples of the Balkans would rise up against their occupation. There were encouraging signs in this direction the year the war began, when the three key Ottoman principalities of Moldavia, Wallachia and Transylvania each acquired new rulers, and each opposed the Ottomans. Very soon these princes were in command of the lower Danube, thereby depriving the Ottomans not only of forts and territories but also of the food supplies they were accustomed to draw from the coastal lands of the Black Sea. Of the three the Transylvanian leader Sigismund Bathory, nephew of Stephen, was the most aggressive. A force of Ottomans was thoroughly routed at Sissek in Croatia in 1593. This battle provided the opening shots of a long conflict called the Thirteen Years War, described by a Christian commentator as 'the slaughter-house of men'.[1]

An angry Ottoman response soon materialised. On hearing of the defeat at Sissek the Grand Vizier Sinan Pasha threw the Habsburg emperor's ambassador into prison and marched against Hungary with the whole of the sultan's European levies and thirteen thousand janissaries. He first captured Veszprem, the Habsburgs' most outlying fortress, but failed to go any further when the janissaries mutinied against the promise of a winter campaign. Sinan Pasha returned to Hungary the following year (1594) with a much-augmented army, perhaps the largest seen since the days of Suleiman the Magnificent. The move obliged the Austrians to abandon a siege of Gran and retire across the River Danube. Sinan Pasha then laid siege to Komarno, but this powerful base across the river held out long enough for the

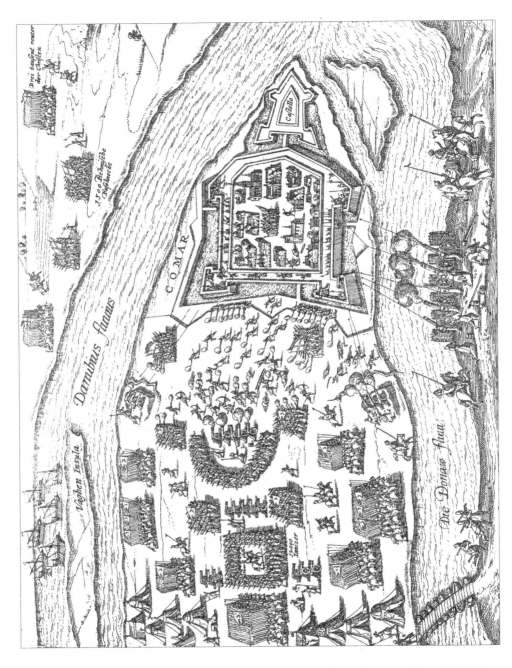

The Siege of Komarno in 1594. Komarno lies on the Danube, and is now in Slovakia. This contemporary print shows the arrangement of angle bastions in great detail

approach of winter to force the Ottomans to withdraw. It was nevertheless a satisfactory outcome for the 1594 campaign.

In 1595 the Ottoman Empire acquired a new sultan who began his reign by eliminating nineteen brothers. The new ruler was Mehmed III, and he had inherited a very dangerous situation because of the defection of the ruler of Transylvania, Sigismund Bathory, to the imperial cause. This had exposed the Ottoman right flank. Sinan Pasha led a counteroffensive as far as Bucharest but was forced back across the Danube.

Elated by this victory the Austrian imperial forces carried the fight down the Danube from Austria and finally succeeded in capturing the great fortress of Gran, which had been in Ottoman hands since 1543. Then Visegrad, high on a mountain peak beside the Danube, also fell to the Austrians and the other northern Hungarian fortresses held by the Ottomans began to collapse like a deck of cards. Soon bands of Christian horsemen could be seen marauding very close to Edirne. The new situation was so grave for the Ottomans that the sultan decided to lead the next campaign in person. His counterattack began in the north-eastern corner of Hungary. Mehmed III accordingly took the field and targeted Erlau (Eger), which lay between the Austrians and their new Transylvanian allies. Erlau fell on 12 October 1596, partly because of treachery from the mercenaries in the garrison. It was nevertheless a gain that must have given immense satisfaction to the Turks, because Erlau had held out so well against Suleiman the Magnificent. But even better was to come.

The Battle of Kerestes

An Austrian army had been on its way to relieve Erlau when the castle capitulated. Archduke Maximilian of Austria and Sigismund Bathory of Transylvania were both present with large armies and decided to risk everything in one huge battle with the Ottoman forces. This was the Battle of Kerestes (modern Mezokeretses in eastern Hungary) (see plate 34). Not only was their army a large one but it was also most unusual in its composition, being predominately cavalry rather than infantry, with an additional large artillery arm. Among the cavalry were many *reiters*.[2]

A force of Ottoman cavalry tried to prevent the imperial army from taking up its position. They were driven off, and when the main body of Turks arrived Mehmed III could see that his enemies had fortified themselves in a field encampment behind a marshy area fed from a tributary of the River Theiss. The sultan sent forward a detachment of light horsemen to try the passage of the marsh. They were forced away, so the Ottoman army drew up in a similar encampment about a mile distant.

On 24 October the Turkish attack began, but was driven off with losses on both sides. Two days later another attack was launched. The sultan was disinclined to lead it and suggested that he should move to the rear, but this was felt to be bad for morale. The Ottoman light horsemen began an outflanking movement while the main body crossed the marsh. One detachment was kept out of sight.

The imperial army had made themselves ready for the expected Ottoman attack, and when the clash came their cavalry charged out to meet it. On the right wing the Ottoman horsemen were driven back in disarray across the marsh. The Austrian archduke had ordered that the Ottomans were not to be pursued beyond the river, but his orders fell on deaf ears when his commanders on the field realised the opportunity that had come their way. As their right wing rolled back the Turks their centre companies advanced to join them and destroyed a force of janissaries holding out in a ruined church. The sultan bravely did not flee, but took up a position behind the abandoned camp.

It was then that the position changed dramatically in favour of the Ottomans, because the victorious imperialists on the right wing abandoned their pursuit of the fleeing Turks for an orgy of plunder within the sultan's camp. So rich were the pickings that the greedy knights dismounted to ransack the tents more effectively. This was the moment that the hidden unit had been waiting for. In they charged against the totally disordered mob that had once been the pride of the imperial cavalry. The routed troops bolted back across the marsh, causing utter confusion among the imperialist rear ranks and soon the archduke had no one left on the field. All their guns were abandoned to the Turks and thousands were cut down. So serious was the defeat at Kerestes that Emperor Rudolf of Austria forbade all Christmas festivities that year as a sign of respect.

Castles and Mercenaries

Had the Ottomans followed up their victory then the war would not have lasted thirteen years, but siegework now became the order of the day, and in spite of the slaughter at Kerestes the Habsburgs managed to put two armies into the field by the following summer. One, under the Archduke Maximilian captured Papa and Totis (Tata), while the Transylvanians besieged Temesvar (Timisoara). In 1598 matters deteriorated even further for the Ottomans when the Austrians recaptured Raab (Gyor) and Veszprem. They even laid siege to Buda but failed to capture it by the winter, and a Turkish attack on Grosswardien (Oradea in present-day Romania) was thwarted. The embarrassments of 1598 stung the Ottomans into mounting a more vigorous response in 1599, but the subsequent advance ended with a feeble effort to threaten Gran and the army pulled back to Belgrade for the winter.

The Ottomans also realised that they were faced with a far more professional force of soldiers than others they had encountered in the past; they included mercenaries who had been schooled in the harsh laboratory of the Low Countries. These men were experienced and well armed, and lived a life that seems incredible these days. A soldier of fortune in about 1600 crossed international boundaries with an ease that modern travellers might well envy in order to sell his skills to the highest bidder. The Spanish army of 1595, for example, included in its ranks a certain Guy Fawkes. On many occasions these men fought for one side one day and for their former enemy the next. Take the case of one Roger Williams, who fought for the Dutch rebels between 1572 and 1573, for the Spanish against the Dutch rebels between 1574 and 1577, and then from 1578 to 1587 for the Dutch – apparently with no complaints from either employer!

When the 1600 campaign started the Ottomans recaptured Papa owing to the treachery of such mercenaries. The garrison was French, and they simply sold the fortress to the besiegers! Not daring to move against Gran, the grand vizier then besieged Kanicsa (modern Nagykanisza), where he was to come up against one of the most famous English mercenaries in history – a certain Captain John Smith. Long before he ventured to the Americas, where his association with Pocahontas was to create a legend, Smith had already achieved a formidable reputation as a soldier of fortune. He first served in the Low Countries, then entered on a journey to the east that was to provide him with some stirring adventures with which even his future exploits in America could scarcely compete.[3]

The Siege of Kanicsa was Smith's first taste of action in Hungary (see plate 35). In charge of the castle's defence was 'Lord Ebersbaught' (as Smith calls him), one of a number of 'brave gentlemen of good quality' whom Smith had met in Austria. It would appear that during their first meeting in Graz Smith had given Ebersbaught instruction in the art of torchlight signalling, a technique Smith may have picked up in the Low Countries. It was soon to be put into operation, because John Smith was assigned a position in the army that marched to relieve Kanicsa. Ten thousand men set out under the French Duc de Mercoeur, whom Smith refers to in his account of the operations as the 'Duke of Mercury'. But the Ottomans were firmly entrenched around the town in lines that proved impossible to break.

A combined operation involving a sortie out of the town synchronised with an attack from the rear seemed to be the only hope of success. Smith therefore went to the Duc de Mercoeur and suggested that he should try to communicate with Ebersbaught inside the town that very night using torches. The commander was willing to let him try, and supplied the Englishman with torches and men. But could Ebersbaught's attention be secured by the sight of apparently random lights flashing from the distant hills? Smith certainly believed that it was worth a try, because he was confident that Ebersbaught would have their agreed code with him. For some time the energetic Smith, stationed on a mountain, waved and worked his torches in vain, till at last he was overjoyed to see his efforts rewarded. From seven miles away Ebersbaught had grasped the situation, and Smith was in a position to flash the following message, recorded in his diary (in somewhat un-necessarily stilted words), 'On Thursday night I will charge at the east. At the alarum sally you.' Ebersbaught answered that it would be done.

Captain
John Smith,
the English soldier
of fortune who fought in
Hungary against the Ottomans before leaving
for America and his best-known exploits

The inventive Smith then prepared another contrivance ready for the combined attack. He tied several thousand matches on a long cord at the distance apart of soldiers in line, and then lit them with small fuses of gunpowder. The Ottoman army was divided in half by a river, and, while the relieving army made its attack at the hour agreed with Ebersbaught, the Ottomans on the far bank were kept in their place by Smith's line of flickering matches, which they took for another large army. The result was that two thousand troops were able to gain access to the town. As relief had arrived, the Ottomans raised the siege.

John Smith's Flaming Dragons

In recognition of the contribution he had made to the Siege of Kanicsa Smith received command of a troop of two hundred and fifty horsemen, and with these men Smith rejoined the Duc de Mercoeur for a siege of their own. This one was to be directed against the Ottoman-held fortress of Stuhlweissenberg (Szekesfehervar) in 1601. The polyglot nature of the Habsburg's mercenary army is shown by the fact that of the three fierce sorties made by the Ottomans against the besiegers the first killed five hundred Germans, the second killed five hundred Hungarians, while a third was repulsed by an army of Frenchmen. Some deserters from the town then appeared with information about where the Ottomans had arranged their densest concentration of troops. The intelligence reached the ears of John Smith, who begged to be allowed to try another novelty on their enemy. Smith's devices, which he called 'fiery dragons', were nothing particularly new. They consisted of delayed action bombs flung into the city by primitive catapults. They were filled with bullets and shards of iron to make them into anti-personnel weapons. But they were enough of a novelty in Hungary in 1600 for Smith to write about their efficacy as follows:

> It was a fearful sight at midnight to see the short flaming course of their flight in the air, but presently after their fall the lamentable noise of the miserable slaughtered Turks was most wonderful to hear.

Besides the loss of life caused by the bombs themselves and their deadly contents (which may not have been very great) the missiles caused fires inside the town. Had an attack been launched at that very moment it may well have succeeded. Instead some more time was to pass before Stuhlweissenberg surrendered, and before that happened Smith was engaged in a major battle with an Ottoman relief army. The Duc de Mercoeur underestimated the force brought against him, and soon Smith and his men were surrounded by 'half-circular regiments of Turks' and thought that they were lost. But by a great effort they cut their way through the Ottoman lines and made such headway 'that it was a terror to see how horse and man lay sprawling and tumbling, some one way, some another on the ground'. Smith's immediate commander, Earl Meldritch, 'made his valour shine more bright than his armour, which was painted with Turkish blood'. Half his regiment was slain. Smith was badly wounded and had lost his horse, but not for long, as he reminds us that there 'were many riderless horses that day'. After this excitement Smith and his colleagues, secure in the possession of Stuhlweissenberg, retired to winter quarters.

John Smith the Champion

The next we hear of our hero is the year 1603, and the place a castle that Smith calls Reigall, probably identified with Rudaly, a minor fortress near Sighisoara in present-day Romania. In 1601 the pro-Ottoman Stefan Bocksai had been elected Prince of Transylvania. His support helped in a final flourish of Turkish success so that in the course of 1603 the Ottomans retook Gran, Visegrad and Veszprem. In Transylvania itself honours were more evenly matched, and in one of these encounters fought Captain John Smith.

The Siege of Rudaly proved so tedious for both sides that the Turkish garrison challenged the Christian besiegers to what can only be described as a tournament. This was a common occurrence during the Middle Ages, but was an almost unheard of anachronism during the reign of King James I. The challenge was delivered in fine style: the besiegers were invited to put forward a champion who would engage a 'Turk' in single combat. The choice of whom to send was settled by drawing lots, and the lucky name out of the hat was Smith's, so our hero rode forth – transformed from soldier of fortune into chivalrous knight.

Whatever chivalric gloss may have been given to the bout, the single combat was in deadly earnest and was to be fought to the death. The fatal joust was brief, because on the first charge Smith drove his spear straight through the helmet and head of the Ottoman, who fell dead to the ground. Smith, in a rather unnecessary and bloodthirsty extension to the affair, promptly cut off the man's head and returned with it to the Christian camp. A comrade of the fallen man then issued a further challenge to Smith to fight him in revenge for his friend. Smith accepted, but this time both lances shattered on first impact. The Ottoman was almost unhorsed but regained his balance. The encounter then 'fast-forwarded' into the seventeenth century when pistols were drawn and each fired a bullet at the other. The Ottoman bullet struck home on Smith, but missed any vital area. Smith's bullet was better on target and hit his enemy on his bridle arm. He could no longer control his horse and fell to the ground. As the agreement had been to fight without quarter Smith finished him off.

It was a bloody end to a very serious contest, and a far cry from the chivalrous contest that many of the onlookers may have been expecting. But there was another combat in store for Smith as the siege dragged on. This time his Turkish opponent named his choice of weapons as pistols and battle axes. Both pistol shots missed, so the combat continued with battle axes from horseback. The two opponents rained blows on each other until Smith lost his grip and his axe fell to the floor. The besieging side gave him up for dead, but Smith managed to draw his sword and ran his opponent through. The town of Rudaly eventually fell, but Smith's triumph was more personal, and expressed through heraldry as he acquired the coat of arms of three 'Turk's heads'. Smith's adventures then took him to the neighbouring province of Wallachia, where he had another opportunity to put into operation one of his stratagems:

> . . . for having accommodated two or three hundred trunks with wild fire upon the heads of lances, and charging the enemy in the night, gave fire to the trunks, which blazed forth such flames and sparkles that it so amazed not only their horses but their foot also and their own horses, by means of this flaming encounter, turned tails with such fury as by their violence.

But this time Smith's stratagem proved to be little more than a gimmick as the Turks triumphed and slaughtered their opponents. Smith lay among those left for dead on the battlefield. Happily for posterity, when camp followers were plundering the bodies he was found to be still breathing. The quality of his armour suggested a man worth ransoming, so he was taken from the field and nursed back to health. After more adventures of a less martial kind he returned to England.

Smith's active military life in Turkey was now over, but the war had anyway not long to run. Both sides were now ready for a settlement, and the result was the Peace of Zsitva–Torok, signed in 1606, which brought to an end the bloody Thirteen Years War – the 'slaughterhouse of men'.

Epilogue

'Some new trick . . .'

The first decade of the seventeenth century saw a number of prolonged armed conflicts come to an end. The war between the Dutch Republic and Spain was interrupted in 1609 by a twelve-year truce, while the Thirteen Years War with the Ottomans ended with the Treat of Zsitva–Torok in 1606. But the peace was uneasy, and much war was to come.[1]

The new flashpoint turned out to be the city of Prague. In 1617 Emperor Matthias placed his heir-apparent, Ferdinand, on the throne of Bohemia. Ferdinand was a staunch Catholic, but he ignored the entreaties of his advisers to enact religious edicts aimed against Protestants. In spite of their monarch's generosity, in May 1618 a group of Protestant nobles broke into Hradcany Castle in Prague and threw Ferdinand's advisers out of a window. This act, the 'Second Defenestration of Prague' – a similar outrage having launched the Hussite Rebellion in 1419 – is regarded as marking the outbreak of the Thirty Years War.

This long and sanguinary contest is often seen as a turning-point in military development. With so much at stake it could hardly have been otherwise: any successful commander had to be thoroughly conversant with new developments, but, just as was seen during the sixteenth century, many of these supposed innovations were soundly based on what had gone before. The European Countermarch system of the Dutch is a case in point. Sweden had experienced a disastrous 'false start' prior to the Battle of Kircholm. Proof of its efficacy came two decades later under Sweden's King Gustav II Adolf, better known as Gustavus Adolphus of Sweden, who made the system his own, to devastating effect. That, to many writers, was the essence of the military revolution.[2]

Yet Sweden was not the only state to have received advice and help from the Dutch Republic. Their advisers had also worked in such places as Brandenburg, Baden and Saxony.[3] Furthermore, although respect for the Dutch system was almost universal, there was a clear recognition that it could only succeed with good-uality troops and leaders. Poor-quality troops, who either could not or would not be drilled, were still manoeuvred in *tercios* during the Thirty Years War. This may appear to be an act of desperation, but it is important to note that *tercios* had shrunk in size since the 1580s, and although clumsy did not require the complex training in the Dutch system to execute a move to receive an attack in flank.[4] They could also 'crash into action, though at a foot pace'.[5]

In 1626, at the Battle of Mewe (now Gniew in Poland), Gustavus Adolphus's infantry took on the Polish cavalry whom he admired so much, and beat back four charges over three days of fighting. Only one Polish cavalry offensive succeeded, and that was when their charge was launched after the first Swedish salvo, before the musketeers had time to reload. The Swedish success was due partly to drill, partly to the increased hitting power of their muskets (although remarkably few Polish hussars were actually killed) and partly to Gustavus Adolphus's stubborn refusal to allow the Polish cavalry any opportunity to fight on ground of their own choosing. This latter tactic involved the use of field fortifications in a tradition that went back to Cerignola.[6]

Gustavus Adolphus is also credited with reviving the offensive role of cavalry, requiring them to attack at the gallop, fire their pistols and then draw their swords, the inspiration for which he is said to have received from seeing the Polish hussars in action.[7] But such a glorious demonstration was not always to be seen when the Swedes were in action. Gustavus Adolphus still used the *caracole* on occasions, and on others the ideal cavalry attack was delivered in a much-diluted form. The front ranks discharged one pistol each, while the second rank went in with their swords, retaining their pistols for close-quarter use within the mêlée.[8] With all these qualifications, it is not surprising that Roberts's initial theory about Gustavus Adolphus and his military revolution has come in for some criticism. Unfortunately, several of these critics have overlooked the fact that Roberts was aware of these points and in fact discussed them at great length.[9]

In spite of all these notes of caution, however, it is clear that warfare in the 1620s looked very different from the picture it had presented in 1453. In that year gunpowder had achieved its most public, if not its most devastating, triumph to date. To the popular mind this one innovation – gunpowder – is credited with destroying feudalism single-handed by laying low castle wall and mounted knight alike, ending the romantic Middle Ages in a clap of thunder.[10] Certainly, the progression via Mons Meg, Charles VIII's artillery train, angle bastions, wheel-lock pistols and Dutch drill manuals indicates that by the first decade of the seventeenth century the stench of gunpowder was everywhere.

It is, however, also abundantly clear that by the age of Gustavus Adolphus expressions of regret at gunpowder's introduction had long since ceased – a small, though telling, footnote involving attitudes towards a military revolution. Here we see a very marked contrast to the previous century, when such negative views echoed the experiences of many of those who suffered personally from its effects. To them, gunpowder appeared to be a device of the devil invented by foreigners, heretics, monks or anyone else whom the writer regarded as an accomplice in the black arts. A certain element of social snobbery came into it, too, because it was reckoned that gunpowder destroyed noble knights by hands that were often anonymous and cowardly.

As we noted earlier, arquebus balls propelled by gunpowder cut short the lives and careers of the *Chevalier* Bayard, Miklos Zrinyi and François de la Noue. Yet, while mourning their particular loss, we may also give thanks that out of the scores of bullets that must have headed in the direction of a particular Spanish galley during the Battle of Lepanto in 1571, only one struck home against the person of Don Miguel de Cervantes. It lost him the use of his hand, but allowed him to survive to bring us the fictional knight Don Quixote, whose role as a symbol for the decline of knightly values and behaviour surpasses any living exemplar. Not even Blaise de Monluc, the eloquent Gascon who denounced the invention that removed half his face,[11] can quite equal the torrent of hatred against guns that Cervantes puts into the mouth of his ill-made knight:

> Blessed were the times which lacked the dreadful fury of those diabolical engines, the artillery, whose inventor I firmly believe is now receiving the reward for his devilish invention in hell; an invention which allows a base and cowardly hand to take the life of a brave knight, in such a way that, without knowing how or why, when his valiant heart is full of courage, there comes some random shot – discharged perhaps by a man who fled in terror from the flash the accursed machine made in firing – and puts an end in a moment to the consciousness of one who deserved to enjoy life for many an age.[12]

This supreme fictional condemnation of that which was too horrible to own, and yet too important to reject, found genuine echoes in the real world. In 1537 Vanuccio Biringuccio wrote the first detailed treatise on artillery and was so shocked by the picture his analysis presented that he burned the manuscript – only to write it out again quickly and send it to the printers when rumours reached him of Sultan Suleiman's latest advance towards Vienna. The manuscript was eventually published as *De la Pirotechnia* in 1540 in Venice.[13]

This *realpolitik* of artillery was always a powerful counter to the Quixotic view, and no commander could ignore the potential of guns. The argument always came down to this, that if the Turks/Protestants/Corsairs etc had them, then we, as the forces of righteousness, would be failing in our moral duty if we did not match them bullet for bullet, round for round. If any moral qualms remained, then the Church's teaching could always be invoked, particularly that inspired choice that had given artillerymen their own patron saint. St Barbara was chosen because, at the moment of her martyrdom, her father who denounced her was struck down by thunder and lightning. Gunners were encouraged to invoke the name of St Barbara when loading their cannons. Other warriors wore images of her on their armour, presumably in the belief that any ball that was fired after two opposing invocations might be expected to deviate considerably from its chosen flight path.[14]

Guns may have been the weapons of cowards and poltroons, discharged without thought, aim or honourable intent, although only the greater range of an arquebus ball made it any less anonymous or random than an arrow. But this argument did not lead to arms control. The successful commander may have condemned firearms in public, but he embraced them in private. Leaders of men had, after all, been advised as early as 1502 by a certain Robert de Balsac that when a prince went to war his first consideration should be that his cause was just; the second consideration was whether or not he had enough artillery.[15] Thus it is that on the bas-relief on the outside walls of the palace in Granada of the Holy Roman Emperor Charles V there are images of cannons, arranged as gracefully as any classical montage of Corinthian helmets or Roman spears. They are also to be found on the side of the tomb of his arch-enemy and rival, King Francis I France, in the Basilica of St Denis. Next to the king's cannons are carvings of Swiss pikemen, the arquebusiers and the fully armoured knights that a lead Francis used alongside his artillery in ways that showed his understanding the strengths and weaknesses of any military technology, old or new. To position of decision-making, the essence of a military revolution consist the resources at your disposal in a way that your opponent's persona prevented him from anticipating. Revolutions are unexpected. So, is defeat or victory.

The French king's appreciation that the military revolution process subject to environment, technology and human natu identified by the skilled commander and used to his advant was not overlooked by others. Perhaps therefore the last w tain Krzystof Radziwill, who, in addition to fighting for its terrifying cavalry, had also witnessed western warfa observed the 1603 Siege of s'Hertogenbosch by Mauric his king that:

Antiquity has its virtues; domestic methods have great value, but in military affairs less than in others: every century teaches soldiers some new trick; every campaign has its own discoveries; each school of war seeks its own remedies.[16]

The century and a half between 1453 and 1618 had seen many a 'new trick'. More were to be played in the years that lay ahead.

Notes

Introduction

1 A. Vasiliev, 'Pero Tafur, A Spanish Traveller of the Fifteenth Century and His Visit to Constantinople, Trebizond and Italy', *Byzantion*, 7 (1932), pp. 75–122.
2 Vasiliev, pp. 115–16.
3 J. R. Hale, *Artists and Warfare in the Renaissance*, Yale, 1990.
4 J. R. Hale, *War and Society in Renaissance Europe 1450–1620*, London, 1985.
5 Stephen Turnbull, *The Knight Triumphant*, London, 2001.
6 Hale, *War and Society*, p. 13.
7 Michael Roberts, *Essays in Swedish History*, London, 1967, pp. 56–81.
8 Geoffrey Parker, *The Military Revolution: Military Innovation and the Rise of the West 1500–1800*, Cambridge, 1988.
9 Jeremy Black, *European Warfare, 1494–1660*, London, 2002, p. 57.

Chapter 1 A Tale of Two Cities

1 The 1422 siege is covered in N. H. Baynes, 'The Supernatural Defenders of Constantinople' in N. H. Baynes, *Byzantine Studies and Other Essays*, London, 1955. D. M. Nicol, *The Last Centuries of Byzantium*, London, 1972. E. Pinto (trans. and ed.), *Giovanni Cananos: De Constantinopolis Obsidieone*, Naples, 1968.
2 Franz Babinger, *Mehmed the Conqueror and His Time*, Princeton, 1978.
3 Dorothy M. Vaughan, *Europe and the Turk: A Pattern of Alliances 1350–1700*, Liverpool, 1954, p. 53.
4 Edwin Pears, *The Destruction of the Greek Empire and the Story of the Capture of Constantinople by the Turks*, London, 1903, p. 176.
5 Richard Vaughan, *Philip the Good: The Apogee of Burgundy*, Harlow, 1970.
6 Dorothy M. Vaughan, p.45.
7 Stephen Turnbull, *The Walls of Constantinople AD 324–1453*, Oxford, 2004.
8 Babinger, p. 75.
9 For a very thorough discussion see Kelly de Vries, 'Gunpowder Weapons at the Siege of Constantinople, 1453' in Yaacov Lev, *War and Society in the Eastern Mediterranean, Seventh to Fifteenth Centuries*, Leiden, 1997. See also Gabor Agoston, 'Ottoman Warfare in Europe 1453–1826' in Jeremy Black (ed.), *European Warfare 1453–1815*, Basingstoke, 1999.
10 De Vries, p. 356.
11 De Vries, p. 356.
12 De Vries, p. 357.
13 Babinger, p. 86.
14 Steven Runciman, *The Fall of Constantinople 1453*, Cambridge, 1965, p. 133.
15 Dorothy M. Vaughan, p. 70.
16 Richard Vaughan, p. 121.

17   R. N. Bain, 'The Siege of Belgrade by Muhammad II, July 1–23, 1456' *English Historical Review*, VII (1892), pp. 235–52. Camil Mureşanu, *John Hunyadi: Defender of Christendom*, Iasi, 2001. Joseph Held, *Hunyadi: Legend and Reality*, New York, 1985.

18   Konstantin Mihailovic, *Memoirs of a Janissary* (translated by Benjamin Stolz; historical commentary and notes by Svat Soucek), Ann Arbor, 1975.

19   Bain, pp. 243–24.

20   Mihailovic, p. 107.

21   Mihailovic, p. 107.

22   Held, p. 159.

23   Mureşanu, p. 196.

24   Mihailovic, p. 108.

Chapter 2 Of Powder and Pikes

1   Robert D. Smith and Ruth Rhynas Brown, *Bombards: Mons Meg and Her Sisters*, Royal Armouries Monograph 1, London, 1989.

2   Cited in Kelly de Vries, *Medieval Military Technology*, Peterborough, Ontario, 1992, p. 145. Unfortunately Odruik cannot be precisely located.

3   Richard Vaughan, *Philip the Good: The Apogee of Burgundy*, Harlow, 1970, p. 34.

4   De Vries, p. 148.

5   Richard Vaughan, *Charles the Bold: The Last Valois Duke of Burgundy*, London, 1973, pp. 300–01.

6   Smith and Brown, p. 5.

7   Vaughan, *Charles the Bold*, p. 76.

8   Kelly de Vries, 'Gunpowder Weaponry and the Rise of the Early Modern State', *War in History*, 5 (1998), p. 138.

9   Benjamin Geiger, *Les Guerres de Bourgogne: La Bataille de Grandson, 1476, La Bataille de Morat, 1476*, Bern, 1996.

10   Geiger, pp. 12–16.

11   Vaughan, *Charles the Bold*, p. 375.

12   Vaughan, *Charles the Bold*, pp. 377–8.

13   Vaughan, *Charles the Bold*, p. 389.

14   Geiger, pp. 17–24.

15   Vaughan, *Charles the Bold*, p. 403.

Chapter 3 The Guns of Granada

1   William H. Prescott, *The Art of War in Spain: The Conquest of Granada 1481–1492* (edited by Albert D. McJoynt), London, 1995.

2   Gerald de Gaury, *The Grand Captain: Gonzalo de Cordoba*, London, 1955.

3   Bert S. Hall, *Weapons and Warfare in Renaissance Europe: Gunpowder, Technology and Tactics*, Baltimore, 1997, pp. 123–30.

4   Prescott, p. 140.

5   Prescott, p. 142.

6   De Gaury, p. 19.

7   Hall, pp. 125–6.

8   Quoted in Hall, pp. 125–6.

9   Prescott, pp. 197–214.

10   Hall, p. 127.

11   Prescott, pp. 234–52.

12   De Gaury, pp. 34–5.

Chapter 4 Breaking the Square

1   Charles Oman, *A History of the Art of War in the Middle Ages, Volume Two 1278–1485*, London, 1924, p. 274.

2   Frederick Taylor, *The Art of War in Italy 1494–1529*, Cambridge, 1921. Charles Oman, *A History of the Art of War in the Sixteenth Century*, London, 1937, pp. 105–207. J. R. Hale, 'War and Public Opinion in Renaissance Italy' in J. R. Hale (ed.), *Renaissance War Studies*, London, 1983, pp. 359–87. Jeremy Black, *European Warfare, 1494–1660*, London, 2002, pp. 71–80.

3   Simon Pepper, 'Castles and Cannon in the Naples Campaign of 1494–95' in D. Abulafia (ed.), *The French Descent into Renaissance Italy, 1494–95: Antecedents and Effects*, Aldershot, 1995, pp. 263–93.

4   Black, p. 71.

5   Hale, p. 359.

6   Gerald de Gaury, *The Grand Captain: Gonzalo de Cordoba*, London, 1955.

7   Taylor, p. 37.

8   Charles Oman, *A History of the Art of War in the Sixteenth Century*, London, 1937, p. 53. Taylor, pp. 44–5.

9   Oman, *A History of the Art of War in the Sixteenth Century*, pp. 53–4.

10 Black, p. 72.

11 Oman, *A History of the Art of War in the Sixteenth Century*, pp. 130–50.

12 Blaise de Monluc, *Commentaires 1521–1576* (edited by Jean Giono and Paul CourtrJault), Paris, 1964, p. 158.

13 Black, p. 74.

14 Oman, *A History of the Art of War in the Sixteenth Century*, p. 168.

15 Oman, *A History of the Art of War in the Sixteenth Century*, pp. 173–16. David Eltis *The Military Revolution in Sixteenth-Century Europe*, London, 1995, p. 52.

16 Oman, *A History of the Art of War in the Sixteenth Century*, p. 44.

17 Michael Roberts, *Essays in Swedish History*, London, 1967, p. 58.

18 Ian Roy (trans. and ed.), *Blaise de Monluc*, London, 1971, pp. 104–17. Oman, *A History of the Art of War in the Sixteenth Century*, pp. 231–40.

Chapter 5 The Laboratory of Siege Warfare

1   David Eltis, *The Military Revolution in Sixteenth-Century Europe*, London, 1995, p. 77.

2   Kelly de Vries, *Medieval Military Technology*, Peterborough, Ontario, 1992. A. Curry and M. Hughes (eds.), *Arms, Armies and Fortifications in the Hundred Years' War*, Woodbridge, 1994. J. R. Hale, 'Gunpowder and the Renaissance: An Essay in the History of Ideas' in J. R. Hale (ed.), *Renaissance War Studies*, London, 1983, pp. 389–420. Volker Schmidtchen, 'Castles, Cannon and Casemates', *Fortress*, 3 (1992), pp. 3–10.

3   Simon Pepper, 'Castles and Cannon in the Naples Campaign of 1494–95' in D. Abulafia (ed.), *The French Descent into Renaissance Italy, 1494–95: Antecedents and Effects*, Aldershot, 1995, pp. 263–93. Ben Cassidy, 'Machiavelli and the Ideology of the Offensive: Gunpowder Weapons in The Art of War', *Journal of Military History*, 67 (April 2003), pp. 381–404.

4   Francesco Guicciardini, *The History of Italy* (trans. Chevalier Austin Parke Goddard), Vol. 1, London, 1754, p. 148.

5   Guicciardini, p. 148.

6   Eric Brockman, *The Two Sieges of Rhodes*, London, 1969. Walter J. Karcheski Jr and Thom Richardson, *The Medieval Armour from Rhodes*, Leeds, 2000. B. H. St. J. O'Neil, 'Rhodes and the Origin of the Bastion', *The Antiquaries Journal*, 45 (1966), pp. 44–54. Anna–Maria Kasdagli and Katerina Maoussou–Delta, 'The Defences of Rhodes and the Tower of St John', *Fort*, 24 (1996), pp. 15–35. Quentin Hughes and Athanassios Migos, 'Rhodes: The Turkish Siege', *Fort* (1993), pp. 3–17. Athanassios Mignos, 'Rhodes: the Knights' Battleground', *Fort*, 18 (1990), pp. 5–28.

7   O'Neil, p.53.

Chapter 6 'God gave the sea to the infidels . . .'

1   Quoted in Andrew C. Hess, 'The Road to Victory: The Significance of Mohacs for Ottoman Expansion' in Janos M. Bak and Bela K. Kiraly (eds.), *From Hunyadi to Rakoczi: War and Society in Late Medieval and Early Modern Hungary*, New York, 1982, pp. 179–88.
2   Robert Gardiner (ed.), *The Age of the Galley: Mediterranean Oared Vessels Since Pre-Classical Times*, London, 1995. John F. Guilmartin, *Gunpowder and Galleys: Changing Technology and Mediterranean Warfare at Sea 1500–1650*, Cambridge, 1974. J. R. Hale, 'Men and Weapons: The Fighting Potential of Sixteenth-Century Renaissance Galleys' in J. R. Hale (ed.), *Renaissance War Studies*, London, 1983, pp. 309–31. Gregory Hanlon, *The Twilight of a Military Tradition: Italian Aristocrats and European Conflicts 1560–1800*, Halifax, Nova Scotia, 1998.
3   Hale, p. 324.
4   Hale, p. 323.
5   Andrew C. Hess, *The Forgotten Frontier: A History of the Sixteenth-Century Ibero–African Frontier*, Chicago, 1978.
6   E. H. Curry, *Sea Wolves*, London, 1962, p. 159.
7   Hale, p. 327.
8   Angus Konstam, *Lepanto 1571*, Oxford, 2003.

Chapter 7 '. . . and the land to the Muslims'

1   Andrew C. Hess, 'The Road to Victory: The Significance of Mohacs for Ottoman Expansion' in Janos M. Bak and Bela K. Kiraly (eds.), *From Hunyadi to Rakoczi: War and Society in Late Medieval and Early Modern Hungary*, New York, 1982, pp. 179–88. Laszlo M. Alfoldi, 'The Battle of Mohacs, 1526' in Bak and Kiraly (eds.), pp.190–203. Leslie S. Domonkos, 'The Battle of Mohacs as a Cultural Watershed' in Bak and Kiraly (eds.), pp. 204–24.
2   Roger Bigelow, *Suleiman the Magnificent 1520–1566*, London, 1978. André Clot (tr. Matthew J. Reisz), *Suleiman the Magnificent*, London, 2005.
3   Bigelow, p. 54.
4   Bigelow, p. 91.
5   Bigelow, p. 92.
6   Bigelow, p. 92.
7   Bigelow, p. 93.
8   Lajos Ruzsas, 'The Siege of Szigetvar of 1566: Its Significance in Hungarian Social Development' in Bak and Kiraly (eds.), pp. 251–60.

Chapter 8 The Bastion Wars

1   R. E. Role, 'Le Mura: Lucca's Fortified Enceinte', *Fort*, 25 (1997), p. 83.
2   A. N. Waldron, 'The Problem of the Great Wall of China', *Harvard Journal of Asian Studies*, 43, 2 (1983), p. 659.
3   David Parrot, 'The Utility of Fortifications in Early Modern Europe – Italian Princes and Their Citadels 1540–1690', *War in History*, 7 (2000), p. 127.
4   Jeremy Black, *European Warfare, 1494–1660*, London, 2002. p. 95.
5   John Childs, *Armies and Warfare in Europe 1648–1789*, Manchester, 1982, p. 136.
6   John A. Lynn, 'The *Trace Italienne* and the Growth of Armies: The French Case', *The Journal of Military History*, 55 (July 1991), pp. 297–330.
7   Christopher Duffy, *Siege Warfare: The Fortress in the Early Modern World 1494–1660*, London, 1979, p. 125.
8   J. R. Hale, *Renaissance Fortification: Art or Engineering?*, London, 1977. J. R. Hale, 'The Early

Development of the Bastion: An Italian Chronology *c.*1450–1534' in J. R. Hale (ed.), *Renaissance War Studies*, London, 1983, pp. 1–29.

9   Hale, *Renaissance Fortification*, p. 12.

10 Hale, 'The Early Development of the Bastion', p. 2.

11 Robert I. Frost, *The Northern Wars 1558–1721*, London, 2000, p. 23.

12 Sir George Hill, *A History of Cyprus*, Cambridge, 1948, is the major source for the account of the Cyprus operations.

13 Jeremy Black (ed.), *European Warfare 1453–1815*, Basingstoke, 1999, p. 32.

14 Hill, p. 998.

15 Thomas Arnold, 'War in Sixteenth-Century Europe: Revolution and Renaissance' in Jeremy Black (ed.), *European Warfare 1453–1815*, Basingstoke, 1999, p. 33.

Chapter 9 Knights Old and New

1   Hans Delbrück, *History of War: Within the Framework of Political History. Volume IV The Modern Era*, London, 1985, p. 117.

2   Delbrück, p. 118.

3   Charles Oman, *A History of the Art of War in the Sixteenth Century*, London, 1937, p. 146.

4   Charles Cruikshank, *Henry VIII and the Invasion of France*, Stroud, 1990. Mark Charles Fissel, *English Warfare 1511–1642*, London, 2001.

5   A. H. Burne, *The Battlefields of England*, London, 2002, p. 313.

6   Oman, p. 295.

7   Blaise de Monluc, *Commentaires 1521–1576* (edited by Jean Giono and Paul Courtréault), Paris, 1964. Ian Roy (trans. and ed.), *Blaise de Monluc*, London, 1971.

8   Roy, p. 53.

9   Roy, p. 53.

10 Roy, p. 117.

11 Oman, p. 347.

12 Roy, p. 164.

13 Roy, p. 165.

14 Roy, pp. 53, 178–94.

15 John A. Lynn, 'Tactical Evolution in the French Army, 1560–1660', *French Historical Studies*, 14 (1985), pp. 176–91.

16 Roy, p. 208.

17 Roy, p. 223.

18 J. R. Hale, 'Gunpowder and the Renaissance: An Essay in the History of Ideas' in J. R. Hale (ed.), *Renaissance War Studies*, London, 1983, p. 397.

19 François de la Noue, *Discours Politiques et Militaires* (ed. F. E. Sutcliffe), Geneva, 1967.

20 Delbrück, p. 123.

21 James B. Wood, *The King's Army: Warfare, Soldiers and Society During the Wars of Religion in France, 1562–1576*, Cambridge, 1996, pp. 246–74.

22 François de la Noue, *The Politicke and Militarie Discourses of the Lord de la Noue*, London, 1587.

Chapter 10 Black Knights and Devilish Weapons

1   François de la Noue, *The Politicke and Militarie Discourses of the Lord de la Noue*, London, 1587.

2   Bert Hall, *Weapons and Warfare in Renaissance Europe: Gunpowder, Technology and Tactics*, Baltimore, 1997, p. 191.

3   Charles Oman, *A History of the Art of War in the Sixteenth Century*, London, 1937, p. 85.

4   Michael Roberts, *Essays in Swedish History*, London, 1967, p. 57.

5   Quoted in Hall, p. 195.

6   Hans Delbrück, *History of War: Within the Framework of Political History. Volume IV The Modern Era*, London, 1985, p. 121.
7   See Chapter 14 below and Robert I. Frost, *The Northern Wars 1558–1721*, London, 2000, p. 68.
8   Hall, p. 196.
9   Delbrück, p. 121.
10   Hall, p. 197.
11   Hall, p. 198.
12   Delbrück, p. 124.
13   Oman, p. 249.
14   William S. Maltby, *Alba: A Biography of Ferdinand Alvarez de Toledo Third Duke of Alba 1507–1582*, Berkeley, 1983, p. 61.
15   Maltby, p. 62.
16   Jeremy Black, *European Warfare, 1494–1660*, London, 2002, p. 104.
17   Oman, p. 474–9.
18   Oman, p. 497.
19   Black, p. 104.

Chapter 11 Fire, Ice and Flood

1   Geoffrey Parker, *The Dutch Revolt*, London, 1985. J. H. Elliot, *Imperial Spain 1469–1716*, London, 1963. John L. Motley, *The Rise of the Dutch Republic: A History* (New Edition in One Volume), London, 1865.
2   Geoffrey Parker, *The Army of Flanders and the Spanish Road 1567–1659: The Logistics of Spanish Victory and Defeat in the Low Countries' Wars*, Cambridge, 1972.
3   Charles Oman, *A History of the Art of War in the Sixteenth Century*, London, 1937, p. 553.
4   Olaf van Nimwegen, 'Maurits van Nassau and Siege Warfare' in Marco van der Hoeven (ed.), *Exercise of Arms: Warfare in the Netherlands (1568–1648)*, Leiden, 1998, pp. 113–31.
5   Motley, p. 495.
6   Motley, p. 496.
7   Motley, p. 497.
8   Motley, p. 499.
9   Motley, p. 502.
10   Motley, p. 508.
11   Motley, p. 515.
12   Motley, p. 525.
13   Oman, pp. 561–3.

Chapter 12 Innovators and Enemies

1   Christopher Duffy, *Siege Warfare: The Fortress in the Early Modern World 1494–1660*, London, 1979, p. 68.
2   John L. Motley, *The Rise of the Dutch Republic: A History* (New Edition in One Volume), London, 1865, p. 639.
3   Duffy, p. 69.
4   Motley, p. 742.
5   Geoffrey Parker, *The Dutch Revolt*, London, 1985, pp. 193–4.
6   The source for the Antwerp siege is John L. Motley, *The United Netherlands*, Vol.1, London, 1875, pp. 147–245.
7   Jeremy Black, *European Warfare, 1494–1660*, London, 2002, p. 111.
8   Parker, *The Dutch Revolt*, p. 228.
9   Parker, *The Dutch Revolt*, p. 228.

10 Parker, *The Dutch Revolt*, p. 229.
11 Marco van der Hoeven (ed.), *Exercise of Arms: Warfare in the Netherlands (1568–1648)*, Leiden, 1998.
12 Geoffrey Parker, *The Military Revolution: Military Innovation and the Rise of the West 1500–1800*, Cambridge, 1988, p. 19.
13 Hans Delbrück, *History of War: Within the Framework of Political History. Volume IV The Modern Era*, London, 1985, p. 157.
14 Michael Roberts, *Essays in Swedish History*, London, 1967, p. 60.
15 Parker, *The Military Revolution*, p. 20.
16 Delbrück, pp. 158, 169.
17 Parker, *The Military Revolution*, p. 21.
18 Charles Oman, *A History of the Art of War in the Sixteenth Century*, London, 1937, pp. 580–2.

Chapter 13 Cavalry and Curiosities
1   Robert I. Frost, *The Northern Wars 1558–1721*, London, 2000, p. 47.
2   Norman Davies, *God's Playground: A History of Poland Volume I*, Oxford, 1981, p. 421.
3   Frost, p. 17.
4   Quote from Michael Roberts, *Essays in Swedish History*, London, 1967, p. 58. See also Michael Roberts, *Gustavus Adolphus, A History of Sweden 1611–1632, Vol. 2 1626–1632*, London, 1958, p. 180.
5   Davies, p. 429.
6   Frost, p. 1.
7   Frost, p. 23.
8   Davies, p. 429.
9   Davies, p. 429.
10 Alexander Ivanov, *Pskov: Ancient Russian City*, Pskov, 2003, p. 15.
11 Davies, p. 430.
12 George Vernadsky, *The Tsardom of Moscow 1547–1682*, London, 1969, p. 164.
13 Frost, p. 52.
14 Serge A Zenkoysky (trans.), *Medieval Russia's Epics, Chronicles and Tales*, New York, 1963, pp. 277–88.
15 Zenkoysky, p. 278.
16 Zenkoysky, p. 280.
17 Ivanov, p. 44.
18 Zenkoysky, p. 282.
19 Zenkoysky, p. 285.
20 Zenkoysky, p. 288.
21 Frost, p. 62.
22 Frost, p. 61.
23 Frost, p. 60.
24 Quoted in Christopher Duffy, *Siege Warfare: The Fortress in the Early Modern World 1494–1660*, London, 1979, p. 168.
25 Davies, p. 432.
26 Vernadsky, p. 165.

Chapter 14 The Shock of the New
1   Michael Roberts, *Gustavus Adolphus, A History of Sweden 1611–1632, Vol. 2 1626–1632*, London, 1958, p. 196. Michael Roberts, *The Early Vasas: A History of Sweden 1523–1611*, Cambridge, 1968, p. 407.
2   Robert I. Frost, *The Northern Wars 1558–1721*, London, 2000, p. 63.
3   Frost, p. 64.

4   Stanislaw Zolkiewski, *Expedition to Moscow: A Memoir* (translated from the original Polish by M. W. Stephen; introduction and notes by Jedrzej Giertych; preface by Robert Bruce Lockhart), London, 1959.
5   Zolkiewski, p. 62.
6   Zolkiewski, p. 64.
7   Zolkiewski, p. 72.
8   Zolkiewski, pp. 77–8.
9   Zolkiewski, p. 79.
10 Frost, p. 67.
11 Zolkiewski, p. 79.
12 Quoted by Frost, p. 68.
13 Michael Roberts, *Gustavus Adolphus*, p. 180.
14 Michael C. Paul, 'The Military Revolution in Russia 1550–1682', *Journal of Military History*, 68 (2004), pp. 9–46.
15 Norman Davies, *God's Playground: A History of Poland Volume I*, Oxford, 1981, p. 458.

Chapter 15 Mercenaries and Marvels

1   Dorothy M. Vaughan, *Europe and the Turk: A Pattern of Alliances 1350–1700*, Liverpool, 1954, pp. 183–6.
2   Charles Oman, *A History of the Art of War in the Sixteenth Century*, London, 1937, pp. 747–51.
3   A. G. Bradley, *Captain John Smith*, London, 1905.

Epilogue 'Some new trick . . .'

1   Ronald G. Asch, 'Warfare in the Age of the Thirty Years' War' in Jeremy Black (ed.), *European Warfare 1453–1815*, Basingstoke, 1999, p. 45.
2   Geoffrey Parker, *The Military Revolution: Military Innovation and the Rise of the West 1500–1800*, Cambridge, 1988, p. 23.
3   John Childs, *Warfare in the Seventeenth Century*, London, 2001, p. 45.
4   Michael Roberts, *Essays in Swedish History*, London, 1967, p. 62.
5   Michael Roberts, *Gustavus Adolphus, A History of Sweden 1611–1632, Vol. 2 1626–1632*, London, 1958, p. 247.
6   Robert I. Frost, *The Northern Wars 1558–1721*, London, 2000, pp. 104–6.
7   Roberts, *Gustavus Adolphus*, pp. 255–6.
8   A. Åberg, 'The Swedish Army from Lutzen to Narva' in M. Roberts (ed.), *Sweden's Age of Greatness*, London, 1973, pp 265–87. Asch, p. 53.
9   Roberts, *Gustavus Adolphus*, pp. 169–271.
10 J. F. C. Fuller, The *Decisive Battles of the Western World and Their Influence Upon History* (2 Vols), London, 1954–5, Vol I, p. 470.
11 Blaise de Monluc, *Commentaires 1521–1576* (edited by Jean Giono and Paul Courtréault), Paris, 1964.
12 Miguel de Cervantes, *Don Quixote* (English translation by J. M. Cohen), London, 1950, p. 344.
13 J. R. Hale, 'Gunpowder and the Renaissance: An Essay in the History of Ideas' in J. R. Hale (ed.), *Renaissance War Studies*, London, 1983, p. 399.
14 J. R. Hale, 'War and Public Opinion in Renaissance Italy' in Hale (ed.) *Renaissance War Studies*, p. 367.
15 From his *Nef des Princes de Batailles* quoted in Hale (ed.), *Renaissance War Studies*, p. 401.
16 Frost, p. 107.

Bibliography

Åberg, A. 'The Swedish Army from Lutzen to Narva' in M. Roberts (ed.), *Sweden's Age of Greatness*, London, 1973, pp. 265–87.

Abulafia (ed.), D. *The French Descent into Renaissance Italy, 1494–95: Antecedents and Effects*, Aldershot, 1995.

Agoston, Gabor 'Ottoman Warfare in Europe 1453–1826' in Jeremy Black (ed.) *European Warfare 1453–1815*, Basingstoke, 1999.

Alfoldi, Laszlo M. 'The Battle of Mohacs, 1526' in Janos M. Bak and Bela K. Kiraly (eds.), *From Hunyadi to Rakoczi: War and Society in Late Medieval and Early Modern Hungary*, New York, 1982, pp. 190–203.

Arnold, Thomas 'War in Sixteenth-Century Europe: Revolution and Renaissance' in Jeremy Black (ed.) *European Warfare 1453–1815*, Basingstoke, 1999, pp. 23–44.

Asch, Ronald G. 'Warfare in the Age of the Thirty Years' War' in Jeremy Black (ed.) *European Warfare 1453–1815*, Basingstoke, 1999, pp. 45–68.

Babinger, Franz *Mehmed the Conqueror and His Time*, Princeton, 1978.

Bain, R. N. 'The Siege of Belgrade by Muhammad II July 1–23, 1456', *English Historical Review*, VII (1892), pp. 235–52.

Bak, Janos M. and Kiraly, Bela K. (eds.), *From Hunyadi to Rakoczi: War and Society in Late Medieval and Early Modern Hungary*, New York, 1982.

Baynes, N. H. 'The Supernatural Defenders of Constantinople' in N. H. Baynes, *Byzantine Studies and Other Essays*, London, 1955.

Bigelow, Roger *Suleiman the Magnificent 1520–1566*, London, 1978.

Black, Jeremy (ed.) *European Warfare 1453–1815*, Basingstoke, 1999.

Black, Jeremy *European Warfare, 1494–1660*, London, 2002.

Bradley, A. G. *Captain John Smith*, London, 1905.

Brockman, Eric *The Two Sieges of Rhodes*, London, 1969.

Burne, A. H. *The Battlefields of England*, London, 2002.

Cassidy, Ben 'Machiavelli and the Ideology of the Offensive: Gunpowder Weapons in The Art of War', *Journal of Military History*, 67 (April 2003), pp. 381–404.

Childs, John *Armies and Warfare in Europe 1648–1789*, Manchester, 1982.

Warfare in the Seventeenth Century, London, 2001.

Clot, André (tr. Matthew J. Reisz) *Suleiman the Magnificent*, London, 2005.

Coles, Paul *The Ottoman Impact on Europe*, London, 1968.

Cruikshank, Charles *Henry VIII and the Invasion of France*, Stroud, 1990.

Curry, A. and Hughes, M. (eds.) *Arms, Armies and Fortifications in the Hundred Years' War*, Woodbridge, 1994.

Curry, E. H. *Sea Wolves*, London, 1962, p.159.

Davies, Norman *God's Playground: A History of Poland Volume I*, Oxford, 1981.

De Cervantes, Miguel *Don Quixote* (English translation by J. M. Cohen), London, 1950.

De Gaury, Gerald *The Grand Captain: Gonzalo de Cordoba*, London, 1955.

De la Noue, François *Discours Politiques et Militaires* (ed. F. E. Sutcliffe), Geneva, 1967.

The Politicke and Militarie Discourses of the Lord de la Noue, London, 1587.

De Monluc, Blaise *Commentaires 1521–1576* (edited by Jean Giono and Paul Courtréault), Paris, 1964.

De Vries, Kelly *Medieval Military Technology*, Peterborough, Ontario, 1992.

'Gunpowder Weapons at the Siege of Constantinople, 1453' in Yaacov Lev, *War and Society in the Eastern Mediterranean, Seventh to Fifteenth Centuries*, Leiden, 1997.

'Gunpowder Weaponry and the Rise of the Early Modern State', *War in History*, 5 (1998), pp. 127–47.

Delbrück, Hans *History of War: Within the Framework of Political History. Volume IV The Modern Era*, London, 1985.

Domonkos, Leslie S. 'The Battle of Mohacs as a Cultural Watershed' in Janos M. Bak and Bela K. Kiraly (eds.), *From Hunyadi to Rakoczi: War and Society in Late Medieval and Early Modern Hungary*, New York, 1982, pp. 204–24.

Duffy, Christopher *Siege Warfare: The Fortress in the Early Modern World 1494–1660*, London, 1979.

Elliot, J.J. H. *Imperial Spain 1469–1716*, London, 1963.

Eltis, David *The Military Revolution in Sixteenth-Century Europe*, London, 1995.

Esson, D. M. R. 'The Italian Campaigns of Gonsalvo de Cordoba', *Army Quarterly*, 80 (1959–60), pp. 235–46.

Fissel, Mark Charles *English Warfare 1511–1642*, London, 2001.

Frost, Robert I. *The Northern Wars 1558–1721*, London, 2000.

Fuller, J. F. C. The *Decisive Battles of the Western World and Their Influence Upon History* (2 Vols), London, 1954–5.

Gardiner, Robert (ed.) *The Age of the Galley: Mediterranean Oared Vessels Since Pre-Classical Times*, London, 1995.

Geiger, Benjamin *Les Guerres de Bourgogne: La Bataille de Grandson, 1476, La Bataille de Morat, 1476*, Bern, 1996.

Guicciardini, Francesco *The History of Italy* (trans. Chevalier Austin Parke Goddard), Vol. 1, London, 1754, p. 148.

Guilmartin, John F. *Gunpowder and Galleys: Changing Technology and Mediterranean Warfare at Sea 1500–1650*, Cambridge, 1974.

Hale, J. R. *Renaissance Fortification: Art or Engineering?*, London, 1977.

'The Early Development of the Bastion: An Italian Chronology c.1450–1534' in J. R. Hale (ed.), *Renaissance War Studies*, London, 1983, pp. 1–29.

'Men and Weapons: The Fighting Potential of Sixteenth-Century Renaissance Galleys' in J. R. Hale (ed.), *Renaissance War Studies*, London, 1983, pp. 309–31.

'War and Public Opinion in Renaissance Italy' in J. R. Hale (ed.), *Renaissance War Studies*, London, 1983, pp. 359–87.

'Gunpowder and the Renaissance: An Essay in the History of Ideas' in J. R. Hale (ed.), *Renaissance War Studies*, London, 1983, pp. 389–420.

War and Society in Renaissance Europe 1450–1620, London, 1985.

Artists and Warfare in the Renaissance, Yale, 1990.

Hall, Bert *Weapons and Warfare in Renaissance Europe: Gunpowder, Technology and Tactics*, Baltimore, 1997.

Hanlon, Gregory *The Twilight of a Military Tradition: Italian Aristocrats and European Conflicts 1560–1800*, Halifax, Nova Scotia, 1998.

Held, Joseph *Hunyadi, Legend and Reality*, New York, 1985.

Hess, Andrew C. *The Forgotten Frontier: A History of the Sixteenth-Century Ibero-African Frontier*, Chicago, 1978.
　'The Road to Victory: The Significance of Mohacs for Ottoman Expansion' in Janos M. Bak and Bela K. Kiraly (eds.), *From Hunyadi to Rakoczi: War and Society in Late Medieval and Early Modern Hungary*, New York, 1982, pp. 179–88.
Hill, Sir George *A History of Cyprus*, Cambridge, 1948.
Hughes, Quentin and Migos, Athanassios 'Rhodes: The Turkish Siege', *Fort*, 1993, pp. 3–17.
Hunczak, Taras *Russian Imperialism from Ivan the Great to the Revolution*, New Brunswick, NJ, 1974.
Ivanov, Alexander *Pskov: Ancient Russian City*, Pskov, 2003.
Karcheski Jr, Walter J. and Richardson, Thom *The Medieval Armour from Rhodes*, Leeds, 2000.
Kasdagli, Anna-Maria and Maoussou-Delta, Katerina 'The Defences of Rhodes and the Tower of St John', *Fort*, 24 (1996), pp. 15–35.
Konstam, Angus *Lepanto 1571*, Oxford, 2003.
Lynn, John A. 'Tactical Evolution in the French Army, 1560–1660', *French Historical Studies*, 14 (1985), pp. 176–91.
　'The *Trace Italienne* and the Growth of Armies: The French Case', *The Journal of Military History*, 55 (July 1991), pp. 297–330.
Mallet, Michael *Mercenaries and Their Masters*, London, 1974.
Maltby, William S. *Alba: A Biography of Ferdinand Alvarez de Toledo Third Duke of Alba 1507–1582*, Berkeley, 1983.
Mignos, Athanassios 'Rhodes: the Knights' Battleground', *Fort*, 18 (1990), pp. 5–28.
Mihailovic, Konstantin *Memoirs of a Janissary* (translated by Benjamin Stolz; historical commentary and notes by Svat Soucek), Ann Arbor, 1975.
Motley, John L. *The Rise of the Dutch Republic: A History* (New Edition in One Volume), London, 1865.
　The United Netherlands, Vol. 1, London, 1875.
Mureşanu, Camil *John Hunyadi: Defender of Christendom*, Iasi, 2001.
Nicol, D. M. *The Last Centuries of Byzantium*, London, 1972.
Oman, Charles *A History of the Art of War in the Middle Ages Volume Two 1278–1485*, London, 1924.
　A History of the Art of War in the Sixteenth Century, London, 1937.
O'Neil, B. H. St. J. 'Rhodes and the Origin of the Bastion', *The Antiquaries Journal*, 45 (1966), pp. 44–54.
Parker, Geoffrey *The Army of Flanders and the Spanish Road 1567–1659: The Logistics of Spanish Victory and Defeat in the Low Countries' Wars*, Cambridge, 1972.
　The Dutch Revolt, London, 1985.
　The Military Revolution: Military Innovation and the Rise of the West 1500–1800, Cambridge, 1988.
Parrot, David 'The Utility of Fortifications in Early Modern Europe – Italian Princes and their Citadels 1540–1690', *War in History*, 7 (2000), pp. 127–53.
Paul, Michael C. 'The Military Revolution in Russia 1550–1682', *Journal of Military History*, 68 (2004), pp. 9–46.
Pears, Edwin *The Destruction of the Greek Empire and the Story of the Capture of Constantinople by the Turks*, London, 1903.
Pepper, Simon 'Castles and Cannon in the Naples Campaign of 1494–95' in D. Abulafia (ed.), *The French Descent into Renaissance Italy, 1494–95: Antecedents and Effects*, Aldershot, 1995, pp. 263–93.
Pinto, E. (trans. and ed.) *Giovanni Cananos: De Constantinopolis Obsidieone*, Naples, 1968.
Prescott, William H. *The Art of War in Spain: The Conquest of Granada 1481–1492* (edited by Albert D. McJoynt), London, 1995.

Roberts, Michael *Gustavus Adolphus, A History of Sweden 1611–1632 Vol. 1 1611–1626*, London, 1953.
  Gustavus Adolphus, A History of Sweden 1611–1632, Vol. 2 1626–1632, London, 1958.
  Essays in Swedish History, London, 1967.
  The Early Vasas: A History of Sweden 1523–1611, Cambridge, 1968.
Role, R. E. 'Le Mura: Lucca's Fortified Enceinte', *Fort*, 25 (1997), pp. 83–110.
Roy, Ian (trans. and ed.) *Blaise de Monluc*, London, 1971.
Runciman, Steven *The Fall of Constantinople 1453*, Cambridge, 1965.
Ruzsas, Lajos 'The Siege of Szigetvar of 1566: Its Significance in Hungarian Social Development' in
  Janos M. Bak and Bela K. Kiraly (eds.), *From Hunyadi to Rakoczi: War and Society in Late Medieval
  and Early Modern Hungary*, New York, 1982, pp. 251–60.
Schmidtchen, Volker 'Castles, Cannon and Casemates', *Fortress*, 3 (1992), pp. 3–10.
Smith, Robert D. and Rhynas Brown, Ruth *Bombards: Mons Meg and Her Sisters*, Royal Armouries
  Monograph 1, London, 1989.
Stewart, P. 'The Santa Hernandad and the First Italian Campaign of Gonzalvo de Cordoba,
  1495–1498', *Renaissance Quarterly*, 28 (1975), pp. 29–37.
Taylor, Frederick *The Art of War in Italy 1494–1529*, Cambridge, 1921.
Turnbull, Stephen *The Knight Triumphant*, London, 2001.
  The Walls of Constantinople AD324–1453, Oxford, 2004.
Van der Hoeven, Marco (ed.) *Exercise of Arms: Warfare in the Netherlands (1568–1648)*, Leiden, 1998.
Van Nimwegen, Olaf 'Maurits van Nassau and Siege Warfare' in Marco van der Hoeven (ed.), *Exercise
  of Arms: Warfare in The Netherlands (1568–1648)*, Leiden, 1998, pp. 113–31.
Vasiliev, A. 'Pero Tafur, A Spanish Traveller of the Fifteenth Century and His Visit to Constantinople,
  Trebizond and Italy', *Byzantion*, 7 (1932), pp. 75–122.
Vaughan, Dorothy M. *Europe and the Turk: A Pattern of Alliances 1350–1700*, Liverpool, 1954.
Vaughan, Richard *Philip the Good: The Apogee of Burgundy*, Harlow, 1970.
  Charles the Bold: The Last Valois Duke of Burgundy, London, 1973.
Vernadsky, George *The Tsardom of Moscow 1547–1682*, London, 1969.
Waldron, A. N. 'The Problem of the Great Wall of China', *Harvard Journal of Asian Studies*, 43, 2
  (1983), pp. 643–63.
Wood, James B. *The King's Army: Warfare, Soldiers and Society During the Wars of Religion in France,
  1562–1576*, Cambridge, 1996.
Zenkovsky, Serge A (trans.) *Medieval Russia's Epics, Chronicles and Tales*, New York, 1963.
Zolkiewski, Stanislaw *Expedition to Moscow: A Memoir* (translated from the original Polish by M. W.
  Stephen; introduction and notes by Jedrzej Giertych; preface by Robert Bruce Lockhart),
  London, 1959.

Acknowledgements

I would like to thank all who helped me in the primary research and supply of illustrations for this book. In particular I acknowledge the help of my colleagues at Leeds University Department of History. Some of the work prepared as part of my MA course in Military History appears here. The Royal Armouries Museum in Leeds was also very generous, as usual, in allowing me to use photographs of objects in its collection, particularly the life-sized diorama of the Battle of Pavia. I thank in particular Philip Abbott and the staff of the library.

While on my field-work trips my visits were greatly helped by the staff of the Legermuseum in Delft; the Citadel at Pskov; the Topkapi Palace, Istanbul; the Polish National Military Museum, Warsaw; the National Museum of Hungary, Budapest; and the Military Museum in Belgrade. I also acknowledge the helpful comments along the way by Jeremy Black, David Nicolle and John Childs. Last, but by no means least, was my late wife who accompanied me to most of the places covered in this book.

Index